# Parrot Culture

# Parrot Culture

## Our 2,500-Year-Long Fascination with the World's Most Talkative Bird

### Bruce Thomas Boehrer

University of Pennsylvania Press
Philadelphia

Copyright © 2004 University of Pennsylvania Press
All rights reserved
Printed in the United States of America on acid-free paper

10  9  8  7  6  5  4  3  2  1

Published by
University of Pennsylvania Press
Philadelphia, Pennsylvania 19104-4011

Library of Congress Cataloging-in-Publication Data

Boehrer, Bruce Thomas
    Parrot culture : our 2,500-year-long
fascination with the world's most talkative bird /
Bruce Thomas Boehrer.
        p.   cm.
    ISBN 0-8122-3793-5 (alk. paper)
    Includes bibliographical references and index.
    1. Parrots.   I. Title.
SF473.P3 B59   2004
636.6'865—dc22                          2004043014

This book is dedicated to the birds I love,
to Jerry Singerman, who gave me permission to write about them,
and to Linda Hall, who helped me to find the words

# Contents

# Prologue: Circa 40 Million B.C.

The oldest parrot known to humankind lived in the south of England. Or, to be more precise, it lived in what we now call the south of England. When this particular bird flourished—some 40 million years ago, in the middle Eocene epoch—there was no one around to call the place anything.

There was no one around to call the bird anything, either. But people being what they are, we've made up for that failure by naming it after the fact. We call it *Palaeopsittacus georgei* (Juniper and Parr 15), a typically intimidating scientific name that, when translated, yields a typically banal meaning: "George's Very Old Parrot." The George in question, a Mr. W. George, who is credited with discovering the bird (Harrison 205), is not the first man to use a parrot as vehicle for his name and reputation.

We found out about this bird as one usually finds out about prehistoric creatures: through fossils, in this case "11 associated and incomplete bones" including, most important, some pieces of the bird's foot. George's Very Old Parrot was "about the size of the Recent *Poicephalus senegalus*" or Senegal parrot, which is to say about twenty-three centimeters (Harrison 204, 205). Through similar remains, researchers have placed parrots in Germany and Australia roughly 40 million years ago; in France some 26 million years ago; in Africa between 1.5 and 7 million years ago; and in South America some 1.5 million years ago.[1]

But the European fossils stand as a special irony. Within recorded history, parrots have lived on five of the six continents inhabited by human beings; Europe, their apparent place of origin, is the single exception. It is the people of Europe, however, who have had the most powerful impact on the world's parrots, and for that reason you could also argue that parrots have made a deeper—or at least a different—impression on the people of Europe and their descendants than on any other segment of the human race.

This is the story of the resulting interaction. It is the story of what these people have meant to the birds, and of what the birds have meant to these people. It's a story with clear beginnings, but with no certain ending, and with certain, but by no means predictable, consequences for our world.

At heart, it is the story of an ongoing process of acquisition, played out on both the material and intellectual levels. It unfolds through the products of European cultural expression: poetry, drama, fiction, philosophy, painting, sculpture, travelogues, natural history, legal records, joke-books, clothing and textiles, and so forth. As it is a story about the global ascendancy of western culture, and since that culture's dominant forms have come to be Anglocentric, English-language materials assume special prominence in this book. Nonetheless, the artifacts surveyed here range from ancient Greece and Rome; through England, France, Italy, Germany, the Netherlands, Portugal, and Spain; to North, South, and Central America.

Since first coming to western attention, parrots have served as zoo specimens and objects of research, as emblems of status, as mythic marvels and artistic subject-matter, as pets and pests, as objects of affection and satirical scorn, and as licit and illicit merchandise of great value. In each of these respects, parrot culture participates in the character and development of human culture: how we see ourselves against the natural world, how we make use of that world to enrich our own lives, and how we make sense of our own spiritual, intellectual, and moral condition in the process. Most recently, however, these birds have come to stand both as a challenge to the ways we distinguish culture from nature and as a marker of the price we have paid for this act of distinction. In this sense, *Parrot Culture* is about the ties that bind us to a particular, and marvelous, piece of our world, and about how that piece of our world can reveal us to ourselves.

Most broadly, parrot culture reveals both our fascination with and our intolerance for the exotic. Western civilization's engagement with parrots, as reflected in 2,500 years of art, literature, and historical evidence, stands as a transcontinental illustration of the adage that familiarity breeds contempt. The very qualities that render these birds sublime from a distance have arguably made them ridiculous at close quarters. Of course this process, like many historical trends, admits of exceptions, and it has developed unevenly. But it has developed nonetheless, with the result that parrots today are more familiar in the home and yet more endangered in the world, more coveted and yet more taken for granted, than ever before. Biologists have catalogued more than 350 species of the bird, with major populations in South and Central America, Australia, Indonesia, India, and West Africa. But a third of these species are now threatened with extinction, and many have already ceased to exist. Less than two centuries ago, parrots inhabited North America in vast numbers. Today the continent's indigenous parrots are gone. In the meantime, exotic parrot species have been imported to North America from elsewhere. Now these birds, too, are increasingly threatened in their homelands.

Historically, the peoples of the western hemisphere have been unable to resist owning parrots. While other birds, such as ravens and jackdaws, can imitate human speech, parrots receive special treatment, both good and bad, due to the unique range of their vocal abilities. These abilities also raise questions about the intelligence of parrots, questions that remain unresolved to the present day, and that have led people to view the birds in sharply contrasting ways. Of course, other animals, too, have been traditionally credited with intelligence; one medieval bestiary, for instance, claims that "there is no creature cleverer than the dog" (*Bestiary* 71). But the idea of parrot intelligence inspires a peculiarly broad range of reactions, from religious reverence to contemptuous dismissal. And the association of parrots with exotic locales has led to further associations as well, especially with the conquered peoples of those same locales.

But in 40 million B.C., the historical processes that would produce these developments were still far in the offing, and parrots lived in Britain long before any human being. They were there more than 39 million years earlier than the original Britons, and some 33 million years before the earliest known hominids roamed the earth. They held forth in the cradle of English-speaking culture, where they fed and flocked and nested and reproduced long before that culture itself could even be described as in its infancy. Then, as climates changed and rivers altered their course and tectonic plates shifted, parrots abandoned this corner of the world, and people arrived in their place. When these two groups finally encountered one another for the first time, it would be in an act of war.

# Chapter 1

# *Invasion of the Parrots*

Early in 327 B.C., after completing his conquest of the Persian Empire, Alexander the Great maneuvered his army across the Hindu Kush and into India. When he finally returned homeward, he brought with him, among other things, specimens of a rare, magical bird. Alexander's major ancient biographer, Arrian, writing some four and a half centuries after the event (c. A.D. 130–140), mentions it as follows: "Nearchus [Alexander's friend and the admiral of his fleet] describes, as something miraculous, parrots, as being found in India, and describes the parrot, and how it utters a human voice. But I having seen several, and knowing others acquainted with this bird, shall not dilate on them as anything remarkable. . . . For I should only say what everyone knows" (8.15.8–9). Nearchus' eyewitness account of the birds is lost,[1] and already, in Arrian's treatment of them, we can see the original wonder they elicited give way to something more like ennui. What was marvelous for a Greek of the fourth century B.C. has become old news for a Roman citizen of the second century A.D. But by discrediting Nearchus, Arrian points to what has changed between Alexander's day and his own. If things that once seemed miraculous have now devolved into the commonplace, this can only be because Nearchus' birds were indeed extraordinary—at least enough so for the people of ancient Greece and Rome to want to own them. Before the birds of India can become boring in Europe, they must first become familiar.

This book is about the group of birds thus introduced to Europe, from India, by Alexander and his followers: the order of parrots, called *Psittaciformes* by biologists. It is also about the process that has rendered these birds commonplace and that now, ironically, bids fair to make them rarer than ever before. The story of their acquisition by the peoples of Europe is lengthy and involved, covering nearly two and a half millennia, and yet in the end it may be as simple as Arrian's dismissive remarks. At first parrots are exotic and astonishing, credited with marvelous abilities and even associated with the gods themselves. Then they become trivial and ordinary and even annoying. Now they are becoming extinct. Whether or not they actually do so will say as much about us and the world we have created as it does about them.

There is a great deal we do not know about Alexander's campaign in India; in some cases we do not even know what route he took as he moved through the region. But as it happens, we have a good idea what kinds of parrot he encountered there.[2] India is home to only a handful of the parrot species that have proven most popular with bird-owners over the centuries. One of these, and one of only three species that seem to have reached ancient Europe, is a true parakeet (not to be confused with the budgies known by that name in American pet stores). The bird is about two feet in length if you count its foot-long tail, with feathers of a pleasing powder-green color highlighted by a broad collar of black and rose-pink, and a very large, plum-colored beak. As with all parrots, its upper beak is hinged, and its feet are four-toed and zygodactylic—that is, arranged in yokelike fashion, with the outer toes pointing backward and the inner toes pointing forward, giving it the avian equivalent of an opposable thumb. Although it does mimic human speech in captivity, by current standards it is not a terribly gifted talker. Its native range extends from Jalalabad in the northwest to the Mekong Delta in the southeast. Biologists have given it the scientific name *Psittacula eupatria* (Forshaw 324–35). In English we call it the Alexandrine parakeet.

I think it fitting that this bird bears the name of Alexander the Great, for the story of parrots in the west is connected, from its very beginning, with Europe's conquest and absorption of other territories. The first part of that story, which is the subject of this chapter, coincides with the initial phase of European military expansion from Alexander to the collapse of the Western Roman Empire in the late fifth century. During this period—as again later—parrots serve, among other things, to mark European civilization's successful confrontation with the world beyond its frontiers. This fact helps to explain both the wonder with which Alexander's Greeks first encounter these birds in India and the casual dismissal the same birds receive from Arrian, for any successful act of conquest and absorption demands that one reduce the foreign to the familiar. Indeed, that very reduction is contained within the name of the Alexandrine parakeet, which transforms it from an exotic beast into part of the legacy of Europe's first great conqueror.

\* \* \*

Alexander was the only European ruler to establish a military presence in India before the Renaissance. After his death, the classical world's contact with south and east Asia was mediated by the merchants and peoples of the Silk Road, a lengthy, convoluted network of trade routes that connected Rome in the west with the Han Dynasty of China in the east. Although the great empires at this road's extremities never met directly, a wide range of goods, parrots among them, traveled it in both directions. Indeed, given the brevity of the ancient European incursion into India, it makes sense that luxury goods from south and east Asia should prove attractive in classical Rome. For apart from their use-value, these goods also perform a kind of symbolic reconquest of lost territory. Lacking an actual Roman administrative presence in India, one might nonetheless recover a piece of India, in the form of its exotic goods, for display within Rome itself. Given the wonder with which Alexander's Greeks first encountered India's parrots, the birds naturally become prime candidates for this kind of reacquisition.

And from the first, these birds were associated specifically with India. In fact, no records of parrot species like the African gray and the Senegal survive from classical Europe. These species were both plentiful in sub-Saharan Africa, theoretically well within the trading range of the Roman Empire at its height. But for whatever reason, the "psittacus" of ancient Greece and Rome was understood to be an Indian bird: either the rose-ringed parakeet, the Alexandrine parakeet, or another related species. This fact would lead to a good deal of geographical confusion in the late fifteenth century, when European explorers searching for a sea route to the East Indies encountered parrots in the New World and thus mistook the Americas for Asia. But in the meantime, the peoples of ancient Europe associated parrots specifically with the luxury and wonder of the East.

So, from Alexander's day forward, parrots serve as an exotic fixture of the classical world, and the records of Greek and Roman civilization reflect this fact in three main ways: through the writing of philosophers interested in natural history, through the work of literary artists, and through what remains of the Greco-Roman visual and spectacular arts. To begin with the first of these, ancient philosophers take a keen interest in parrots and begin trying to make sense of them as soon as they appear in Europe. Aristotle provides the first widely accepted scientific mention of the birds—although his is not quite the earliest mention of them by a western author. His *History of Animals* (344–342 B.C., with probable later additions) concludes a discussion of the eared owl by noting that "in general all the crook-taloned birds are short-necked and flat-tongued and given to mimicry. For such too is the Indian bird, the parrot, that is said to be human-tongued (and it becomes even more outrageous after drinking wine)" (597b.25–30). This brief remark is likely a later addition to Aristotle's work, either by the philosopher himself or by another hand. In any case it is grounded in hearsay rather than direct experience. The allegation of drunkenness, as one classicist has remarked, is "a criticism no bird ever deserved from a human being" (Dalby 193). But hearsay or not, Aristotle's mention of parrots proves most durable, both in its details (the observation about wine is echoed for centuries to come) and in its general features.

Among the latter, Aristotle's tendency to anthropomorphize parrots proves especially influential, most obviously in the remark about wine. Parrots may eat fermented fruit in the wild, and in past centuries have been fed a mixture of wine-soaked bread called "parrot soup," but when given a choice, they don't seem given to drink. I've even put the matter to the test (purely in the interests of scholarship, of course) by tempting my two Amazon parrots with a small but discerning selection of red and white wines, including an Australian chardonnay, a Chilean cabernet, an Oregon pinot noir, and a vernaccia from San Gemignano. They turned up their beaks at the lot.

But beyond the question of parrots and alcohol, Aristotle describes the bird as "human-tongued," while nonetheless noting that other birds, too, are capable of mimicry. This fact implies a lasting distinction; mynahs, jackdaws, and jays may be able to imitate human speech, but historically the parrot emerges as western culture's articulate bird par excellence, its eloquence rendering it by coincidence more human than the rest. Why should this be so? In part, perhaps, this status derives from the exceptional degree of the parrot's ability as mimic, which extends in present-day cases to the singing of opera and the conduct of seemingly meaningful conversation.[3] But other things, too, render many parrot species exceptional. Their gaudy appearance immediately captures attention, as does their exoticism (from the western point of view, at least). Their longevity endows them with a life-cycle of human proportions. Around A.D. 425, the historian Olympiodorus wrote with wonder about a parrot "with whom he had lived for twenty years, so that it had learned almost every human action that could be imitated" (Müller 4:65; my translation). And then there is their obvious intelligence. In Aristotle, for the first time, we see certain of these factors (the articulateness and exoticism) combine to produce a bird that also seems to participate, to a limited extent, in the human condition.

So if it becomes possible to view parrots as in some ways almost human, it also becomes possible, in the process, to view them as possessing, and as typifying, a supposedly inferior humanity. In the context of ancient imperial aspirations, the parrot can emerge by this calculus as a sort of servant-figure, offering a symbolic compensation for the existence of unconquered foreign lands (we don't have India, but its birds pay us homage) and also offering an apparently natural model for the inferiority of foreign and subordinate peoples (they're more like parrots than like us and therefore should obey us). Following Aristotle in this spirit, Pliny the elder declares in his *Natural History* (completed A.D. 77) that

> above all else, parrots mimic the human voice and indeed are even capable of conversation. India sends us the bird, which the Indians call "siptacis." Its entire body is green, set off with a vermilion collar about its neck. It salutes emperors and repeats the words it hears, being especially outrageous in its speech when drunk with wine. Its head is as hard as its beak, and is beaten with an iron rod when one teaches the bird to speak, for it feels no other blows. When it flies down from a perch, it catches and supports itself with its beak, making itself lighter because of the weakness of its feet. (10.58.117; my translation)

The description here is sketchy, but it seems to be aimed at depicting parrots as miniature people. Aristotle's anecdote about psittacine drunkenness persists, supplemented by other observations that implicitly cast the bird as a servant. It greets emperors, sports a collar about its neck that might call to mind the similar collars worn by Roman slaves, and sustains regular beatings with an iron rod, without which it would prove impervious to learning. And in fact, far from being a confirmable detail, this last point—like Aristotle's charges of drunk and disorderly behavior—flies in the face of experience. Parrots are wild animals at heart even now, when many are bred in captivity, and they most certainly were so in Pliny's day. Training them well cannot be done by physical violence, which will drive them into terror and psychosis. To teach a parrot to talk, one must on the contrary form a close personal bond with it, and the resulting intimacy can easily defy any distinction between master and pet. Over the years I have taught various parrots to whistle, speak, and sing. In turn, they have encouraged me to cluck, squawk, and hiss—responses to which I now find myself instinctively resorting in sometimes inappropriate circumstances, as for instance during faculty meetings. But for Pliny, the articulate birds of India exist in large part to confirm the cultural ideals of the Roman *imperium*, and these have more to do with hierarchy and subordination than with intimacy and mutuality.

Likewise, in another passing mention of the birds (*Letters* 4.2.3), Pliny notes that the unscrupulous advocate Marcus Aquilius Regulus has lost his son, whom he treated while alive with "a disgusting show of indulgence, quite unnatural in a parent. . . . Now that his son is dead he mourns with wild extravagance. The boy used to possess a number of Gallic ponies for riding and driving, also dogs of all sizes, and nightingales, parrots, and blackbirds; Regulus had them all slaughtered round his pyre. That was not grief, but parade of grief." Pliny disapproves of the ostentation with which Regulus mourns his son, but the funerary slaughter of animals nonetheless makes sense in a mental environment that views them as living property. The inappropriateness of such slaughter in this case becomes a matter of decorum, not of social, political, ethical, or ecological principle. Regulus is guilty not of despotism or cruelty or wanton destructiveness, but of bad taste.

For its part, Pliny's discussion of parrots in the *Natural History* is echoed and enlarged by later writers of natural history such as Apuleius (c. A.D. 165) and Solinus (early third century A.D.). For instance, Apuleius observes that

the parrot is a bird of India. Its height is very slightly smaller than that of doves, but its color is not that of doves, for it is not milk-white or lead-grey or both, or speckled pale yellow, but the parrot's color is green from its innermost feathers to its outermost wing-tips, except that it is distinguished by its neck alone. For its neck is collared and crowned with a crimson band as bright as a circle of twisted gold. Its beak is of the first order of hardness; when it flies down in excitement upon a rock from a very high perch, it catches itself with its beak as with an anchor. But the hardness of its head is equal to that of its beak. When it is compelled to imitate our language, its head is struck repeatedly with an iron rod so that it might begin to perceive the authority of its teacher; in teaching, this is called a ferrule.

However, as a young bird it learns quickly until it reaches two years of age, while its mouth is soft so that it might be adapted to speech, and while its tongue is tender so that it might be taught to echo; but an old bird, when captured, is intractable and forgetful. In truth, a parrot is more easily brought to learn human speech when it eats nuts and when its feet, like those of a man, bear five little toes. For that is not a characteristic of all parrots, but it is proper to all of them to have a broader tongue than other birds, and they pronounce human words with their more open plectrum and palate. Indeed, what the parrot has learned, it sings, or rather speaks, so similarly to us that if you were to hear its voice, you would think it a person. On the other hand, if you were to hear a crow, it would approximate, not speak, the words. Yet both the crow and the parrot say nothing more than what they have learned. If you teach it to curse, it will curse by day and by night, making a great clamor with its railing; this is a song to it, and it thinks it is singing. When it has run through all the curses it has learned, then it starts the song all over again. If you want it not to speak, its tongue must be cut out, or it must be sent back to its forests as soon as possible. (12; my translation)

To my mind, this is the best description of parrots to survive from ancient times, and it corrects a certain amount of the misinformation that precedes it. For instance, although Apuleius, like Pliny, maintains that parrots must be beaten while learning to talk, he nonetheless connects their acquisition of language more realistically to positive reinforcement with food. Also, he notes the dramatic difference between language acquisition in young parrots and in older specimens that have matured in the wild—a difference of which neither Aristotle nor Pliny seems aware. Moreover, his allusion to the raucous and repetitive character of parrot chatter, now detached from rumors of avian alcoholism, suggests familiarity. Still, Apuleius' fondness for parrots with five toes betrays an innocence of the birds' anatomy, there being no such thing as a five-toed parrot; however, a five-toed parrot is more like a human being than is a four-toed parrot, so it might stand to reason that the former would have a better command of human speech. And as a general rule, Apuleius follows Aristotle and Pliny in presenting the birds from an anthropomorphic viewpoint. In repeating Pliny's remarks about parrot-training, he draws a direct connection between the beating of animals and the beating of schoolchildren, and in echoing Pliny's description of the colorful band that encircles the necks of most Indian parrot-species, Apuleius depicts this marking both as a collar and as a crown. This last point comes as a surprise in a passage that generally follows Aristotle and Pliny by presenting parrots as inferior and subordinate creatures. It suggests a second vein of classical nature-writing on parrots, to which I will turn in a moment. As for Solinus' later work, it combines Pliny's observations with those of Apuleius, adding that the birds' articulateness "made the Romaines to have so much pleasure and delight in [them], that the barbarous people made a merchandise of their Poppinieyes" (sig. 2E1v).

In Aristotle, Pliny, and their followers, we can see the beginnings of a western tendency to treat parrots not just as a material but also as a conceptual resource. They prove valuable, in other words, not only because of their rarity, but because they exemplify both nature's subservience to culture and the subservience of certain social groups (slaves, women, the poor, barbaric foreigners, etc.) to others. Submitting as it does to human rule, echoing the "Hail, Caesar!" of the governed, the parrot seems to provide a basis in nature for the acquiescence of social inferiors to their so-called betters. This acquiescence, in turn, helps explain the literary impulse to trivialize and denigrate the very qualities that rendered parrots marvelous and valuable in the first place.

Alongside this impulse, however, there also persists a fascination with the beauty, rarity, and exoticism of parrots, which leads some authors to associate these birds not with the low and the commonplace, but rather with the exalted and the sacred.

This tendency originates in the very first surviving reference to parrots by a western author, predating Aristotle by roughly fifty years. Sometime after 398 B.C., Ktesias of Cnidus, who had just returned to his home in Greece after seventeen years as a physician to the king of Persia, composed a geographical account of India which now survives only in an abstract made by Photius, the Patriarch of Constantinople, in the late ninth century A.D. This brief narrative is full of fabulous, incredible material, among which Ktesias mentions "the kind of bird called the parrot . . . : it has a tongue and voice like the human, is of the size of a hawk, has a red bill, is adorned with a beard of a black colour, while the neck is red like cinnabar, it talks like a man in Indian, but if taught Greek can talk in Greek also" (1.3). Ktesias was describing a bird the Greeks hadn't yet generally seen, and given the fantastic content of his work, it may have been easy to dismiss his report out of hand. Yet he seems to be referring to a species of parrot otherwise unreported by classical authors: the blossom-headed parakeet (*Psittacula roseata*), whose neck and entire head are a deep and pleasing violet. In any case, Ktesias describes a bird that does not mimic but instead "talks like a man," and he thus gives later authors a precedent for viewing parrots not as minions or toys but as marvels, worthy of wonder and even veneration.

On this point, his attitude opposes the tradition of nature-writing descending from Aristotle and Pliny, and the Greek historian/philosopher Plutarch (A.D. 45–125), for one, clearly understands as much. In his massive and influential *Moralia* appear two essays, entitled "Beasts Are Rational" and "Whether Land or Sea Animals Are Cleverer," which together make an unusual case for displaying respect to the creatures of the natural world. There Plutarch claims that beasts reason, that they teach their young as humans do, and that they are capable of personal attachments and loyalties. Then, taking dead aim at Aristotle's insistence that the "power [of speech] is peculiar to man" (*History of Animals* 536b.1–2), he adds that

> as for starlings and crows and parrots which learn to talk and afford their teachers so malleable and imitative a vocal current to train and discipline, they seem to me to be champions and advocates of the other animals in their ability to learn, instructing us in some measure that they too are endowed both with rational utterance and with articulate voice; for which reason it is quite ridiculous to admit a comparison of them with creatures who have not enough voice even to howl or groan. (972f–973a)

Plutarch's reading of avian mimicry stands in sharp contrast to other treatments of the subject and draws attention to the uncertain meaning of such behavior. For Aristotle, Pliny, and Apuleius it emerges as a marker of difference, demonstrating how short all birds fall of possessing full human consciousness. Hence Apuleius stresses the mindless and repetitive character of parrot chatter, while Aristotle and Pliny describe it as a kind of verbal license and associate it with strong drink. In each of these cases, psittacine mimicry figures as an index of mindlessness; what matters most is not the similarity of parrot speech to human language, but the intellectual difference that underlies the two. But for Plutarch, as for Ktesias before him, the speech of birds suggests their abiding affinity with humankind. They remind us of humanity's intimate connection to the surrounding world even as they lay claim to their own peculiar dignity.

In similar spirit, Aelian's *On the Characteristics of Animals* (c. A.D. 200) associates parrots with the marvels of eastern royalty and spirituality. Aelian remarks that

> in the royal residences in India where the greatest of the kings of that country lives, there are so many objects for admiration that neither Memnon's city of Susa with all its extravagance, nor the magnificence of Ecbatana is to be compared with them. . . . The remaining splendours it is not the purpose of this narrative to detail; but in the parks tame peacocks and pheasants are kept, and they live in the cultivated shrubs to which the royal gardeners pay due attention. . . . There too Parrots are kept and crowd around the king. But no Indian eats a Parrot in spite of their great numbers, the reason being that the Brahmins regard them as sacred and even place them above all other birds. And they add that they are justified in so doing, for the Parrot is the only bird that gives the most convincing imitation of human speech. (13.18)

In its way, this description proves as influential among later writers as do those of Aristotle and Pliny. Among other things, its association of parrots with royal opulence and its treatment of them as objects of religious veneration find unexpected parallels in the Middle Ages. Although he writes roughly half a century after Arrian, Aelian does not wholly share his predecessor's cavalier view of the parrot world; instead, he voices something very much like the admiration and wonder that Arrian has already rejected as naive.

Elsewhere, in contrast, Aelian seems more cavalier about the birds in question, noting that they "learn like children" and that while they speak in captivity, in the wild they "are unlearned and cannot talk" (16.2). Recent historians have traced a connection between the growth of opposition to animal cruelty and the decline of corporal punishment in the classroom over the past four centuries (Thomas 45). In Aelian's comparison of parrots to children, and in Pliny's and Apuleius' observation that the birds must be beaten when taught to speak, we encounter traces of older views on both subjects.[4] But in general, the natural historians of Greece and Rome seem to be of two minds about the parrots of India, inclined both to extol them as miraculous and to dismiss them as pedestrian, to associate them with gods and kings on the one hand and with servants and children on the other. The tension between these attitudes remains constant, in various ways, to the present day.

While the practitioners of ancient science were busy studying parrots, others embraced the birds with enthusiasm. When Alexander the Great died, his officers divided his empire into a series of smaller kingdoms, and the richest of these, Egypt, went to his former lieutenant Ptolemy. By 285 B.C., the aging Ptolemy decided to share the realm with his son, also named Ptolemy, and to celebrate the accession of Ptolemy II he produced an immense public pageant. Among the costly fabrics, the incense, the massed soldiers, the banqueting, and the other splendors of this affair, there appeared columns of servants carrying parrots in cages (Athenaeus 5.201b). Apart from the obvious luxury of this spectacle, it conveyed a political point, for the elder Ptolemy had accompanied Alexander to India and back. The birds that returned with him served as a reminder of that connection, and perhaps as a way of linking the new Ptolemy with Alexander's achievements.

If this was the intended effect of the display, it seems to have worked, at least in the long run. Alexandria became the center of the parrot trade for the classical Mediterranean (Wotke 931), and parrots became a popular marker of privilege in ancient society, increasingly associated with kings and emperors. When the news spread that Julius Caesar's adopted nephew Octavian had defeated Mark Antony at the battle of Actium (31 B.C.), thereby ensuring that he would become the emperor Augustus, at least one parrot appeared among his well-wishers, greeting him with the words "Hail Caesar, conqueror and leader!" (Macrobius 3.30; my translation). This was a calculated appeal to the victor's largesse, of course; it takes a long time to teach a parrot to say anything, so the bird's greeting offered powerful evidence of its owner's loyalty. In this case, the ploy worked, and Octavian bought the bird from its owner for a handsome sum. But another fortune-hunter used a raven for the same purpose, with less than ideal results:

> It happened that a man appeared before Caesar with a raven, which he had taught to say, "Hail Caesar, conqueror and leader!" Caesar, marveling, bought the dutiful bird for twenty thousand coins. But a companion of the bird's trainer, who had received nothing of this generosity, declared that the trainer had another bird, too, which Caesar demanded to see as well. When brought forward, it greeted him with the words "Hail Antony, conqueror and leader!" (Macrobius 3.30; my translation)

The bird-trainer evidently had been hedging his bets.

Not to be outdone by such yokels, Greek and Roman poets also began to employ the parrot in the endless derby for imperial patronage. Writing in the first century B.C., the Greek Crinagoras set the tone here with an effusive epigram:

> The parrot that talks with human voice, taking leave of his wicker cage, flew to the woods on his many-coloured wings, and ever assiduous in greeting famous Caesar, did not forget that name even in the mountains. All the birds, sharpening their wits to learn, strove among each other which should be the first to say "Chaire" [Hail] to the god. Orpheus made the beasts obey him in the hills, and now every bird tunes its voice for thee, Caesar, unbidden. (9.562)

The parrot's praises are a projection of the poet's own sycophantic ambitions, which others strove to outdo in their turn. Petronius (d. A.D. 66), for instance, amidst his duties as Roman magistrate and party-companion of the emperor Nero, took time to compose an epigram spoken by a parrot whose wondrous abilities associated it not only with the Latin language but with the gods themselves: "My birthplace was India's glowing shore, where the day returns in brilliance with fiery orb. Here I was born amid the worship of the gods, and exchanged my barbaric speech for the Latin tongue. O healer of Delphi, now dismiss thy swans; here is a voice more worthy to dwell within thy temple" (18). And, capping these performances in turn, in A.D. 85 the poet Martial flattered the emperor Domitian by composing a deft couplet uttered by a parrot that had *taught itself* to sing Caesar's praises.

Like the philosophers of their day (and Martial, at least, had clearly been reading Pliny), these poets seem torn between wonder at the parrot's powers of speech and an urgent desire to put the bird in its place. As an eastern miracle, it becomes a proper companion for Caesar and Apollo, even displacing the sun-god's swans. But it is also in dire need of domestication, exchanging its "barbaric speech" for Latin, learning to praise Caesar or to name others at Caesar's direction. As it happens, this exquisite combination of eminence and inferiority gives perfect expression to the circumstances of a poet in pursuit of royal patronage. The parrot's marvelous eloquence sets it apart from other beasts, thereby marking the poet's own aspirations to distinction and uniqueness. But its status as a pet of the powerful marks, at the very same time, the humiliation of the poet's own life of service. Like the parrot, the poet is an articulate beast torn between two incompatible images of himself.

In practice, this conflict could lead to painful consequences. Despite the advantages of his friendship with Nero, and despite—perhaps even because of—his own energy and talent, Petronius was eventually forced to commit suicide by his imperial patron. Likewise, despite their beauty and value, Marcus Aquilius Regulus had his son's parrots slaughtered at his funeral pyre. To serve well, one must please well. That, at least, is one implication of a fable by Aesop (c. 600 B.C., with many later attributions, of which this tale is one) that again casts a parrot in the role of household servant, having to deal with the inevitable politics of the workplace:

> A man who had bought a parrot let it fly freely in his house. The parrot, who was tame, jumped up and perched in the hearth, and from there began to cackle in a pleasant way. A house-ferret, seeing him there, asked him who he was and from whence he came. He replied:
>
> "The Master went out to buy me."
>
> The house-ferret replied:
>
> "And you dare, most shameless creature—newcomer!—to make such sounds, whereas I, who was born in this house, am forbidden by the Master to cry out, and if sometimes I do, he beats me and throws me out of the door."
>
> The parrot replied:
>
> "Oh, go for a long walk [i.e., get lost]! There is no comparison to be made between us. My voice doesn't irritate the Master as yours does."
>
> *This fable concerns all malevolent critics who are always ready to throw the blame on to others.* (355)

Figure 1. A wall painting from Roman North Africa, depicting a parrot with cherries

And for the most part, parrots seem to have pleased the ancient Greeks and Romans surpassingly, so much so that one classicist has claimed "there was a fashionable cult of parrots in Imperial Rome" (Douglas 90). No doubt the birds were popular, and not just for their voices. They seem to have been a standard feature of public ceremonies, along with "white blackbirds, and other unusual things of that sort" (Varro 3.9.17). Pliny records that a talking raven received a public funeral in Rome in A.D. 36 (*Natural History* 10.122–123); no such accounts of public parrot funerals survive, but the raven's example suggests their possibility. And the stunning appearance of parrots made them a standard subject of pictorial representation, so that they begin to turn up regularly in the ancient visual arts. Often they appear simply as eye candy, as in a wall painting from El-Djem in Tunisia that depicts a parrot on a tree branch, reaching forward with its beak to grasp a cluster of cherries (Figure 1). In like spirit, a mosaic from Naples shows two parrots and a dove perched on a bowl of water, being eyed covetously from below by a cat; among his other fantasies, Pliny believed that parrots and doves enjoyed a special friendship (Pliny 10.207).

But elsewhere, painters and artisans encourage the association of parrots with India and its mythic wonders, which they transform in the process into a species of household ornament. The silver-gilt Dish of Lampsacus, for instance, is decorated with an elaborate relief depicting at its center an enthroned female figure whose headdress and clothing identify it as India personified (Toynbee

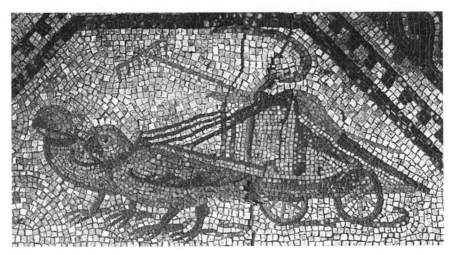

Figure 2.  Detail of the Dionysus Mosaic from Cologne, showing two parrots harnessed to a miniature cart (courtesy of the Romisch-Germanisches Museum, Cologne)

59–60). Surrounding this figure is a variety of exotic fauna, including apes, leopards, and, immediately to the left of the figure, a parrot. The result is an allegorical grouping in which the beasts of India serve as attendants upon a queen or goddess representing the region as a whole. As a luxury item, the dish embodies a desire to possess the exotic, even if only at second hand, and to turn it into domestic property.

Then again, there is the so-called Dionysus Mosaic, now in the Römisch-Germanisch Museum in Cologne. This decorative pavement formed part of a Roman villa dating from the third century A.D. It consists of a complex geometrical pattern enclosing a series of illustrations that relate to the worship of the god Dionysus: musical instruments and theater masks reflecting the god's status as patron of music and the drama; bunches of grapes referring to his invention of wine; and so forth. Among these images there appears a pair of rose-ringed parakeets harnessed to a miniature cart loaded with farm implements (Figure 2). The farm tools are a seasonal reference; other birds appear on the mosaic as emblems of autumn, winter, and spring, and the parrots in their turn represent summer. But they also illustrate the tradition that Dionysus himself visited, and in some accounts conquered and governed, India. This tale was influential enough to prompt Alexander, during his own invasion of India, to seek out a local shrine that he believed to have been dedicated to the god (Arrian 5.2.5–7), and the parrots on the Dionysus Mosaic serve as reminders of this geographical association.

Yet at the same time that this mosaic associates parrots with the pagan gods, it also transforms them into toys, harnessed like draft animals to a diminutive wagon. This motif of birds in harness is a fairly common one in Roman visual art: a "jeu d'esprit" (Toynbee 280) that Roman painters and their audiences seem to have found oddly engaging. For instance, another such image survives in which a parrot pulls a chariot guided by a grasshopper.[5] In illustrations of this sort we see parrots taking their place, very early on, in the cultural province of the Cute, where they have remained, to one extent or another, ever since.

Less cute—but just as enduring—is the use ancient satirists made of the birds. Where patronage poets like Crinagoras and Martial employed them to flatter the powerful, writers of social invective used them to denounce the contemptible, thus paving the way for centuries of parrot-insults to come. Perhaps the earliest pioneer in this vein was the Greek Callimachus (fl. 280–240 B.C.), who employed an otherwise-lost fable of Aesop's as mordant social commentary:

> Just is Zeus, yet unjust was his ruling when he deprived the animals of their speech, and—as though we were not in a position to give part of our voice to others—[diverted it], to the race of men [defective in this way?]. Eudemos, therefore, has a dog's voice, and Philton a donkey's, [the orators] that of a parrot, and the tragedians have a voice like the dwellers in the sea. And for this cause, Andronicus, all men have become loquacious and wordy. Aesop of Sardis told this, whom the Delphians did not receive well when he recited his tale. (Iambus 2.4–17)

Even in the fragmentary form in which it has survived, one can see why this tale might have displeased the Delphians. It introduces, for perhaps the first time in European history, the enduring tendency to compare mindless chatter to the mimicry of a parrot. And at the same time, it also implements a startling (and perhaps even more insulting) reversal of roles. The parrot's chatter, which early nature writers like Pliny and Apuleius present as an imperfect imitation of human speech, reemerges here as an object of human imitation. As a result, the rhetoricians of ancient Alexandria—as famed in their day for babbling nonsense as are certain politicians in our own—function as a cheap copy of the animal world. Nature is more cultured than culture.

Such patterns of association seem to have caught on quickly in ancient satire. As a result, by A.D. 62 the poet Persius poses a question that has already become rhetorical:

> I have not bathed my lips in the horse's spring, Helicon, nor do I recall dreaming on two-headed Parnassus in order to spring up so suddenly as a poet. . . . Who

instructed the parrot to say hello, and who taught the magpie to attempt our language? That master of arts and patron of ingenuity, the belly, an expert at mimicking the voices denied to him. Because of him, if any hope of deceitful money glittered, you would think that crow-poets and magpie-poetesses warbled Pegasean nectar. (Prologue 1–3, 8–14)

Yet Persius, unlike Callimachus, seems to view *himself* as a parrot and the objects of his scorn as crows and magpies. His is a literary world afflicted with the defects of the patronage system, in which legions of aspiring poetasters give vent to verbal excess in the name of inspiration. Indeed, some of that excess finds its way cleverly into Persius' own poem, which mockingly coins inflated poetic phrases like "the horse's spring" ("fonte Caballino," for Helicon), "two-headed Parnassus," and "Pegasean nectar." Such stuff, the poem implies, is the province of lesser talents: imperfect imitators who are to Persius what crows and magpies are to the parrot. As for the inspiration to which they lay claim, it's obvious nonsense, and it marks the bad poets indelibly as such: writers whose sense of reality is as defective as their sense of diction. Persius himself, on the other hand, emerges as the dominant figure of his poem not only because of his ability as a mimic, but because his motivation for writing is so refreshingly parrot-like. When set against grandiose vaporizings about poetic afflatus and Pegasean nectar, his cheerful claim that "I'm only in this for the money" provides not just a much-needed dose of realism, but a genuine ethical improvement.

But among classical writers, it is Ovid (43 B.C.–A.D. 18) whose satirical use of parrots proves most outrageous and enduring. This use occurs in the sixth poem of book 2 of his *Amores*: a sixty-two-line elegy for the death of his girlfriend's rose-ringed parakeet. Beginning the exercise in a heroic vein, Ovid summons all feathered creatures to join in the obsequies for Corinna's pet:

> Parrot, winged mimic from the dawn-lands of India, has died: come in flocks, ye birds, to his funeral. Come, pious poultry, and beat your breasts with your wings, and rend your tender cheeks with the unyielding claw. . . . As for the Ismarian tyrant's crime, which you, Philomela, lament, that same lament has been satisfied in its own time; turn now to the sad last rites of a rare bird. Your cause of grief for Itys is great, but it is ancient history. (2.6.1–4, 7–10; my translation)

Both Ovid's occasion and his tone here suggest mockery. Certainly—to compare early things with late—that is how the same subject matter functions in Evelyn Waugh's gleeful trashing of all things American, *The Loved One* (1948). Waugh's protagonist, the English expatriate Dennis Barlow, embraces a career as a pet undertaker in Los Angeles, which career culminates in a parrot funeral reminiscent of Ovid's elegy: "Mr. Joyboy would have an open casket. I advised against it and, after all, I know. I've studied the business. An open casket is all right for dogs and cats who lie down and curl up naturally. But parrots don't. They look absurd with a head on a pillow. But I came up against a blank wall of snobbery" (140). Waugh's humor arises from the discordant juxtaposition of human obsequies with pet care, and this is what Ovid offers us as well, two thousand years earlier.

Moreover Ovid—like Persius with his Pegasean nectar—is clearly engaged in literary parody. And in Ovid's case, the literary victim has a name. By composing a dirge for the death of his beloved Lesbia's pet sparrow, Catullus (c. 58–55 B.C.) influenced generations of Roman love-poets to come with his tender evocation of intimate feelings: "Lament, o Venuses and cupids, and whoever is most charming among men. My girlfriend's sparrow is dead, that sparrow, my girlfriend's delight, whom she loved more than her eyes. . . . It now travels by an obscure way to that place from which no one knows how to return" (3.1–5, 11–12; my translation). This kind of tremulous emotion, however, could not have been farther from Ovid's approach to love and sex. Where Catullus and his imitators leave the reader "convinced of the sincerity and the seriousness of their love and their bitterness at finding that [its] fulfillment is impossible" (Du Quesnay 7), Ovid seems to relish the role of the lover, which he presents not as an emotional abyss but as a game of seduction. Against this background his grief for Corinna's parrot sounds derisive rather than genuine, marking the distance between his experience and his predecessors' innocence. For instance, Ovid's language is a little too grandiose, a little too exaggerated, for the sentiments it conveys. Catullus keeps his verses strictly in the personal register, describing Lesbia's feelings for her sparrow and recalling her behavior with it in intimate detail: "For it was sweet as honey and knew her as well as a girl knows her mother, nor would it move from her bosom, but hopping about this way and that it would chirp to its mistress alone" (3.6–10). Ovid, by contrast, presents the loss of Corinna's parrot as an event of epic magnitude, grander than Philomela's rape or Procne's murder of her own son, Itys. (Likewise, he compares the bird's proverbial friendship with the turtle-dove to Pylades' friendship with Orestes.) As Catullus understands, the relationship between a pet bird and its owner is too fragile a subject to sustain the weight of heroic allusions. For a poet intent upon making that relationship look ridiculous, however, such allusions are perfectly chosen.

Nor does Ovid simply inflate Catullus' diction. He also exaggerates the structure of his poem so that where Catullus offers a delicate eighteen-line lyric, Ovid responds with a full-scale formal elegy. This extends from a call to the proper mourners ("Come, pious poultry"), through an outburst against divine injustice ("The best things are often carried off by greedy hands" [2.6.39]), to a death-bed (death-perch?) scene in which the expiring bird, sensing that its hour is at hand (or at wing?), squawks out a desolate "Corinna, farewell!" (2.6.48). This moment of high bathos, in turn, gives way to a formal consolation in which the parrot finds its place in Elysium, within "a grove of black ilex" (2.6.49) designated as "the good birds' home" (2.6.51). As the classicist John Ferguson has remarked of Ovid's poem, "the whole thing is amusing and utterly unfeeling" (353). It's also brilliantly pitched, employing the death of a natural mimic as the occasion for a barbed exercise in literary mimicry.

Even so, Ovid handles his subject so deftly as to leave many readers doubtful of his insincerity. Even a near-contemporary of Ovid seems to have taken his poem quite seriously. I refer in this case to the poet Statius (c. A.D. 40–96), who produced his own parrot-elegy (*Silvae* 2.4) in obvious (but to my mind misguided) imitation of the master. *Silvae* 2.4 bewails the demise of a parrot belonging to Statius' patron Atedius Melior, and this shift away from parody turns his poem into a fawning thing. Yet his obsequiousness extends still further, for the poem is not just a token of respect to Statius' patron, but also, in a way, an act of literary ancestor-worship. Imitating Ovid as he does, Statius abandons the attitude of irreverence essential to satire, and he replaces it with a bookish kind of bowing and scraping:

> Flock hither all ye scholar fowl, to whom Nature has given the noble privilege of speech; let the bird of Phoebus [the raven] beat his breast, and the starling, that repeats by heart the sayings it has heard, and magpies transformed in the Aonian contest [the maidens who challenged the Muses and were turned into magpies], and the partridge, that joins and reiterates the words it echoes, and the sister that laments forlorn in her Bistonian bower [Philomela]: mourn all together and bear your dead kinsman to the flames. (2.4.16–23)

In Statius, the parrot has ceased to be a vehicle for satire and has become once again an instrument of flattery, including the sincere form of flattery born of imitation. For poets, as for natural historians, the bird remains both a servile and a transcendent creature. Efforts to fix its meaning in one category or the other seem hopeless.

Yet while poets and painters pursue their work, parrots become subject to still another strange tension, this time centering on the dinner-table. We eat many things in America today, but parrots are not among them. Not that one would expect the parrots to complain, of course. Given all of the other indignities to which they had already been exposed in ancient Europe—capture, transportation and sale, beating with iron rods, satirical mockery, and so forth—it seems only fair that people should at least refrain from eating them. And their chances at first seem good in this respect. As we've seen, Aelian notes in his description of India that "no Indian eats a Parrot in spite of their great numbers, the reason being that the Brahmins regard them as sacred and even place them above all other birds." This standard of treatment might give reasonable cause for optimism. After all, parrots have a number of qualities that could well be expected to save them from meeting their maker on a bed of wild rice. They are rare. They are beautiful. They are associated with the gods. They are intelligent and amusing. They are not eaten in their native land. They are popular as pets. And most of all, they are articulate.

Rarity alone might discourage one from eating an animal for practical reasons; to eat it is to risk losing its kind. The birds' beauty might appeal to one's aesthetic sense; their association with the gods to one's sense of holy dread; their intelligence to one's potential respect for other sentient beings; the fact that they are not eaten to one's respect for tradition. As pets, they enter into a special relationship with their owners that cuts across the barrier of species, placing them in a sense inside the human family unit. By defining our pets as "surrogate family members" (Shell 123), we turn them into honorary human beings, under the safeguard of the prohibition against cannibalism.

In the case of parrots, this protection is extended still further by the ability to speak, which redoubles the kinship between owner and beast. The Beat novelist and composer Paul Bowles, writing in 1953 of his own longstanding attachment to parrots, noted that for the Central American Indians "the parrot can be a temporary abode for a human spirit" (159). For others, too, the parrot's voice presents a special challenge to the distinction between people and animals. In eating such a bird, we seem to be eating a piece of ourselves.

And on the whole western society has proven reluctant to treat parrots as foodstuffs. But if we were therefore to consider them completely exempt from the demands of the table, we would ignore the invincible perversity of human nature. In fact, people—Europeans among them—*have* eaten parrots, in most cases as a matter of necessity. The peoples of pre-Columbian America consumed the birds, as did those of West Africa, and T'ang China (Schafer 100), and as did some European explorers faced with starvation. In the nineteenth century, parrot pie became a classic pioneer dish in the Australian outback.

But the ancient Romans are to my knowledge unique among western peoples in treating the parrot as a culinary delicacy rather than as an entree of last resort. They have even left us recipes for preparing the birds. Here is one from Apicius' celebrated cookbook, *On the Art of Cookery* (late third century A.D.):

> For Flamingo [and Parrot] *in phoenicoptero* [flamingo style]
> Scald the flamingo, wash and dress it, put it in a pot, add water, salt, dill, and a little vinegar, to be parboiled. Finish cooking with a bunch of leeks and coriander, and add some reduced must to give it color. In the mortar crush pepper, cumin, coriander, laser root, mint, rue, moisten with vinegar, add dates, and the fond of the braised bird, thicken, [strain] cover the bird with the sauce and serve. Parrot is prepared in the same manner. (231–232)

Never having tried this dish, I can hazard no opinion as to its quality. Nor is it clear just how widely such recipes were made in their own day. But used they were, specifically by the rich and privileged.

We know, for instance, that parrots were a part of the diet of the late Roman boy-emperor Elagabalus (A.D. 218–222). As one historian noted in tight-lipped disgust, he even fed parrots to his lions; as for his palace staff, he regaled them with "huge dishes filled with mullets' innards, flamingoes' brains, partridge eggs, thrushes' brains, and the heads of parrots, pheasants and peacocks" (*Lives of the Later Caesars*, Elagabalus 21.2; 20.6). Such banquets seem to have earned him little admiration; on the contrary, they survive as evidence of his softness, profligacy, and corruption. Eating parrot and similar things, Elagabalus transforms himself into an emblem of epicurism run amuck.

He makes a lasting impression in the process. Nearly fourteen hundred years after the young emperor's death, Ben Jonson recalls Elagabalus' dining habits in his dramatic masterpiece, the comedy *Volpone* (1606). There Jonson's depraved, eponymous protagonist attempts to seduce the virtuous Celia in part through a miscalculated appeal to her sense of gourmandise:

> The heads of parrats, tongues of nightingales,
> The braines of peacoks, and of estriches
> Shall be our food. (3.7.200–204)

But Jonson is a latecomer with his loathing of psittacophagy. Within two centuries of Elagabalus' demise, his eating habits were the stuff of legend, appearing in the verse satire *Against Eutropius* by the late Roman poet Claudian (A.D. 370–c. 404). This is a venomous political lampoon aimed at its title character, the powerful eunuch, consul, and chamberlain of the eastern Roman emperor Arcadius, whom Claudian imagines summoning his favorites to a council of war as follows: "Their hunger is only aroused by costly meats, and they tickle their palates with foods imported from overseas, the flesh of the many-eyed fowl of Juno, or of that coloured bird brought from farthest Ind that knows how to speak" (2.328–331).

We know, from records like these, that in ancient times parrot was regarded as an upper-class delicacy like caviar, the food of only the highest stratum of Roman society. But the same records also show that even in classical Rome the practice of eating these birds suffered from a very mixed press. Psittacophagy is associated with the effete and idle rich, with jaded palates, and with something like oriental luxury. This last fact is ironic, given Aelian's insistence that parrots were not eaten in ancient India. Elagabalus, for one, was closely connected with eastern forms of worship and culture, and for Claudian the eating of parrots seems somehow deeply un-Roman: something a degenerate eunuch would do at the court in Constantinople. This most distinctive of Roman dietary practices is already, at least for some Romans, outlandish and loathsome and beyond the pale.

So what should we make of this contradiction? The opponents of parrot-eating are perhaps easy enough to understand. They have no shortage of reasons to regard the parrot as forbidden flesh. Yet the very qualities that should have rendered it exempt from eating seem somehow to have attracted the parrot-eaters, who seized on it precisely because of its scarcity and beauty and association with foreign lands. And perhaps also because of its voice. It is as if some impulse compelled Roman society to kill and consume the very things it found miraculous.

Nor has that impulse disappeared, although it takes different forms in contemporary America. We still consume parrots, at least symbolically. A quick visit to online auctions yields mountains of parrotphernalia on sale to the highest bidder, including items depicting the macaws that have become the mascot for Corona beer. In convenience stores we can slake our thirst with cups of a fruit-slush drink called Parrot Ice. Psittacine-theme taverns and eateries range across the United States, from the Green Parrot Bar, founded in 1890 in Key West, Florida, to the Blue Parrot Restaurant in Avalon, California.

And the urge to kill remains with us too, as illustrated by the case of Chad Alvarez, a twenty-three-year-old senior at the University of Wisconsin. In May 1999, Alvarez, angry at fraternity brother Corey Greenfield for circulating an email at which he took offense, seized Greenfield's Quaker parrot and placed it in the fraternity's microwave oven, which he activated with sixty minutes on the timer. The bird, named Iago, exploded before other fraternity members could rescue it. According to Greenfield, the parrot had a vocabulary of about twenty words. When animal-rights activists responded to Alvarez's deed with outrage, his attorney, Charles Giesen, declared, "Chad has never hurt anybody or anyone before in his life. . . . He's a good kid" (Murphy). Two weeks earlier, Alvarez had been arrested on a charge of drunk driving, to which he had entered a plea of no contest. He also pled no contest to charges of theft and animal cruelty for cooking Iago (Chaptman).

# Chapter 2

# *Mysteries and Marvels*

The Holy Roman Emperor Frederick II, avid bird-fancier and leader of the Sixth Crusade, received a diplomatic gift from the Sultan of Babylon that was probably unique in thirteenth-century Europe: an umbrella cockatoo (*Cacatua alba*) from Indonesia (Streseman 25). Charles IV of France (1322–1328) kept an Alexandrine parakeet in his royal menagerie (Loisel 1:169). By the fifteenth century, parrots inhabited the Vatican.

These were exceptional cases, however. As a rule, living parrots seldom appear in the historical records of medieval Europe. One ornithologist claims that after the glut of Indian parakeets in Roman times, "all trace of them disappears until the fifteenth century" (Streseman 25). No medieval naturalists complain about the birds' abundance. No accounts of royal processions involve them. There is, of course, no sign of them being eaten. The story of parrots in medieval Europe is in large part the story of their absence.

Yet, paradoxically, as they grow less available in the feather, they loom larger in the cultural imagination, often in ways that bear no discernible relation to biological reality. So the story of medieval parrots is one of art, literature, and the birth of a marvelous fiction. Where the ancient Greeks and Romans viewed these birds as somehow both sublime and ridiculous, in the Middle Ages they become less commonplace, less servile, and more magical.

Of course, it's easy to overstate the changes that occur from classical times to the Middle Ages. Parrots remained available in medieval Europe and were still prized as pets, although their availability diminished. Likewise, the Middle Ages preserved classical parrot culture but also reinterpreted it in the process, so that the birds of India come increasingly to figure as emblems of the mythic and supernatural.

For a good example of this process, consider the medieval legacy of Pliny's *Natural History*. This is partly what we would now call a work of zoology, but partly also a work of geography. In the Middle Ages, these two aspects of Pliny's history split into separate literary forms: the bestiary and the travel-narrative. In the process, Pliny's remarks about parrots undergo embellishment at the same time that they are preserved and repeated.

On the whole, the bestiaries remain quite faithful to what Pliny wrote, given their complicated history. In design, they served as zoological encyclopedias, dealing with animals both real and imaginary. In the typical bestiary, entries on the hedgehog and weasel and frog stand side by side with those on the parander, monoceros, and manticore, and the parrot's scarcity in medieval Europe tends to ally it with these latter, fantastic creatures. In derivation, the bestiary is a compendium of beast-lore without identified authors, developing by transmission of material from one copyist to another. The main sources for the form were the great classical works of natural history, especially those by Aristotle and Pliny, supplemented by versions of a late Roman-Greek treatise on beasts, now lost, attributed to a writer called the Physiologus (c. 100–140 A.D.). By the twelfth century, bestiaries circulated throughout Europe, combining the opinions of Aristotle, Pliny, and their fellows with variations on the Physiologus' work and passages from post-classical authors such as Isidore of Seville and Hugh of Fouilloy.

Two entries on parrots drawn from English manuscripts typify the bestiary form. In a twelfth-century description:

> It is only from India that one can get a PSITIACUS or Parrot, which is a green bird with a red collar and a large tongue. The tongue is broader than in other birds and it makes distinct sounds with it. If you did not see it, you would think it was a real man talking. It greets people of its own accord, saying "What-cheer?" or "Toodle-oo!" It learns other words by teaching. Hence the story of the man who paid a compliment to Caesar by giving him a parrot which had been taught to say: "I, a parrot, am willing to learn the names of others from you. This I learnt by myself to say—Hail Caesar!"
>
> A parrot's beak is so hard that if you throw down the bird from a height on a rock it saves itself by landing on its beak with its mouth tight shut, using the beak as a kind of foundation for the shock. Actually its whole skull is so thick that, if it has to be taught anything, it needs to be admonished with blows. Although it really does try to copy what its teacher is saying, it wants an occasional crack with an iron bar. While young, and up to two years old, it learns

what you point out to it quickly enough, and retains it tenaciously; but after that it begins to be distrait and unteachable. (Cambridge University MS II.4.26, in *Book of Beasts* 112–114)

And from the thirteenth century:

The parrot is only found in India. It is green in colour with a pumice-grey neck and a large tongue which is broader than those of other birds, and which enables it to speak distinct words, so that if you could not see it, you would think that a man was speaking. It will greet you naturally, saying "Ave" or "Chere" (the Latin and Greek words for "Hail"). It learns other words if it is taught them. As the poet says: "Like a parrot I will learn other words from you. I have taught myself to say 'Hail, Caesar'" [Martial xiv.73]. Its beak is so hard that if it falls from a height on to a stone, it presses on it with its beak and uses it as a kind of protection of extraordinary firmness. Its head is so strong that if you have to teach it with blows while it is learning how to speak to men, you have to strike it with an iron rod. For as long as it is young, not much over two years old, it learns what it is taught quickly and remembers it longer; if it is a little older it is forgetful and difficult to teach. (Oxford University MS Bodley 764, in *Bestiary* 129)

These passages offer a literary pastiche that transcends any idea of individual authorship. Both manuscripts clearly refer to Pliny with his tales of parrot corporal punishment and the firmness of the parrot's beak. (This latter story, by the way, misconstrues fact. Parrots do rely heavily upon their beaks for mobility, but not, as Pliny believes, "because of the weakness of [their] feet" [10.58.117]; on the contrary, their legs and beak are strong and together make them such excellent climbers that they are more at home in the forest canopy than on the wing. The specialized use of their beak for climbing is an adaptation to this preferred habitat.) Likewise, both manuscripts cite Martial, who was also referring to Pliny, so the manuscripts already find themselves performing three distinct acts of literary reference: one to Pliny, one to Martial, and one to Pliny again *via* Martial. And that is just the beginning. For instance, these bestiaries also report that parrots learn best when young—an observation that doesn't appear in Pliny but does show up in later writers like Apuleius and Solinus, both of whom also rely upon Pliny. So once again we encounter a wide range of potential acts of literary allusion: to Apuleius, to Solinus, to Pliny through Apuleius, to Pliny through Solinus, to Apuleius through Solinus, to Pliny through Apuleius through Solinus. The number of possible sources and cross-sources, borrowings and cross-borrowings, multiplies at an alarming rate. Nor have we even considered the manuscripts' possible indebtedness to postclassical sources like Isidore of Seville (c. 630). Like the bestiaries after him, Isidore contributes to a corporate text that transcends time and individuals, reencountering and reproducing version after version of itself. Through this rage for allusion and compilation, the medieval bestiary preserves a remarkable lot of classical nature-lore, but it does so by becoming a fabulous genre, in the root sense of the word: a kind of writing more preoccupied with the act of writing, the process of story-telling itself, than with any of its declared subjects.

Yet even as these works preserve the classical heritage, they also introduce novelties. At least two innovations occur in the bestiary entries cited above. One has to do with the parrot's appearance: in Pliny it is described as possessing a "vermilion collar," and other classical writers preserve Pliny's exact diction on this point. But for Isidore, Pliny's vermilion collar has already become a band of pumice-gray; of the two later bestiary manuscripts, in turn, the Cambridge version follows Pliny, while the Bodley version follows Isidore. As it happens, this variation might have some basis in experience. Closely related to the Alexandrine and the rose-ringed parakeet are several other species of Indian parrot, of similar overall appearance, in which the rose-red of the collar-band has been replaced by various patterns of gray and black. These include the Malabar parakeet (*Psittacula columboides* [Forshaw 338–339]), the emerald-collared parakeet (*Psittacula calthorpae* [Forshaw 339]), and perhaps most impressively, the slaty-headed parakeet (*Psittacula himalayana* [Forshaw 330–331]), in which the collar is surmounted by a full head of feathers that could easily be called pumice-gray. As parrots became less plentiful in medieval Europe, a few stray specimens of one of these breeds might have found their way into captivity, thus confusing the record of their appearance. Perhaps (this is a bigger stretch) this confusion might have influenced the visual record too. As medieval painters stylize the birds, they introduce various anatomical variations, including peculiarities of color. In the Holkham Bible Picture Book (early fourteenth century; British Library MS Add. 47682, fol. 10r), for instance, a parrot with green breast and blue-gray head and wings perches on a family tree of Jesus Christ (Figure 3). This image may reflect the medieval understanding of parrots as gray-collared or even gray-headed.

But a second change is far more important: the idea that parrots can speak on their own. Isidore and both of the bestiaries cited above agree on this point: the parrot speaks to people "of its own accord" and "naturally"—although all three works also agree that parrots need human instruction to utter more than a

Figure 3. The Holkham Picture Bible (B.L. MS Add. 47682, fol. 10r), with a family tree of Christ depicting a parrot perched on the far left, above King Solomon (courtesy of the British Library)

simple greeting. In each case the bestiaries cite the same authority for this view: Martial 14.73, whose psittacine narrator claims to have taught itself to say "Hail, Caesar!" It is as if the bestiarists, in their preoccupation with collecting the observations of older authorities, had lost any sense of the difference between such literary genres as natural history and epigram, so that Martial's outrageous flattery can now somehow pass for fact. Likewise, where the speech of Martial's parrot originally marks it as a very clever servant, the bestiaries generalize that parrot's talent to its species as a whole, thereby producing a race of birds that seem less servile than magical. Consider, for instance, these anecdotes from Thomas of Cantimpré's *On the Nature of Things* (1240):

> [The parrot] has from nature a voice with which it greets emperors. It so happened that when Charlemagne was traveling through the deserts of Greece he was met by some parrots, who greeted him, as it were, in the Greek language, saying: Farewell, Emperor. Later events were to prove the truth of this expression, almost like a prophecy, because at that time Charles was only king of France. In the subsequent period he became Emperor of the Holy Roman Empire. There is also a story in the life of Pope Leo, that a certain nobleman had a talking parrot, which he sent to Pope Leo as a present. When the parrot was on its way there and met passers-by, it cried out: I am going to the Pope, I am going to the Pope. And as soon as it reached the presence of the Pope, it cried out: Pope Leo, hail! (5.109)

"At this," the story concludes, "the Pope was rightly delighted, and often afterwards, as a relaxation from the labours of the day, he would talk to the parrot." What pope and parrot said to one another has not been recorded, but the clear implication is that they shared some sort of meaningful conversation on a regular basis.

Of course, the Romans had already imagined parrots as companions of princes or as associates of the sacred. So to transfer the bird's intimacies from emperor to pope may seem a small enough adjustment. Still, the shift has huge implications, for it endows the bird with a specifically Christian sanctity. This, in turn, is enlarged by the parrot's reputation for saying meaningful, even prescient things, as in the anecdote about Charlemagne. Such stories combine and proliferate, generating a medieval view of the parrot as sentient, sacred, and prophetic.

Sometimes this reputation can carry ambiguous moral overtones. In his *On the Nature of Things* (c. 1180), for instance, Alexander Neckam remarks, like Thomas of Cantimpré, that the parrot is "admired of the Pope" (1.36). In fact, Neckam explains the origin of the parrot's common medieval name—"popinjay" in English, "papagallo" in Spanish, "Papagei" in German, and so forth—in this same phrase, *papae gabio* (1.36). Such false etymologies provide a popular way of relating the names of things to their supposed natures. But Neckam declares that the parrot "has great ingenuity and is most prone to falsehood" (1.36) and illustrates this remark with a story:

> In Great Britain there lived a knight of great generosity who owned a parrot and loved it most dearly. The knight, having set out on a journey around the mountains of Gilboa, saw a parrot there, and recalling the one that he had at home, said to it, "Our captive parrot, identical to you, sends greetings." Hearing these words, the bird fell down as if dead. The knight grieved at this, being deceived by the bird's trickery, and, having completed his journey and returned home, brought the tale back with him. The knight's parrot listened attentively to his master's words and then, feigning grief, fell from its perch as if dead, too. The entire household marveled at this sudden onset of grief, but the knight commanded that the bird be placed out in the open, so that it might be revived by fresh air. As soon as the opportunity presented itself, the parrot then flew off maliciously, never to be caught again. The master groaned and the entire household complained loudly that they had been tricked. (1.37; my translation)

Having thus deceived its master, the parrot presumably headed straight back to Mount Gilboa, which was becoming the preferred haunt of parrots in some bestiaries. After the Philistines had killed Saul and Jonathan there, King David prayed that no dew or rain should fall upon the place (2 Samuel 1.21). For whatever reason, the bestiarists had begun to insist that parrots could not stand to touch water (Neckam 1.36; Cantimpré 5.109).[1]

Of course, giving parrots a home in the Holy Land illustrates how well the bestiaries had absorbed these birds into the Christian tradition. Writers like Neckam might view parrots as too clever, but in general they were being reimagined as miraculous and even sacred. For instance, one Jaco (perhaps Jacques de Vitry),[2] the author of a fifteenth-century bestiary called *The Waldensian Physiologus*, explains the birds' supposed intolerance of water by claiming that "they love purity above all other things, so that in the parts of the orient where they live there is neither dew nor rain," and he concludes that "every Christian should observe this nature and quality devoutly so as to preserve his purity and integrity and follow them without sin" (Mayer 403–404; my translation).

While the bestiaries develop this distinctive view of parrots as fabulous birds with sacred associations, something similar happens in the geographical and mythographical writing of the Middle Ages. Pliny's *Natural History* provides a source not only for medieval zoology but also for medieval geography. In Pliny, as in almost every classical writer to deal with the subject, the parrot is an Indian bird. As a result, the earliest European map to include an illustration of a parrot also identifies the bird with India: this is the so-called Ebstorf Map, attributed to Gervase of Tilbury and dating from about 1235 (Figure 4). This map divides the world into the three continents known to scholars in the Middle Ages: Europe, Africa, and Asia. In the process, it also provides numerous richly detailed illustrations of each region's flora and fauna. In a time before cartography as we know it, maps functioned less as an independent mode of representation than as a subspecies of painting, and the Ebstorf Map makes an outstanding case in point. It is blanketed with pictures of birds and beasts, many of them mythical or semimythical, many of them drawn from Pliny, each one supposedly representing a specific region. Africa, for instance, holds not only an elephant, a leopard, and a hyena, but also a mirmicaleon, a cameleopardalis, and a tarandrius. Europe offers us not only lions and tigers and bears, but also an aurochs, a bonacus, and a gryphe. And in Asia, along with chameleons and antdogs and saiga antelopes, we encounter our parrot.

It's right where it should be, on a mountain in India (Figure 5). But India itself may prove hard for a modern reader to recognize. For one thing, it's covered

Figure 4. The Ebstorf Map of the World, c. 1235, from the Miller reproduction (courtesy akg-images, London)

with strange pictures. For another, there's no wedge-shaped peninsula jutting into the expanse of the Indian Ocean, no island of Sri Lanka suspended from the tip like a teardrop. And even worse, India itself isn't where we expect it to be; it occupies the upper right-hand quadrant of the map, roughly where modern maps locate Outer Mongolia.

Part of the problem here involves the principle by which the map is organized. Although medieval navigators and cartographers understood that India lay to the east and south of them, Gervase did not therefore feel obliged to organize his map by the traditional points of the compass. Instead, he oriented it in the root sense of the term: toward the east. As a result, Asia occupies the entire

Figure 5. Detail of the Ebstorf Map, depicting the earliest appearance of parrots on a western map, just below and to the right of Christ's head (courtesy akg-images, London)

upper half of the map, with Europe on the lower left and Africa on the lower right. East is up, south is right, west is down, north is left. And this entire rotation, haphazard as it may seem, is superimposed upon an anatomical model that lends method to the design; the body of Christ, feet at the Pillars of Hercules, head on the eastern horizon, spans the entire earthly creation. The parrot appears immediately below and to the right of Christ's head, its placement there marking not only the geographical location of India on this topsy-turvy map, but also the medieval belief that parrots are created in the earthly paradise.

This idea survived the end of the Middle Ages, appearing in Conrad Gesner's *History of Animals* (1551–1558): "The parrot surpasses other birds in cleverness and understanding, because it has a large head and is brought into India from the true heaven, where it has learned not only how to speak but even how to think" (2P1r; my translation). It also appears in Giovanni Boccaccio's *Bucolicum Carmen* (1370), where the Kingdom of Naples under Queen Joan and Louis of Taranto is a second Eden, for which the world's parrots leave their home on Mount Gilboa:

> Here the bright birds made their nests;
> The parrot, much enraptured with the land,
> Came all the way here from her dried-up fields. (5.43–45)

And in John Mirk's book of homilies *Festial* (c. 1450), we learn that Saint Matthew included among the joys of paradise "popinjays and birds evermore singing, love, and rest, and all manner of comfort" (256; text modernized).

Over the course of the Middle Ages, parrots are identified not just with India, but with biblical and mythical locales as well. Perhaps the most striking example of this trend appears in *Mandeville's Travels* (c. 1357–1366). This notorious book, supposedly written by a peripatetic English knight, became one of the most popular medieval travelogues. Among its extraordinary tales appears an account of the marvelous realm of Prester John, the emperor of India, whose kingdom "is situated on islands because of the great floods that come from Paradise, and that depart all the land in many channels" (195; text modernized). There, we learn, the country is so rich that "they find . . . of popinjays as great plenty as men find here of geese" (196; text modernized). If one proceeds deep into these territories, one arrives at an arid plain between mountains. "And there be many popinjays, that they call *psitakes* in their language. And they speak of their own nature and greet men that go through the deserts and speak to them as fluently as though it were a man. And they that speak well have a large tongue and have five toes upon a foot. And there be also another sort that have but three toes upon a foot, and they speak not or but little, for they do nothing but cry" (198). The idea of five-toed parrots comes, as we've seen, from Apuleius; the idea of inarticulate three-toed specimens would seem, in turn, to be a medieval addition to the record. In both cases, the record is wrong by one digit.

But the most remarkable thing about this account remains the extraordinary gift of speech with which it credits the parrots of India. This gift has long since transcended ideas of mere imitation. Like the bestiarists, Mandeville insists that the birds "speak of their own nature." Moreover, he also gives them a fully human capacity for conversation, a misconception easily traced to its source.

After all, classical writers like Pliny and Apuleius insist that if one heard a parrot speaking without actually seeing it, one would mistake the bird for a human being. As first advanced, this comment applied to the quality of the bird's voice, not its conversation. But taken out of context, it might easily seem to describe much greater abilities. If we add to this the parrot from Martial, who proudly declares itself a self-taught Latinist, we get the medieval parrot, with its miraculous command of language and its fully developed human consciousness.

And if a parrot can speak and think like a man, perhaps it might even once have *been* a man. Boccaccio takes this obvious next step in the chain of association in his influential encyclopedia of classical mythology, the *Genealogia Deorum* (1374). Here, under the entry for "Psittacus," Boccaccio traces the race of parrots back to an ancestry both human and divine:

> Psittacus was the son of Deucalion and Pyrrha. . . . Having been imbued with the learning of his grandfather Prometheus, he traveled among the Ethiopians, where he was held in the greatest veneration after he had passed a long time there. He then prayed to the gods that he be withdrawn from human affairs, and, moved by his prayers, the gods readily transformed him into the bird of his name. I believe the basis of this tale to be the fame of his strength and name, which endured in his perpetual green color; these birds are generally green. There are some people who believe this to be the Psittacus who is said to have been one of the seven wise men. (4.49; my translation)

Boccaccio's reference to the seven wise men marks one more bizarre medieval misunderstanding of classical lore. As it happens, Pittacus of Mytilene (c. 650–570 B.C.) was one of the Seven Sages of Greece. His name differs from the Greek word for parrot (*psittakos*) only in its initial consonant. So it becomes easy enough to confuse the letters pi and psi, which makes possible a tale in which the races of people and parrots become genealogically related.

And the relationship is an exalted one. Parrots don't simply wander into the world as an undistinguished afterthought; they embody a direct line of descent from one of the wisest of the ancients, in a form given to him by the gods as acknowledgment of his eminence. Elsewhere, we have seen parrots casually endowed with prophetic powers, uncanny articulacy, sacred origins, and more. It's tantalizing, and challenging, to imagine the mental environment these stories must have produced, and to imagine how they must have affected the way men and women viewed the few forlorn parakeets that somehow made their way into European aviaries during the Middle Ages. These birds must have seemed a feeble approximation of their wondrous and distant relatives, who spoke like human beings, foretold the future, lived almost forever, and flew freely from branch to branch among the trees of paradise.

Such supposedly factual matters—what manner of bird the parrot might be, where it hailed from, how it behaved, and so forth—affect more imaginative treatments of the bird, both literary and visual. These, too, transform parrots into miraculous and supernatural beings. Hence over the course of the Middle Ages, parrots become a prominent feature of medieval European cultural life.

The parrot is one of the "commonest" birds to appear in medieval illuminated manuscripts (Yapp 75)—so common that paintings of parrots occur in manuscripts of bestiaries that don't mention the bird, such as Hugh of Fouilloy's *Aviarium* (twelfth century). In the process, too, parrots become associated with certain standard visual motifs. For instance, they become a beloved element of marginal decoration, frolicking in vines and knotwork around many a block of calligraphy. And more prominently, they sometimes appear in illustrations of biblical events.

For instance, the early fourteenth-century Queen Mary Psalter (Figure 6; MS Royal 2 B.VII, fol. 2, in the British Library) depicts a parrot amidst God's creation of the animals (Genesis 2.19), where its beauty, exoticism, and association with paradise make it automatically at home. Here God sits enthroned among his new creation, dominating the picture plane, with the beasts of land and air surrounding him in adoration. In typical medieval fashion, the artist has made no effort at establishing perspective or proportion. The animals encircle God in a two-dimensional ring, perhaps suggesting his transcendence of earthly space at the very same time that earth's creatures place him at the center of their being. Both of God's hands are raised in blessing. And the parrot appears immediately at God's right hand, in a scale that makes it larger than the goat just beneath it. In fact, the parrot in this illustration seems to leap from the page with special exuberance. Not only is it rendered in remarkable size and accurate detail, but its coloring, too, makes it more prominent than every other figure in the illustration except God himself.

A parrot appears in another manuscript of the early fourteenth century, this time illustrating a scene not from Genesis but from Revelation (Figure 7; MS Royal 19 B.XV, in the British Library). This image represents the "Summoning of the Birds" at the Apocalypse, from Revelation 19.17–18: "And I saw an angel

Figure 7. Early fourteenth-century illumination depicting the gathering of the birds from Revelation 19.17–18 (B.L. MS Royal 19 B.XV, fol. 37v; courtesy of the British Library)

standing in the sun: and he cried with a loud voice, saying to all the fowls that fly in the midst of heaven, Come and gather yourselves together unto the supper of the great God; That ye may eat the flesh of kings, and the flesh of captains, and the flesh of mighty men, and the flesh of horses, and of them that sit on them, and the flesh of all men, both free and bond, both small and great." This Hitchcockian moment might seem like reasonable payback for the culinary excesses of ancient Rome, but the artist has made the scene sedate and even reassuring. The angel stands to the left, a vague smile playing on his features and his hands half-outstretched, as if he were making a point about the price of livestock. Standing on the ground or perched on the usual stunted tree, a dozen birds and a rabbit regard him with something like mild curiosity. There is a certain amount of incidental scratching and grooming. The entire montage reminds me of one of my undergraduate Milton lectures. On the ground, in the dead middle of the

Figure 6. The Creation of Birds and Beasts, from the Queen Mary Psalter (BL MS Royal 2 B.VII, fol. 2), early fourteenth century (courtesy of the British Museum)

painting, stands another supersized parrot, poised as attentively as an honors student.

Then again, a parrot appears as marginal ornament in another Biblical scene, this time from the London Hours of René of Anjou (Figure 8; MS Egerton 1070, British Library, c. 1410). This volume, illustrated in gorgeous detail by an artist now known as the Egerton Master, contains an extraordinary full-page Adoration of the Magi, with the Virgin Mary seated inside an open animal-stall that has been turned into an impromptu bedroom. As she dandles the infant Christ on her knee, the Magi approach with their gifts. One removes his crown and kneels before the infant, while Joseph greets the second. Behind these figures appear various animals (a bull, an ass, two horses), an attendant, and a bit of landscape. But as much of the page is devoted to marginal decoration as to the miniature itself. The picture is framed by a marvelous tangle of vines and flowers, in which five birds perch at various intervals. Among these, the parrot appears at lower left, directly across from the Virgin Mary.

This placement may not be accidental. As it happens, parrots come to be associated often with the Virgin during the high Middle Ages. The *Oxford English Dictionary* notes that the medieval word "popinjay" is often used "in a eulogistic sense in allusion to the beauty and rarity of the bird" (sb. "Popinjay" 4.a.). The *Middle English Dictionary* is more specific, defining "papejai" first as "a parrot" and then, figuratively, as "a lady, the Virgin Mary" ("Papejai" sb. a.). Given this relationship, the parrot in the Egerton Master's painting is right where it should be.

The relationship itself seems to have grown out of the parrot's reputation as a rare and luxurious creature. In one of his few references to the bird, Chaucer (c. 1343–1400) describes the popinjay as "ful of delicasye" (*Parliament of Fowls* 359), fond of elegance and daintiness. From that point it becomes easy to identify one precious creature devoted to luxury with another of similar disposition. Parrot and lady emerge as birds of a feather, and the Virgin, most precious and delicate lady of all, stands in for all others.

For instance, one anonymous Middle English lyric begins, "I have a bird in a bower, as bright as beryl" (Luria and Hofman 21, text modernized): But before we mistake this poem for a panegyric to a green bird, we learn that the bird's "rode is as rose that red is on ris;/ With lilie-white leres lossum he is" (21), meaning that her complexion is as rosy as red on a twig, and she is lovely, with lily-white cheeks. The poem views woman through bird and vice versa, praising both

Figure 8. The Egerton Master's Adoration of the Magi, c. 1410, with a parrot in the marginal decoration to the lower left (B.L. MS Egerton 1070, fol. 34v; courtesy of the British Library)

in the process. Finally, it becomes evident that the bird-woman in question has more than normal abilities:

"Her face is a flower, fairest under fine linen with celandine and sage, as you yourself see. He who looks upon that sight is brought to bliss. . . . She is the parrot who relieves my suffering when I am in pain" (21, text modernized). As the bird merges into the woman, so the woman metamorphoses into a spiritual comforter. The poem works both as a love-lyric and as a devotional exercise.

Elsewhere, the parrot elides with Mary more directly. Around 1450, the poet John Lydgate could compose a "Balade in Commendation of Our Lady" in which the Virgin is addressed as a "popynjay, plumed in clennesse" (81). And around 1481, Vittore Crivelli painted an exquisite altarpiece whose center panel depicts a Virgin and Child sumptuously enthroned amidst angels in fifteenth-century attire with lutes and rebecs (Figure 9). The scene is one of great splendor, rich in gold and ornate hangings. A parrot appears on the Virgin's right hand (the viewer's lower left), in the same place where it also perches in the Egerton Master's Adoration of the Magi.

As for the bird's broader association with women, we can see it in the Middle English alliterative poem *Susannah* (late fourteenth century), attributed to a shadowy author named Huchon. This is a verse rendition of the tale of Susannah and the elders from Daniel 13 in the Vulgate Bible. There, as Susannah prepares to take the bath that will expose her to the elders' lust, the Vulgate simply remarks that she entered into a garden with two maidens (Daniel 13.15). Using this as his only instigation, Huchon develops an elaborate and luxurious setting for Susannah's bath, replete with "popyniayes prest / Nightyngales vpon nest / Blithe briddis of [th]e best / On blosmes [so briht]" (75–78). By contrast, Thomas Hoccleve's roundel in "A Humorous Praise of his Lady" (c. 1430) offers some peculiarly uncourtly compliments to the damsel in question:

Hir mowth is nothyng scant/ with lippes gray;
Hir chin unnethe [scarcely]/ may be seen at al;
Hir comly body/ shape as a foot-bal:
And shee syngith/ fol lyk a pape Jay. (17–20)

These lines may seem to contradict the idea that parrots represent something precious and miraculous. After all, Hoccleve's mistress would have plenty of cause to complain about his verses, and the obvious reason he compares her voice to a parrot's is to imply that she won't stop talking. The old classical associ-

Figure 9.  Vittore Crivelli, *Enthroned Virgin and Child, with Angels*, c. 1481 (Philadelphia Museum of Art: purchased with the W. P. Wilstach Fund, 1896)

ations of the parrot with satire don't disappear in the Middle Ages, but they do grow gentler. Likewise, despite its flippancy, Hoccleve's inept but amiable joke of a poem preserves the ghost of a more traditional, serious connection between parrots and ladies.

While parrots acquire a feminine cachet in the Middle Ages through their relation to luxury, the birds' association with opulence acquires a masculine cast, too, at certain moments. The obvious case in point is the long-standing tie between parrots on the one hand and kings, emperors, and popes on the other. But in a poem like William Langland's *Piers Plowman* (c. 1370), this tie leads in the direction of social condemnation. There "the pokok and the popeiay with here proude federes/ By-tokneth ryght riche men" (C-text 15.173–174); reigning on earth, they pursue their earthly appetites at the risk of spiritual perdition. Such opinions don't amalgamate well with medieval conventions of deference to authority, so Langland's remains a minority voice. In contrast, Richard de Holland's beast-fable *The Buke of the Howlat* (c. 1450) describes the "Pacocke of pryce" as the pope of birds, while "the proper Pape Iaye, provde in his apparale," becomes the pope's chamberlain (in Amours 90, 125). If the parrot can be identified *with* the rich and powerful, it can also be identified *as* the rich and powerful.

But among the beast-fables of the Middle Ages, parrots figure most prominently in what may be the most noteworthy of the lot: the anonymous Latin verse narrative called *Ecbasis Captivi* (c. 1150). The lion, king of beasts, has fallen ill. The fox undertakes to cure the lion and to govern his realm during his illness. As the lion recovers, the parrot enters the scene, and along with the nightingale and the swan it sings a song to celebrate the "paschal feast of the one who is undergoing resurrection" (quoted in Ziolkowski 186)—that is, the lion, but also, of course, the spiritual king of beasts, Christ. After the birds sing an Easter hymn for the lion, the parrot reads a lengthy sermon on proper spiritual comportment. Finally, the parrot, the lion, the swan, and the leopard disperse to the four points of the compass, to which they will bear the good news of what has happened at the lion's court. The parrot heads, of course, to India, to disseminate the lion's gospel throughout that region (Ziolkowski 189).

Using a parrot as an evangelist in the medieval context grows out of a tradition that endows the bird with miraculous qualities and sacred connotations. Established through a misreading and embellishment of classical literature and philosophy, this tradition expresses a distinctive way of experiencing the world, in a sense beyond the contemporary distinction between fact and fiction.

Yet one part of the medieval world's classical heritage still involved the parrot's status as a vehicle for satire. Medieval writers respond to this part of the classical legacy by crafting an image of the bird as wily, wise, and humorously deceptive. Part trickster, part jester, this model of the parrot's character enhances the bird's traditional role as an object of entertainment while extending still further the remarkable qualities with which it is credited. As John Trevisa observed in his late fourteenth-century translation of Bartholomaeus Anglicus' *On the Properties of Things*, among the animals meant for man's entertainment were "apes and marmusettes and popyngayes" (2:1110). This view assimilates the classical idea of the ridiculous parrot to later views of the bird as an animal savant.

We've already seen an example of this assimilation in Alexander Neckam's tale of the cunning parrots who prove more than a mental match for the English knight. Likewise, a late fourteenth-century French *fabliau* entitled "The Tale of the Lady and the Three Parrots" produces a parrot that outwits both its master and his wife.

The master in this case is an elderly vavasour (the tenant and liege-man of a feudal baron) married to a young and beautiful lady. This vavasour, in typical fabliau fashion, suspects his wife of bestowing her favors upon another man. To test his suspicion, he places three parrots, each in its cage, in a gallery from which they can see the comings and goings at her chamber door. He commands these birds to keep a eye on his wife, they promise to do so faithfully, and he leaves home.

As the vavasour has feared, when he departs, his wife summons her lover, whom her maid, Margot, conducts into her bedroom for a night of illicit love-making. But when the heat of the moment is past and her lover gone, the lady recalls the three parrots in the gallery. Fearing what they might relate to her husband, she sends for Margot, who advises her to speak to the birds in order to find out what they actually know. After all, they could well have slept through the entire business. So off goes the lady to the parrots, whom she interviews one after the other.

Addressing the first parrot, the lady asks, "Can you tell me of anything new you've seen happen here since yesterday? And be sure you tell me the truth." To this the bird replies that it has witnessed the entire sorry spectacle of the evening's entertainment. The lady, thus accused, strangles the parrot, leaving the body in its cage and placing some feathers outside on the floor, to suggest that the cat was the killer. Then proceeding to the next bird, she conducts much the same interview.

When the second parrot has also assured the lady that it knows of her indiscretion, she kills it as well, once again making sure to frame the cat for the crime.

Finally, the lady meets with the third bird. This parrot, we are told, is very wise and of great age, and it says to her:

> O lady kind, with heart so warm,
> Who never did me any harm,
> So must I greatly hold you dear
> And love and honor bring you here.
> Much have I see in my own time,
> Of which have part put out of mind:
> But who wants everything to say
> Often knows for it to pay.
> While he who would have wisdom's art
> Will hold this knowledge in his heart:
> That who speaks not, though hears and sees,
> Gives all great joy but none doth please.

The tale continues: "When the lady heard such a response, she immediately asked if he would say more. The bird replied that he knew nothing else. The lady asked her maiden's advice about what they should do with their popinjay. The maiden responded: 'Surely you must greatly cherish him, for never did parrot make more wise reply'" (Gorra 75–76; translation by Susan Seeley). Finally, the vavasour returns home to a scene of disarray. Two of his parrots lie dead while his wife stands by in great vexation over the cat's misbehavior. Approaching the surviving bird, the lord of the house asks it many questions regarding the events of the previous night; however, the parrot replies only, "But little foresight." The vavasour interprets this as a reference to lack of foresight in protecting the other birds from the cat, and so the tale ends, to the amusement of all, with his blissful ignorance intact.

The most remarkable feature of this narrative is the one that makes its ending possible: the sagacity and eloquence of the third parrot. But the contrast between this bird and its fellows is also noteworthy. If the classical world viewed parrots as miniature, inferior human beings, the first two birds of this tale still retain something of that character. They're extremely talented speakers, to be sure, but nonetheless their behavior remains confined to the role of the obliging servant;

for them, as much as for the parrot of Aesop's fable about the house-ferret, to serve well is to please well. So when required to displease either their master or their mistress, they naturally respond with confusion. The third bird, in contrast, is made of sterner stuff. Understanding that its principal obligation is to serve itself, it contrives to satisfy both human parties without fully pleasing either. As a result, this bird no longer remains wholly inferior to its human companions. Instead, it manipulates both husband and wife and inaugurates, in the process, a long tradition of tales about human beings who are outwitted by parrots—most of them not nearly as clever as this one. Where the wife of the tale emerges as a tart and the vavasour as a cuckold, the parrot achieves a reputation for wisdom.

Moreover, this wisdom is so great as no longer to require the testimony of eloquence. The first two parrots make their claim to distinction by their tongues; they understand and obey their master's commands, engage in elaborate impromptu conversations, and manage the entire business in verse as well. (This last achievement exceeds both the vavasour and his lady, by the way.) But the third parrot not only matches its companions in all of these ways; it has also mastered the virtues of silence, and these, in the end, save its life. This bird proclaims its marvelous nature less by speech than by understanding when to keep its beak shut. Apparently the parrot's reputation for cunning has become so well established as no longer to need verbal confirmation.

Yet verbal confirmation remains abundant in medieval literature. Take, for instance, *The Marvels of Rigomer*, a French Arthurian romance composed in the late twelfth century by a poet identified only as Jehan. Late in this narrative King Arthur's nephew, Sir Gawain, traveling to a tournament at the enchanted castle of Rigomer, finds himself in the company of an Irish knight and a youthful archer. As they come to a fork in their road, a bird appears and sings "so very sweetly that nowhere else in the whole wide world could a song be heard that could match its beauty" (248). The young archer, incensed at the bird, attempts to shoot it with an arrow, which it easily dodges. We then learn its species: "Because the parrot was so valiant, another of its traits became apparent. The Lord God had granted it, as gift and grace, the power to understand and use human speech in the same way as God had caused it to be taught. The bird was so wise that from there to the city of Sens, no other beast or bird could be found as wise. This bird was even able to speak in several tongues" (249).

The parrot scolds the youth for trying to kill it, declaring that "I serve the most skillful, best knight of might and strength there ever was or will be: Gawain,

King Arthur's nephew, the best knight to ever carry a lance, bevore, pennon, or mace" (249). The bird then goes on to identify itself by name as Willeris, the servant of an incomparably fine lady whose identity remains hidden and who, in turn, has sent Willeris to Gawain to conduct him to the castle of Rigomer. When Gawain finally reaches his destination, the lady's identity is disclosed; there Gawain comes upon a splendid tent, constructed of silver and silk and gold, which has been pitched by his own mistress, Lorie. Atop a golden eagle that adorns the highest point of the entire pavilion perches Willeris, who sings a song of unutterable sweetness. The trickster-bird that can speak in tongues and outwit an irate archer folds into the parrot associated with women and delicacy.

Then again, *The Knight of the Parrot* makes its title bird into a major character. This anonymous French romance of the fifteenth century relates the career of young King Arthur, who defeats a tyrannical knight and is rewarded for his pains with a parrot. This, "the best bird in all the world who sings the sweet, pleasant song of love and converses cleverly about matters which warm the hearts of men and women" (5), along with a dwarf who serves as its attendant, accompanies Arthur throughout his adventures. Indeed, once the king and the bird meet, Arthur undergoes a change of identity, appearing thenceforth in the narrative as the Knight of the Parrot.

Although the bird itself has no name in this poem, it's endowed not only with personality, but also with a variety of miraculous gifts. These once more include marvelous eloquence, coupled here with ravishing powers of song. Likewise, the bird is associated with prophecy and enchantment from the very first. For instance, when it meets Arthur it carries on as follows:

> No one can possibly describe to you the noise the parrot made; for he told the dwarf to lead him to the highest place he could, and he cried out: "Dwarf, my dwarf, bring me to see the best knight in the whole world! It is he about whom Merlin spoke so much in his prophecy. . . . Bring me quickly to him, for he has won me." When the parrot came near the king, he began to relate sweetly all the events which had come to pass from the time of Merlin up to the present moment in such a way that the king and the others there marveled greatly about all he said. (10)

Moreover, when Arthur has met the heroine of the poem, a beautiful woman called only the Lady with Blonde Hair, the bird realizes that Arthur is falling in love and does its bit to help him out:

> Now while they [Arthur and the lady] were conversing thus, the parrot who had well understood what they were saying—for no one might ever move his lips so

cleverly that he could not learn what was being said—and so I tell you that the parrot completely understood his lord's intention, like one who is used to manners and fine ways; and so he began to sing a lay of love so sweetly, that the lady broke off speaking to the knight to listen and note in her heart what the parrot was recounting. (23)

Partly as a result of such attentions, Arthur and the Lady with Blonde Hair become lovers. Like Willeris in *The Marvels of Rigomer*, the parrot here is identified with "manners and fine ways." As with Willeris again, this association lends the bird an affinity for the ladies. And like Willeris once more, this parrot has a command of language that not only equals but surpasses the human. Understanding its master's intentions by perfect sympathy, it sings a song that mesmerizes the Lady with Blonde Hair into erotic receptiveness. The bird, in short, is a marvel.

Yet marvelous as it is, it also serves as comic relief. In a rare discussion of *The Knight of the Parrot*, Lori Walters notes that the title-bird occasionally drops out of its miraculous character into "behavior [that is] inappropriate or comic" (335). For instance, when Arthur joins battle with a particularly fierce opponent, the parrot's attendant dwarf runs for cover, leaving his charge in its cage to fend for itself. But this is no bird to suffer in silence: "Ha, dwarf, do not leave me here to die!" Whatever prophecies the parrot may have learned from Merlin, it still loses its composure in the heat of battle. And when Arthur has prevailed and the dwarf returns to duty in disgrace, the bird throws a tantrum:

As soon as the knight had dismounted, the dwarf ran to serve the parrot, just as he was accustomed to, but the parrot did not want anything to do with him or his service, and told him: "Flee from here, you bad, cowardly dwarf, for you are not in the least worthy to touch me, nor do I desire to be served by you any longer." He cried this aloud and shouted it about again and again so that all those, both big and small, who heard it, spoke about nothing else. . . . So much did he cry these words that the knight finally heard him and ordered a young squire to bring the parrot to him, which was done immediately. (20)

In other words, this parrot is both extraordinary and annoying, and this strange combination typifies the role of parrots in medieval comedy and satire as a whole. Rarely do they cease to be wondrous creatures, endowed with precious and prodigious gifts. But in the comic mode they can also appear selfish and guileful, without any sense that these latter qualities might be at odds with the former.

In this way the conventional parrot of ancient satire is assimilated to the marvelous bird of medieval myth. Beginning in the Renaissance, the parrot of satire and ridicule will return in force. For the time being, however, mystery and marvel remain in the ascendant.

Finally, beyond poetry and painting, bestiaries and travelogues, the Middle Ages contributed to the growth of parrot culture in another medium altogether: textile and costume design.

In ancient Rome, of course, parrots had already supplied subject-matter for visual artists in a variety of genres. But during the Middle Ages, for the first time, we encounter evidence that the birds of India have metamorphosed into a fashion statement as well. Given their medieval association with luxury, femininity, and the exotic, this transformation must have been inevitable. And while it has left its mark upon fabric and clothing design even to the present day, much separates the parrot-theme apparel and jewelry of the Middle Ages from their twenty-first century descendants.

For one thing, the parrots of medieval fashion function as a marker of social eminence, not as an element of mass culture. They figure in the richest of fabrics and the most splendid of ceremonial garments. They seem far graver, far more severe, than their offspring in the realm of twenty-first-century costume kitsch. Nowadays, by contrast, the very idea of parrot *gravitas* seems absurd. But *gravitas* is just what we get in *The Wars of Alexander*, an English alliterative romance of the early fifteenth century. There, Queen Candace of Prasiaca pledges obedience to Alexander by presenting him with "a rich treasure, a gem-encrusted crown polished and engraved with pelicans and popinjays whose crests and circlets are all of fine pearl" (5249–5256; my translation). In this poem, at least, it's not only right for the world's greatest conqueror to be greeted by parrots; he should accessorize with them as well. This opinion is shared by the anonymous author of *Sir Gawain and the Green Knight* (c. 1375–1400), which describes its title hero donning a magnificent battle-helmet "with birds on its seams, such as popinjays painted between periwinkles" (605–611; my translation). In the context of the poem, this finery comprises a supreme achievement of the armorer's craft.

Beyond the confines of verse romance, the decorative use of parrots in fabric and clothing extended throughout the more affluent ranks of medieval society. Account books and wills list items like "two coverlets in wrought work with popinjays" and "one bed for trussing, of red, embroidered with a circle, and inside the circle a popinjay." Prominent among such records are references to church

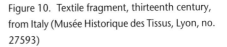

Figure 10. Textile fragment, thirteenth century, from Italy (Musée Historique des Tissus, Lyon, no. 27593)

vestments and related articles, such as a chasuble with a "grunde of White Sylke wt Popynjays of gold" ("Churchwardens' Accounts" 7–14:16:19), and the "white vestment, embroidered with a circle, and, inside the circle, popinjayes" which the priest Henry Snayth dedicated to the high altar at York Minster on February 5, 1380 (Surtees Society 4:111; my translation). These items bespeak yet another bond between parrots and sacred ritual in the Middle Ages.

Moreover, in the fragments of medieval fabric that still survive, doubled parrots abound, comprising a standard motif of medieval textile manufacture. A fragment of Italian taffeta dating from the thirteenth century offers a nice example of this material (Figure 10). The elaborate weave of gold and olive-green depicts a series of paired beasts and floral patterns, with twin parrots, back to back, regarding each other in calm and contemplative fashion. Doubled dragons appear between the pairs of parrots. Together, these beasts give the fabric a distinctly fabulous air, drawn straight from a bestiary or romance. Enough similar samples of textiles survive to suggest the popularity of such designs and the elegance they must have embodied for medieval sensibilities.

Over the years my friends and family have accommodated my mania for parrots by offering me numerous psittacine birthday or Christmas gifts. I have received my share of parrot-theme garments: parrot-festooned ties, parrot-studded socks, parrot-embossed handkerchiefs. But my favorite is a Hawaiian shirt, a gift from my sister, embellished with electric-green tropical foliage and huge, belligerent-looking macaws. It makes you want to close your eyes.

That's the point. In the contemporary fashion vocabulary, parrots lend themselves more or less automatically to such bad taste; they become the perfect embodiment of genial, garish vulgarity. But nothing could be less true of the Middle Ages, and this fact speaks volumes about the changes wrought in western society by five hundred years of colonialism, industrialism, and consumer culture. By 1492, those changes are poised to begin.

# Chapter 3

# *Return of the Parrots*

From a parrot's-eye-view, at least, the Middle Ages stand as the high point of western civilization. People didn't bother them much, tended to view them with reverence and amazement, and credited them with powers far beyond any attributed to them before or since. Recently, scholars have enjoyed challenging the traditional distinction between medieval and Renaissance society, but for anyone writing a cultural history of parrots in the West, this distinction remains a stark one indeed. At the end of the fifteenth century, a series of events begins to render these birds less mysterious, less wonderful, and more available in Europe than ever before. As a result, Roman associations of the parrot with inferior humanity return with a vengeance.

When Christopher Columbus sailed west from Palos across the Atlantic Ocean on his first voyage to the New World, he was in search of gold, silver, precious stones, spices, and silks. Instead, he found parrots. On October 13, 1492, within a day of making his first landfall in the Caribbean, he notes in his log that "other than parrots, I have seen no beast of any kind on this island" (77). But he had already seen people. The inhabitants of the island had rowed out to the Spanish ships that day, in dugout canoes, bearing with them items to trade: "balls of spun cotton, spears, and parrots" (77). On October 17, having put in at the Bahamas, on Long Island, which he named Fernandina, Columbus again remarks that he has "seen no land animals of any sort, except parrots and lizards" (84). Four days later, he adds, "The flocks of parrots that darken the sun and the large and small birds of so many species are so different from our own that it is a wonder" (89).

Columbus must have had reason to wonder at them. My reaction was much the same in 1987, when, on a visit to Mayan ruins in Yucatan, I saw my first flock of Amazon parrots in the wild. Toward sunset, when they return to their nests to roost for the night, I caught myself gazing idly as a great mass of black birds rose up in the distance out of the forest canopy. At first they seemed unremarkable, but as they headed toward me my ears filled with an immense, metallic shrieking. Then, coming nearer, they passed directly across my field of vision, and the entire flock pivoted in mid-flight. At just that moment, catching the sun's declining rays, the mass of birds flashed into a blaze of emerald green. I doubt I shall ever forget that sight, but it would be nothing compared to what must have met Columbus's eyes, five hundred years ago.

Columbus was by no means the only European to note the New World's abundant bird life. The Jesuit missionary José de Acosta (1540–1600) remarks that "There are . . . at the Indies great numbers of Parrots, especially upon the Andes of Peru, and in the Ilands of Port Ricco, and Saint Dominique, where they flie by flocks, as Pidgeons do here" (Purchas 15:130). Nor are these birds the exclusive property of the New World; Sir Richard Hawkins, riding off the coast of West Africa in 1593, remarks that "In [these parts] also are store of . . . Parrots, but of colour different to those of the West Indies; for they are of a russet or gray colour and great speakers" (Purchas 17:72). He is referring, of course, to the African gray parrot (*Psittacus erithacus*), the most brilliant, articulate, and neurotic of all such birds. This species first entered Western awareness in 1402, when the French took possession of the Canary Islands, and by the middle of the fifteenth century, as the Portuguese trade with West Africa expanded, they began to make their way into Europe.

Even so, parrots figure in the records of the Age of Exploration mostly as New World novelties. At first, their presence in America bred understandable confusion; after all, these birds had been associated with India from the time of Aristotle. Noting Columbus's discovery of them on his first voyage, the historian Peter Martyr thus draws the obvious, and wrong, inference: "Albeit the opinion of Christophorus Colonus (who affirmeth these islandes [the West Indies] to be parte of *India*) dothe not in all poyntes agree with the iudgement of auncient wryters . . . , yet the Popingiaies and many other thynges brought from thence, doo declare that these Ilandes sauoure somwhat of *India*, eyther beynge nere unto it, or elles of the same nature" (A3v). This misconception did not long survive, however, and soon parrots became one of the signature beasts of the New World. When Pedro Cabral discovered Brazil in 1500, he christened this "new land . . . that of the parrots [*papaga*], because some are found there which are an arm and a half in length, of various colors" (120). For the time being this name stuck, so that René Laudonnière, writing in 1587, could declare of the Portuguese colony in South America, "This Countrey is named by some, the land of Bresill, and the lande of Parots" (Hakluyt 8:449).

With the inevitable eye for profit, European adventurers and travel writers began to size up the possible value of the exotic birds they encountered, and as they did so, western society briefly flirted once more with the idea of having them for dinner. Martyr's *Decades of the New World*, for instance, mentions Caribbean islanders who raise parrots for the table "as we bring up capons and hennes" (B2r). Martin Fernandez de Enciso (1470–1528) describes the New World as containing numerous "bestes of good mete and savour," including "grete plentie of foules as popingais of dyvers sortes, gret partriches, pecockys, duckys and herings and dyvers other straunge birds" (153). Touring the Aztec capital Tenochtitlan (Mexico City) in 1520, Hernán Cortés saw parrots for sale as food (1:257). And in 1542, while leading the exploration party that would discover the Amazon River, Francisco de Orellana encountered South American natives who gave him "much food, consisting of turtles and parrots in abundance" (Heaton 180). Later, Orellana and his followers came upon a native village where, "praised be Our Lord, there was no lack of [food], because there were many turtles . . . and turkeys and parrots" (Heaton 210). If anything, the gustatory zeal of Orellana's men came to exceed that of the local Indians. One early account of his expedition mentions an encounter with "'guacamayos,' which are parrots of the large sort . . . which the Indians are accustomed to having in their houses for the pleasure they get out of them and [also] in order to pluck their feathers and put these to some use." But "as for us," the narrative goes on, "we wanted them for the pot" (Heaton 415). This seems the enthusiasm of starving men. In similar *extremis*, the crew of Sir John Hawkins's difficult 1567–68 Indies expedition lament the necessity of eating "cats and dogs, mice, rats, parrats, and munkies" (Hakluyt 9:408), and theirs is surely the prevailing view. After the fall of the Roman Empire, Europe never again embraced the parrot for its culinary potential.

Why not? In this case, after all, there is historical precedent for parrot-eating, both from ancient Rome and from the Native Americans themselves. Many New World foodstuffs did gain rapid popularity in Europe; by 1541, for instance, the turkey was so beloved in England that Archbishop Thomas Cranmer "had to forbid his clergy to serve more than one such bird at a banquet" (Stresemann 24). And, if anything, dining had grown into a still more lavish forum for conspicuous consumption than it had been in ancient times. So one might expect the gastronomic excesses of classical Rome to repeat themselves. But they don't.

In general, Renaissance writers who mention psittacophagy simply note that they or somebody else ate the birds, or that somebody might eat the birds. There is no consideration of reasons for and against doing so, and in the absence of any such remarks, all I can offer is a hypothesis: I believe that the earliest accounts of New World exploration incidentally associate parrots and parrot-eating with cannibalism, so that psittacophagy silently begins to elicit the same revulsion as does anthropophagy. Consider, for instance, one of the earliest and most influential accounts of New World cannibalism, Peter Martyr's description of Columbus's second voyage. Upon reaching the island of Guadeloupe, Martyr reports, Columbus sent a landing party ashore, with disturbing results:

> Having entered [the natives'] homes, they found vessels of every sort, earthenware pots, jars, goblets, and other things of every sort, not much different from our own; and in a large cooking vessel they discovered boiled human flesh along with that of parrots and geese, and other body-parts skewered on spits. And in searching through the hiding-places of other homes, they found the bones of human arms and legs carefully preserved, to be fashioned into the points of arrows; for they make these out of bone, because they have no iron. (Martyr, *De Orbe* 1.2, sig. A6v; my translation)

This isn't the only story of American exploration to couple parrot-eating with cannibalism. Indeed, as signature products of the New World, parrots and cannibals might seem irresistibly connected, with the result that the horror inspired by the latter might transfer, in culinary contexts, to the former as well.

Whether or not this was so, one thing remains certain: European adventurers were interested in finding some use for the parrots they encountered in their travels. And even if the birds' culinary prospects proved limited, one could do other things with them. For instance, their feathers were objects of great beauty and therefore of potential decorative value. Again, Native American practices lent this idea precedent; Amerigo Vespucci records early on that the native tribes' "riches consist" in part "of variegated birds' feathers," and that one such tribe presented him with "feathers of very great value, . . . and . . . numberless parrots of different colors" (Waldseemuller 98, 109). Exploring Argentina from 1534 to 1554, Ulrich Schmidel observes that among the natives there, "The men have a little hole in their nose, into the which, for ornament, they put a Parrats feather" (Purchas 17:12–13). André Thevet writes that the inhabitants of Brazil greatly esteem "a kinde of Parats," from which, "three or foure times a yeare, they plucke their fethers for to make hats, garnish bucklers, swordes of woode, and other things requisite" (L3r). John Chilton (1572) reports that the people of Chiapas "pay their tribute to the king [of Spain] all in Cotton wooll and Feathers" (Hakluyt 9:369). Acosta remarks that "In new Spaine there are abundance of birds with excellent feathers, . . . as wee may see by the images of Feathers they bring from thence, [which] have so lively and pleasing a regard, as the Painter cannot exceed it with his pencill and colours" (Purchas 15:135).

Again, however, the decorative use of parrot feathers proves of limited appeal. In a sense it leaves an indirect mark on the rich tradition of European bird painting, of which more later. After all, as Acosta suggests, parrots offer an irresistible appeal to the eye. But in the long run, visual artists find them more congenial as subject-matter than as medium.

Still, parrots remain quite wonderful in and of themselves. As marvelous beasts, they seem to invite human acquisition, and it is as pets, in the end, that they take their definitive place in western culture. Once more, this practice draws precedent from the New World as much as from the Old. Francisco de Orellana had encountered pet parrots among the natives of the Amazon Basin. André Thevet, too, notes that "The *Americans* keepe all these birdes [i.e., parrots] in their lodgings" (L3v), and then goes on to describe how "the women . . . nourishe some, the which they sette suche store by, that they call them their friends. Furthermore our *Americanes* do learne these birdes in their language to aske for meale made of rootes. But they teache them most commonly to say and profer, that they must goe a warfare against their enemies, for to take them, and for to eate them, and other things" (L3v). These grisly sentiments then lead into the subject of diet: "There is a multitude of other Popengayes that are in the wooddes, of the which they kill a great many with their arowes for to eate" (L3v). Somehow it seems right that a race dedicated to cannibalism should eat both human beings and parrots. But the parrots one eats remain "other" than the parrots one raises as "friends." In a society of pet owners, psittacophagy, like cannibalism, entails fine but crucial distinctions.

As for America's European explorers, they began collecting live parrots almost before they did anything else. Parrots have the distinction—or misfortune, depending on how you look at it—of being the first animal to be exported from the New World to the Old. According to Peter Martyr, Columbus on his first voyage carried back to Spain "fortie" parrots "of moste liuely and delectable coloures" (A3v); on his second voyage he returned with even more. Other explorers followed suit, electrifying European spectators with a parade of strange, colorful birds from far away. The Florentine banker Bartolomeo Marchioni found himself in Lisbon in 1501, when Cabral returned in triumph from his discovery of Brazil. That June, he wrote back excitedly to Florence with news of the voyage, remarking, among other things, that Cabral had "brought back two parrots which are an arm [*gomito*] and a half long which are more than an arm and a half of ours. They are marvellous things" (Cabral 148). And marvelous they were. As late as 1578 the great naturalist Ulysse Aldrovandi (1522–1605) could respond with wonder and delight when he first saw live macaws at the court of Duke William of Mantua (Stresemann 25).

In the meantime, a growing demand for New World parrots had developed among the wealthy and privileged of European society. Leading the way, of course, was the nobility. Private menageries and aviaries had already become a feature of courtly life in the Middle Ages, but these collections achieved a whole new level of diversity with the discovery of the New World. King Manuel I of Portugal (c. 1469–1521), governing a realm at the forefront of New World exploration, was ideally situated to cultivate such interests. By 1514, he could offer the new Pope Leo X an inaugural gift drawn from his personal zoo and including "numerous parrots" (Bedini 28). These birds were carried through the city of Rome in a public procession reminiscent of the one produced for Ptolemy II, 1,800 years earlier, in Alexandria (Bedini 48). As for the pope, his predecessors had long been parrot-addled. In 1418 Pope Martin V had employed two servants as traveling attendants for the papal parrot, and half a century later, in 1462, Pope Pius II was still authorizing payments to a "custodian of the parrot" (qtd. in Bedini 82). Leo, in turn, maintained an extravagant papal menagerie in the Vatican, where he kept, among other things, "a multitude of parrots, of diverse colouring" (qtd. in Bedini 84). Likewise, England's Henry VIII (1509–1547) owned a pet parrot of whose exploits we will hear more presently. His distant heir Charles II (1660–1685) established an aviary for exotic birds in St. James's Park, a structure whose presence is still recalled by the name of nearby Birdcage Walk (Church 8). And Charles's mistress Frances Stuart, duchess of Richmond and Lennox (1647–1702), reputedly owned a pet African gray parrot for forty-odd years (Hartmann 248). When she died, the bird followed suit four days later. It was stuffed and still stands next to an effigy of its mistress in the Undercroft Museum of Westminster Abbey, where it is accounted the oldest stuffed bird in the realm (Figure 11).

Ironically, the aristocratic bird collections of Renaissance Europe may have

Figure 11. Stuffed African gray parrot once belonging to Frances Stuart, duchess of Richmond and Lennox (courtesy of the Undercroft Museum, Westminster Abbey. Copyright Dean and Chapter of Westminster)

drawn some of their energy from Native American precedent. Bernal Díaz (1492–1584) writes that when Cortés entered Tenochtitlan, he found a royal zoo containing birds that defied enumeration, including "parrots of many different colours, and . . . so many of them that I forget their names" (212). Cortés himself, in a letter to Holy Roman Emperor Charles V, declared of the Aztec zoo that "there is nothing comparable with [it] in Spain" (1:265). In his brutal campaign to subdue the Aztecs and surrounding tribes, Cortés destroyed this collection, regarding it as a key to demoralizing the native peoples. At the same time, the menageries of European rulers were on the increase.

But parrots did not long remain the special property of European aristocrats. As the number of these birds steadily grew in the Old World, merchants and other prosperous citizens began to acquire them too. By 1564, the English scholar John Caius could write to the naturalist Conrad Gesner that he was familiar with "many kinds of Parrots" in England (qtd. in Stresemann 25). According to historian Keith Thomas, "commercial bird-dealers" first appeared in England "in Tudor times, and in the late seventeenth century there was a large London market in singing-birds, some caught at home by professional bird-catchers, others exotics imported from the tropics" (111). Parrots were prominent among the exotics, as illustrated by an archaeological dig conducted between 1989 and 1991 in Norwich's Castle Mall area. There, as excavators sifted through a pile of seventeenth-century garbage, they came across two parrot bones, the first such relics to emerge from an English historical site (Shepard). Norwich had been the largest city in medieval England, but by the 1600s its population ran a distant second to that of London, where far more by way of exotica could have been found.

And England itself was, if anything, a backwater in the sixteenth and seventeenth centuries. A second-rate European power and a latecomer in the race to the New World, it could not begin to rival nations like Spain and Portugal in collecting foreign marvels. By 1519, Diogo Velho da Chancellaria described Lisbon as a place where "Monsters and talking birds,/Porcelains, diamonds—/All now are quite common" (qtd. in Bedini 161). By 1526, in his *General and Natural History of the Indies*, Gonzalo Fernandez de Oviedo does not include parrots in his discussion of the New World's fauna. His reason for this oversight is simple: "Since so many species have been carried to Spain, it is hardly worth while to take time to describe them here" (65). In this dismissive remark, we can detect an echo of the ennui to which Arrian had given voice more than a thousand years earlier. But where Arrian's attitude arose from almost five centuries of classical contact with the parrots of India, Oviedo's emerges after barely thirty years of Spanish presence in America. Parrots have already been assimilated into Renaissance society to a degree that the ancients could not have imagined. In a way, they have already ceased to be exotic birds.

We can get a graphic sense of this assimilation by considering two famous maps of the New World, one drawn in 1502, the other sixty years later. The first is a Portuguese manuscript map called the Cantino Planisphere after its maker, Alberto Cantino (Figures 12, 13). Drafted in the first flush of excitement following Columbus's return from the West Indies, it preserves the pictorial quality of medieval mapmaking, and it populates both Africa and America with indigenous species. In both cases, the species in question are parrots, and Cantino has carefully noted the difference between the Senegals and African grays of the Old World and the Amazons and macaws of the New. Painted in brilliant hues of red, blue, yellow, and green, these birds regard each other across the intervening space of the Atlantic Ocean, marking their continents with their distinctive presence.

By 1562, however, things had changed a great deal. Diego Gutierrez's New

Figure 12. Details from the Cantino Planisphere, depicting parrots in South America and West Africa, respectively (Biblioteca Estense, Modena—Su concessione del Ministero per i Beni e le Attivà Culturali)

Figure 13. Detail from the 1562 New World map of Diego Gutierrez, depicting giants in Patagonia (Library of Congress, Washington, D.C.)

World map of that year, drawn for King Philip II of Spain and engraved by Hieronymus Cock, continues to embellish the Americas with pictures of indigenous marvels. In Patagonia, for instance, there are giants, while in Brazil a band of cannibals has a companion for dinner (Figures 13, 14). But America's parrots have now been shunted to the margins of the map; their species indeterminate, they appear only in the lower left-hand corner, decorating Gutierrez's colophon (Figure 15). In subsequent maps, they disappear altogether.

In short, from 1492 onward, the parrots of America enter Europe as miracles and gradually degenerate into trifles, just as their Indian cousins had done before them in the Roman Empire. But this time the sheer scale of the degeneration makes it both more emphatic and less reversible.

Of course, even rapid social change takes time and occurs unevenly across broad areas, and this sudden decline in the cultural stock of parrots is no exception. As the sixteenth century progresses, old habits of mind survive in various ways, but bit by bit they either disappear or mutate into unrecognizable forms. As a result,

Figure 14. Detail from the 1562 New World map of Diego Gutierrez, depicting cannibals in Brazil (Library of Congress, Washington, D.C.)

when we encounter parrots in the Enlightenment we find ourselves dealing, in a sense, with an entirely new kind of bird.

The English language itself affords a good example of this shift, for in sixteenth-century English, even the word for parrots begins to change. The change is twofold, affecting both vocabulary and usage. The Middle English noun *popinjay* gradually loses currency, to be replaced by the modern English *parrot*. The new word's origin remains unclear. The *Oxford English Dictionary* conjectures it may derive from the French "*Perrot*: a man's proper name, being a diminutive or derivative of Pierre," and if this were the case, it would mark an ominous return to the old classical association between parrots and inferior people.[1] But what remains certain is that the noun *parrot* comes into usage in the early sixteenth century (c. 1525, according to the *OED*), and that over the next century it steadily muscles the word "popinjay" into archaism. If the parrots of the Enlightenment are in effect new birds, they need a new name. In English, at least, they get one.

The shift in usage is best illustrated by the fate of the older name. After losing currency in its primary sense, as a word for the parrot, *popinjay* survives as a

TROPICVS CAPRICORNI

MARE MAGELLANICVM
SIVE PACIFICVM

REGIO PATALIS

Figure 15. Colophon from the 1562 New World map of Diego Gutierrez, adorned with parrots (Library of Congress, Washington, D.C.)

metaphorical term referring to people. One sees it in this form even today, although the word is rarely heard in speech. And it's no compliment; the *OED* defines this sense of "popinjay" as "a type of vanity or empty conceit." Yet this derogatory usage could not be farther from the original medieval sense of "popinjay" as a metaphor, which was reverent and positive. In effect, the newer meaning replaces the older at the same time that *parrot* replaces *popinjay* as a name for birds. In the 1450s, Lydgate referred to the Virgin Mary as a "popynjay, plumed in clennesse," but by 1528 William Tyndale ridiculed illiterate Catholic priests who "play the popengay with Credo say ye: volo saye ye and baptismum saye ye" (89b).

This same derogatory usage attaches to the new noun *parrot*, too. By 1596 the prolific Elizabethan writer Thomas Nashe, attacking his archenemy, the scholar Gabriel Harvey, could complain that Harvey "would do nothing but crake and parret it in Print, in how many Noble-mens fauours he was" (3:136). In 1590,

Nashe had already published a satirical pamphlet entitled *An Almond for a Parrot*, which has nothing to do with almonds or parrots, but a great deal to do with ridiculing Puritans. And by 1669, a book published in London entitled *Psittacorum regio, the land of parrots, or, The she-lands*, pretends to describe a newly discovered country called "the *She-lands*, or *Womandecoia*," which "lyeth in that part of the Southern continent . . . called *Psittacorum Regio*, the *Land of Parrots*" (63).[2] This region is actually inhabited not by parrots, however, but by mindless women who reverse the order of nature by indulging their every whim and making "men . . . their drudges, to wash, wipe, scoure, and sweep" (83). In short, by the late seventeenth century the parrot has become a proverbial figure not for the marvelous and luxurious and sacred, but for the vacuous and loud and vulgar.

In fact, the older, reverential view of the parrot largely seems to disappear along with the Catholic consensus of the late Middle Ages. In its stead emerges a new kind of bird, associated with America rather than India, with religious conflict rather than harmony, and with idiots rather than kings (not that these last terms need exclude each other). And this new bird also has a preferred literary genre. Abandoning the lyrics and romances of an earlier age, it appears again and again in satirical verse, prose, and drama, often in connection with religious controversy, with race- or class-based ridicule, or with misogynist invective. Ironically, this last fact preserves one bit of contact with the medieval parrot, which was also often associated with women. But in the new order of things, neither birds nor women benefit from the association.

Of these new satirical attachments, the one to religious controversy crops up earliest, in ways that still at first preserve the parrot's wondrous medieval qualities. Sir David Lindsay's *The Testament, and Complaynt, of Our Souerane Lordis Papyngo* (1530) supplies a case in point. This poem is written mostly in the voice of a parrot, belonging to King James V of Scotland, that has suffered a nasty fall from a high tree-branch. Attracted by the parrot's dying words, a magpie, a raven, and a kite gather round and announce themselves as functionaries of the Catholic church: a canon regular, a black monk, and a holy friar, respectively. In their priestly capacity, they offer spiritual solace to the dying parrot, but the parrot responds with an indictment of their covetous and lecherous ways. At last, seeing no other help to be had, the parrot asks them to administer its last testament, in which it bequeaths its possessions generously to others: its green coat to the owl, its beak to the pelican, its eloquence to the goose, its heart to King James, and so forth. The three other birds promise to do as asked, but as soon as the parrot gives up its ghost, they glut themselves on the bird's carcass until nothing but the heart remains. The magpie then declares that it will carry this to the king, but before it can do so, the kite snatches the heart away and flies off, with magpie and raven in hot pursuit.

In many ways, not least of all its treatment of parrots, this poem serves as a holdover from the Middle Ages. The bird of Lindsay's title is still associated with royalty. It remains fabulously articulate. It is wise in the ways of the church, seeing through and denouncing the holy pretenses of the other three birds. And it is associated with holiness itself: a "pure Papingo" (1074, 1130) whose cannibalistic death evokes the Eucharist. But the parrot is also a vehicle for bitter religious invective, and it becomes the dupe of the poem, dying pathetically and giving itself into the clutches of ravenous thieves that consume it whole. I'm tempted to read this death as a metaphor for the demise of the medieval parrot as a cultural stereotype.

Certainly that stereotype has begun to change in John Skelton's *Speke, Parrot* (c. 1525). This, another verse satire on church matters, casts itself as a monologue by the parrot of the title, and the poem develops as a bizarre combination of political lampoon, proverbial wisdom, and sheer tomfoolery. Again, the bird introduces itself through medieval associations with myth and riches and royalty:

My name is Parrot, a byrd of paradyse,
    By nature devysed of a wondrous kynde,
Dyentely dyeted with dyuers dylycate spyce,
    Tyl Euphrates, that flode, dryueth me into Inde;
    Where men of that country by fortune me fynd.
   . . . . . . . . . . . . . . .
With my becke bent, my lyttyl wanton eye,
    My fedders fresh as is the emrawde grene,
About my neck a cyrculet lyke the ryche rubye,
    My lyttyl legges, my feet both fete and clene,
    I am a mynyon to wayt vppon a quene. (1–5, 17–21)

Like Lindsay's Papyngo, Skelton's bird then launches into a diatribe against mismanagement in the church, but unlike Lindsay's poem, Skelton's has a very personal target: Cardinal Thomas Wolsey, Henry VIII's Archbishop of York and Lord Chancellor of England. Skelton's parrot accuses Wolsey of everything from corruption of the criminal justice system ("So many thevys hangyd, and thevys never the lesse" [470]) to the unethical sale of pardons ("So many bullys of pardon puplysshyd and shewyd" [508]). But, perhaps as cover for this audacious attack, it also babbles like a mad thing. Drawing again on medieval traditions, it says it "can mute and cry / In Lattyn, in Hebrew, Araby, and Caldey; / In Greke tong Parrot can both speke and say" (26–30). However, this command of languages makes the bird's own speech almost incomprehensible. In a perverse twist on an ancient truism, the parrot urges moderation in all things, including moderation itself, and its language, ranging from Latin to English to Greek to English to Latin to Italian, can hardly be called moderate. Its own watchword, "Ne tropo sanno, ne tropo mato" (which translates as "Be neither too sane nor too mad"), leaves the bird's own state of mind in even further doubt.

Because of these extremes, one critic has described Skelton's parrot as speaking "as if [it] were a prophet or Christ" (Kinney 16), while another has seen it as a "conventional image of [the] mimic-fool" (Fish 136). Both have a good point. Skelton's parrot is very much a transitional figure, with a claw in two worlds. As it hearkens back to the miraculous and prophetic associations of parrots in the Middle Ages, it also looks forward to a new order of business, in which the same birds become a byword for all that is mindless and trivial and loud.

In religious satire, this road leads straight to Samuel Butler's *Hudibras* (1663), a withering attack on the zealotry of Presbyterians and Puritans during the English Civil Wars. Butler's poem stands the medieval romance on its head by depicting Sir Hudibras, a colonel in Cromwell's army, and his squire Ralph as stupid, bigoted, corrupt, and self-serving. Of Ralph, for instance, we are told that

> He understood the Speech of Birds
> As well as they themselves do Words:
> Cou'd tell what subtlest Parrots mean,
> That speak and think contrary clean:
> What Member 'tis of whom they talk,
> When they cry Rope, and Walk, Knave, walk. (1.1.547–552)

As Butler's poem empties out and parodies the romance genre, it also parodies the parrots that populate that genre. There's no longer any pretense that these birds could be prophets, or linguists, or even able to sustain a meaningful conversation; on the contrary, only someone as vacuous as Ralph might ever believe such things. No more the companion of kings, Butler's parrots consort instead with the small and the base and the stupid. They are more an object than a vehicle for satire.

When it comes to the ridicule of women, foreigners, and social inferiors in Renaissance and Enlightenment writing, parrots undergo much the same transformation once more. But it can be harder to distinguish these three lines of satirical reference, since differences of gender and race tend to entail differences of social position as well. Even so, Shakespeare offers instances of both gender- and rank-based parrot humor. In *Much Ado About Nothing* (c. 1598–99), for instance, Benedick responds to Beatrice's jibes by calling her "a rare parrot-teacher" (1.1.138), implying that her insults are as predictable and repetitive as a bird's chatter. Elsewhere, similar witticisms disparage servants. For example, in *The Merchant of Venice* (c. 1594–98), Lancelot Gobbo indulges some cheesy wordplay about an African woman he has made pregnant: "It is much that the Moor should be more than reason; but if she be less than an honest woman, she is indeed more than I took her for" (3.5.40–42). Despairing at this silliness, the gentleman Lorenzo retorts, "I think the best grace of wit will shortly turn into silence, and discourse grow commendable in none only but parrots" (3.5.44–46). Likewise, in *1 Henry IV* (c. 1596–98), Prince Hal mocks the harried tavern-servant Francis as he responds to his customers with the one-word assurance "Anon" (2.4.97): "That ever this fellow should have fewer words than a parrot," Hal marvels, "and yet the son of a woman!" (2.4.98–99).

Elsewhere, Shakespeare draws contemptuous connections between parrots and the mentally or socially challenged. Salerio refers to the former when, in *The Merchant of Venice*, he speaks of "strange fellows" who "laugh like parrots" at the mournful strains of a bagpipe (1.2.50–53). In *Othello* (c. 1605), Cassio describes his inebriation as a kind of temporary insanity: "Drunk? and speak parrot? and squabble? swagger? swear? and discourse fustian with one's own shadow? O thou invisible spirit of wine, if thou hast no name to be known by let us call thee devil!" (2.3.279–283). And in *1 Henry IV* again, when Hotspur has won the Battle of Holmedon, he refuses to deliver his prisoners into the hands of the king's messenger:

> When I was dry with rage and extreme toil,
> Breathless and faint, leaning upon my sword,
> Came there a certain lord, neat, and trimly dress'd,
> Fresh as a bridegroom, and his chin new-reap'd. . . .
> With many holiday and lady terms
> He questioned me, amongst the rest demanded
> My prisoners in your Majesty's behalf.

> I then, all smarting with my wounds being cold,
> To be so pest'red with a popingay,
> Out of my grief and my impatience
> Answer'd neglectingly, I know not what. (1.3.31–34, 46–52)

Here the association between parrots and subordinate people is so entrenched that it can be used to ridicule someone who is not necessarily a social inferior, at least not by much, and who represents no less an authority than the king. Hotspur belongs to a dying breed, the armigerous gentry of the Middle Ages, for whom social rank is an expression of military rank. Encountering a representative of a new order of privilege, he responds with uncomprehending contempt. After all, this nameless lord doesn't behave like a lord at all. He doesn't fight, he trims his beard, he pays too much attention to his clothing, he uses bewildering, affected language. In fact, he's more like a woman than a man, but he's not a woman, either. So he must be the next worst thing—a popinjay.

But among the playwrights of the English Renaissance, Shakespeare's friend and colleague Ben Jonson gives parrots their most enduring onstage presence. Jonson's masterpiece, *Volpone* (1606), is a surreal and sardonic work, part confidence-game and part beast-fable, whose hero poses as an elderly invalid in order to attract and defraud a group of legacy hunters. Recalling Lindsay's *Testament of the Papyngo,* the legacy-hunters gather around Volpone's bedridden body, and Jonson strengthens the resemblance by giving them the names of carrion-eating birds. Voltore, the vulture, is a wealthy and unscrupulous Venetian lawyer; Corbaccio, the raven, is a greedy old fool, far closer to death than Volpone, who hopes to outlive him and inherit his wealth; and Corvino, the crow, offers Volpone his beautiful wife in an effort to ingratiate himself with the imaginary invalid. And in the midst of this play set in Venice, there is also an English couple, Sir Politic and Lady Would-Be, whom the other characters refer to as Sir and Lady Pol.

Jonson is credited with many contributions to the English language, but one of these has so far escaped notice. To my knowledge, he's the first writer to employ "Pol" or "Poll," as the generic name for any pet parrot: the psittacine equivalent of "Fido" or "Bowser," as it were.[3] He does this most clearly in an epigram to which I'll turn in a minute, but context makes clear that he's doing the same thing in *Volpone* as well. As scholars have long observed, the nicknames of Sir and Lady Pol react upon the play's other charactonyms so that "the Venice of

*Volpone* seems to be populated primarily by birds: the vulture, the raven, the crow, the parrot and the hawk" (Barton 107).

Unlike the play's menacing carrion-birds, the psittacine Would-Bes are more fool than knave. Lady Pol does try at one point to seduce Volpone, but the attempt is rendered comical by its utter ineptitude. Volpone finds her loud, obnoxious, and idiotic, but his own pretense of illness forces him to keep to his bed and endure her advances. The result is a kind of reverse rape scene whose victim must endure verbal rather than sexual violence:

> VOLPONE: The Poet,
>> As old in time, as PLATO, and as knowing,
>> Say's that your highest female grace is silence.
> LADY WOULD-BE: Which o' your Poets? PETRARCH? or TASSO? or DANTE?
>> GVERRINI? ARIOSTO? ARETINE?
>> CIECO *di Hadria*? I have read them all. (3.4.76–81)

Lady Pol may indeed know her Dante and Petrarch, but it makes no difference. Barren of judgment, she seems to hear and repeat everything while understanding nothing; she can't even tell the difference between a request for silence and a classroom discussion-question. Through her congenital inability to keep her mouth shut, and through the empty ostentation of her chatter, she parallels her namesake parrot.

As for Sir Pol, he embodies the same general tendencies, with results that are as much xenophobic as misogynist. Overawed by the sophisticated intrigue of the Italians around him, he has somehow convinced himself that he's a covert political operative—a sort of Renaissance double-agent with informants everywhere. But his cover is blown when another character manages to peek inside his top-secret personal diary, which proves in fact to be a vapid catalogue of daily trivia. Empty-headed amidst the world's infinite variety, Sir Pol responds to his environment as does his wife, by echoing everything without discrimination. To a mind that can't distinguish between the trifling and the momentous, even micturation can become an event of geopolitical import.

Jonson and Shakespeare are often depicted as a study in contrast: two dramatists working in the same place and time while pursuing very different artistic visions. But when it comes to parrots, at least, they seem to be in general agreement. Both see these birds as emblems of mindless inferiority, Where Shakespeare gives this inferiority a spin toward women, the lower social ranks, and figures of effete privilege, Jonson again more or less follows suit. In *Volpone*, moreover, the satire of women and overprivileged ninnies also combines with Jonson's anti-Italian prejudice, so that Sir Pol's reverence for things Italian becomes just another aspect of his complete subservience to his wife. He has come to Venice not on secret state business, but in obedience to "a peculiar humour of [his] wiues,/ . . . to obserue/ To quote, to learne the language, and so forth" (2.1.11–13), and this focus upon "quoting" and "learning the language" transforms Sir Pol into a parrot at the same time that it makes him into his wife's pet. As for Lady Pol, she tries to seduce Volpone in part, at least, because she seems to think it's the custom of the country. Venetian courtesans were famous throughout seventeenth-century Europe for their sexiness, so where Sir Pol aspires to the Italian standard of political cunning, Lady Pol aims at an Italian model of erotic sophistication. Both fail miserably. Far from being a master of intrigue, Sir Pol remains too clueless to realize his wife is trying to cheat on him, and Lady Pol remains so frumpy that she can't cuckold Sir Pol despite her best efforts. Both husband and wife are reduced to self-parody by their eagerness to copy what they can't comprehend.

Elsewhere, Jonson returns to parrot-related satire in his nondramatic verse, specifically in a two-line epigram entitled "On Court-Parrat" (Epigram 71; 1612–1613): "To plucke downe mine, POLL sets up new wits still,/ Still, 'tis his lucke to praise me 'gainst his will." To the lasting discredit of hookbills everywhere, this poem seems to have been aimed at a specific person: the poet Henry Parrot, who flourished between 1606 and 1626, writing satires and epigrams that sometimes drew more closely on Jonson's own work than Jonson himself appreciated. By this unhappy coincidence, the idea of the parrot becomes synonymous not only with vacuous chatter, vulgar ostentation, and uncomprehending mimicry but also with plagiarism. Through his maladroit efforts to preempt Jonson's reputation by stealing his lines, Court-Parrot ironically offers the poet the highest praise of which he's capable. Moreover, Jonson, the same poet who seems to have introduced the word "Poll" into the English language, has given us another coinage: "plagiary," used in the sense of "literary thief." "On Court-Parrat" employs the former of these new words while taking an example of the latter as its subject. In the process, this little poem suggests how these seemingly unrelated neologisms share a common origin in Jonson's concerns about the ownership of literary property. By creating new words for his satirical preoccupations, the poet asserts his status not just as the creator of a poem, but as the inventor of the very language in which it is written.

In composing this epigram, Jonson also paves the way for other poets to write occasional verses on the theme of the bird-brained parrot. In 1630, for instance, John Taylor the Water Poet publishes an epigram all about the idleness of parrot-chatter:

> Why doth the Parrat cry a Rope, a Rope?
> Because hee's cag'd in prison out of hope.
> Why doth the Parat call a Boate, a Boate?
> It is the humour of his idle note.
> O pretty Pall, take heed, beware the Cat.
> (Let Watermen alone, no more of chat)
> Since I so idly heard the Parrat talke,
> In his owne language, I say, Walke, knaue, walke. (*All the Workes*, Epigram 31)

Taylor earned his nickname "the Water Poet" because he started out in life as a Thames boatman, ferrying customers from one side of the river to the other. As it happens, this poem of his responds to an old joke about a boatman and a parrot, in which the latter makes a fool of the former. I'll tell that joke later in this chapter; in the meantime, it's enough that Taylor settles an old score between parrots and his profession by insulting the birds' intelligence. Phrases like "A rope!" and "Walk, knave!" were the nastier seventeenth-century counterpart to "Polly want a cracker!" Taylor turns these expressions back on their speaker, suggesting that the parrot itself is the knave in question, and that it should beware a rope, or a cat, or a ferryman nursing a grudge.

And again following Ben Jonson, in 1648 Robert Herrick published a quatrain entitled "Upon *Parrat*," which offers a contemptuous summary of the old classical wisdom about these birds:

> *Parrat* protests 'tis he, and only he
> Can teach a man the *Art of memory*:
> Believe him not; for he forgot it quite,
> Being drunke, who 'twas that Can'd his Ribs last night. (*Hesperides* 501)

The Greek and Roman tales about psittacine drunkenness and corporal punishment return here in a cheerful, derogatory hodgepodge.

But after Herrick, there are fewer and fewer references to the old classical stories about parrots, because the birds' new associations are so firmly in place.

By 1709, Richard Steele writes with irony of "a fine lady" so attached to her parrot that her gentleman-admirer finds "Poll had her ear, when his sighs were neglected" (*Tatler* 27). Making a virtue of necessity, he woos her by writing love-poetry to the bird. In 1710, Steele describes an elderly lady who has "transferred the amorous passions of her first years to the Love of cronies, petts, and favourites," these being "four of the most mischievous animals that can ever infest a family; an old shock dog with one eye, a monkey chained to one side of the chimney, a great grey squirrel to the other, and a parrot waddling in the middle of the room" (*Tatler* 266). And by 1714, Alexander Pope dismisses "Men, Monkeys, Lap-dogs, [and] Parrots" as the typical, and equally idiotic, denizens of a lady's drawing-room ("The Rape of the Lock" 4.120).

Twenty-five years earlier, John Locke's *Essay Concerning Human Understanding* (1690/1691) repeats a lengthy, amusing parrot-story from Sir William Temple's *Memoirs* (1686), and in doing so Locke makes clear how much the parrot's cultural meaning has changed in the past two centuries. The tale appears amidst Locke's argument that "it is not the *idea* of a thinking or rational being alone that makes the *idea* of a man in most people's sense, but of a body so and so shaped, joined to it" (1:280):

> I had a mind to know from . . . Prince *Maurice's* . . . own mouth . . . of an old *parrot* he had in *Brazil* during his government there, that spoke and asked and answered common questions like a reasonable creature. . . . They asked it what he thought that man was, pointing to the Prince. It answered, *some general or other.* When they brought it close to him, he asked it: *D'ou venez-vous?* It answered: *De Marinnan.* The Prince: *A qui etes-vous?* The parrot: *A un Portugais.* Prince: *Que fais-tu la?* Parrot: *Je garde les poules.* The Prince laughed and said: *Vous gardez les poules?* The parrot answered: *Oui, moi, & je sais bien faire,* and made the chuck four or five times that people use to make to chickens when they call them. (1:279)

It's a cute story, this, about a parrot guarding chickens, and it says a lot about the decline of medieval ideas of psittacine intelligence. For Locke finds it frankly "incredible" and "ridiculous" (1:280) that a parrot could even display this much reasoning ability. And even if it could (which it can't), he goes on, this ability wouldn't make anyone mistake the bird for a person: "The Prince . . . and our author . . . both . . . call this talker a *parrot*; and I ask anyone else who thinks such a story fit to be told, whether, if this *parrot* and all of its kind had always talked, . . . they would not have passed for a race of *rational animals*; but yet for all that they would have been allowed to be men and not *parrots*?" (1:280). Medieval beast-lore not only credits parrots with impressive reasoning ability; it also confuses them with people in various ways, even endowing them with a human ancestry. Locke's commonsense argument rejects such stuff out of hand.

Still—and ironically—while Locke refuses to mistake parrots for people, that doesn't prevent people from doing the reverse, mistaking other people for parrots. As we've again seen, much early modern satire draws on just this kind of willful misrecognition. Nor was this confusion limited to literature alone. Consider, for instance, the story of friar Bernardino de Minaya. In 1536, Minaya was serving as a missionary in the New World when Cardinal Garcia de Loaisa, president of the Spanish Council of the Indies and personal confessor to Emperor Charles V, issued a directive allowing Spanish captains "to enslave Indians at their will" (qtd. in Hanke 84). Appalled at this decree, Minaya returned to Spain and appealed in person to the cardinal on behalf of the Native Americans. But Loaisa ignored this petition, responding that Minaya "was much deceived, for he understood that the Indians were no more than parrots."

By 1719, this assumption is implicit in the structure of Daniel Defoe's masterwork, *Robinson Crusoe*. There Crusoe, catches one parrot, then others, then teaches them to speak, and in time even mistakes their language for that of another human being (141). At length, he can describe his mastery of the island as follows: "Then to see how like a king I dined, too, all alone, attended by my servants; Poll, as if he had been my favourite, was the only person permitted to talk to me" (147). Poll's personhood here confirms Crusoe's sovereignty, and for that reason, if no other, it's worth retaining. And as Crusoe's preeminent "servant," this bird also foreshadows his eventual acquisition of another, human underling who will become Crusoe's "favourite" in his turn. From the structural standpoint, Poll is a man Friday with feathers, and the bird's status as such supplies precedent for Friday's own servitude.

As writers of the Renaissance and Enlightenment transform parrots into comical, subordinate, living property, painters of the same period do much the same thing. In the visual arts, historical developments lead away from the mythic themes and reverential tone of the Middle Ages, toward a much more casual, unastonished view of the creatures.

Medieval themes and motifs persist into the early sixteenth century. Andrea Mantegna's *Madonna della Vittoria* (1496; Figure 16), for instance, preserves the

Figure 16. Mantegna, *Madonna della Vittoria*, 1496 (The Louvre, Paris) Art Resource

medieval association of parrots with the Virgin Mary. Directly above the crucifix that appears by Mary's right shoulder there stands a sulfur-crested cockatoo (*Cacatua galerita*), a particularly rare bird in Renaissance Europe, native not to the New World but to New Guinea and Australia.

Then there is Albrecht Dürer's famous engraving of 1504, *The Fall of Man* (also called *Adam and Eve*; Figure 17). In its Edenic setting and its careful depiction of animals, this work recalls medieval tableaux like the Creation of the Animals in the Queen Mary Psalter (see Figure 6). But in Dürer's engraving it is humanity, not God, that occupies center stage. This fact, like Dürer's painstaking concern with perspective and anatomy and the chilly classicism of the naked Adam and Eve, suggests the new humanist focus of his work. There, above Adam's right shoulder and Dürer's own signature, perches a carefully drawn macaw, reminding us, perhaps, of the old medieval tradition that parrots originate in the earthly paradise.

From here on, parrots begin to appear in paintings more and more frequently as commodities or as figures of inferiority. For an example of the former, look at Jan Davidszoon de Heem's *Elaborate Tabletop Still-Life with Foodstuffs, Precious Objects, and Exotic Animals* (late 1640s; Figure 18), a wonderful example of the seventeenth-century Dutch still-life. A luxury object itself, de Heem's painting revels in the profusion of valuables it depicts. The precious trinkets range from the inert—silk hangings and tableware of gold and silver—to the dead—seashells, a boiled lobster, a plate of oysters, a mass of fruit—to the living. There, at the top of the arrangement, appear two parrots. An African gray stands on a hanging perch, looking down with suspicion as it holds a piece of fruit in its claw. And just beneath it, a green-winged macaw regards it greedily with open beak. This painting is all about the diversity of life's riches, and this fact is mirrored, in turn, by the contrast between these birds. The one small and gray, the other large and red, the one from the Old World, the other from the New—between them they embody the distant reaches of the earth from which the merchants of the Dutch Golden Age drew their nation's wealth.

In Peter Paul Rubens's famed painting *Deborah Kip, Wife of Sir Balthasar Gerbier, and Her Children* (1630; Figure 19), perched on Kip's right shoulder and looking down at her infant inquisitively, there appears an African gray parrot. Its body serves as both an extension of and an accessory to the painting's human subject-matter. Here, as in the later portrait *Rubens, His Wife Helena Fourment, and Their Son Peter Paul* (Metropolitan Museum of Art, New York), Rubens employed

Figure 17. Albrecht Dürer, *Adam and Eve*, 1504, engraving, 24.8 x 19.2 cm (Clarence Buckingham Collection, 1944.614. Reproduction, The Art Institute of Chicago)

Figure 18. Jan Davidszoon de Heem, *Elaborate Tabletop Still-Life with Foodstuffs, Exotic Animals, and Precious Objects,* oil on canvas, 59 ¹/₄ x 46 1/4 inches, SN289 (Bequest of John Ringling, Collection of The John and Mable Ringling Museum of Art, the State Art Museum of Florida)

Figure 19. Peter Paul Rubens, *Deborah Kip, Wife of Sir Balthasar Gerbier, and Her Children* (Andrew W. Mellon Fund, Image © 2003 Board of Trustees, National Gallery of Art, Washington, D.C.)

a parrot both as a kind of visual accent and as an active participant in his work's overall design—in other words, both as an object and as a living being in its own right.

Elsewhere, the pictorial connection between parrots and inferior people becomes central to Jan Steen's great allegorical painting, *The Effects of Intemperance* (1663–65; Figure 20). Steen's work illustrates the biblical adage that "Wine is a mocker" (Proverbs 20.1), and it does so by depicting the havoc alcoholism wreaks on family life. The scene is circular in arrangement, with the mother of the household at the far left, slumped in a drunken stupor, and the misbehaving members of her family surrounding her. Completing the circuit back to the

Figure 20. Jan Steen, *The Effects of Intemperance* (National Gallery, London)

mother, her eldest daughter sprawls on hands and knees across the bottom foreground of the painting, where she gives a glass of wine to an African gray parrot.

Steen has carefully drawn the bird and the mother to mimic each other. Where the mother is drunk, the parrot is drinking; where the mother slumps forward in her stupor, the parrot stretches forward for its wine. But they also represent the different extremes of the family hierarchy. The mother, as an adult, remains distinct from and superior to her children; the parrot, as a pet, remains distinct from and inferior to them. So if wine is a mocker, who's mocking whom here? The painting leaves us with a parrot-and-egg dilemma: does vice evolve from the top or the bottom of the social order, from the better sort parroting the meaner, or the meaner sort parroting the better? As a final irony, this scene recalls Aristotle's claim that parrots are "outrageous after drinking wine"—surely a case of the birds behaving like their so-called betters.

If Steen's painting associates parrots with the lower orders of the family, elsewhere they are identified with an exotic foreign world awaiting European conquest. That is how they figure, for instance, in Anthony Van Dyck's *Portrait of William Feilding, First Earl of Denbigh* (1633–34; Figure 21). Denbigh had visited Persia and India from 1631 to 1633, when he commissioned Van Dyck to com-

Figure 21. Anthony Van Dyck, *Portrait of William Feilding, First Earl of Denbigh* (National Gallery, London)

memorate his travels in this portrait. The painter chose to depict him in Asian dress, on a hunting expedition, and accompanied by a dark-skinned page, who points to a parrot perched in a palm tree. Ironically, given the portrait's eastern setting, the parrot is a green-winged macaw (*Ara chloroptera*), native to northern South America; it cannot be confused with any species of Old World parrot. For Van Dyck, the birds of one colonial region are as good as those of another.

This painting's real interest lies in the arrangement of its figures. These form a triangle that stretches from the bird at the top right, to the page at the bottom right, to Denbigh at the bottom left. Denbigh, in turn, gazes up at the parrot, completing the triangular circuit of the composition. But this design also distinguishes Denbigh, on the left, from the page and parrot, who occupy the same vertical axis—sketched out by the trunk of the palm tree—on the right. In fact, the page and the parrot mirror one another with especial intimacy. "The guide's lips, like the parrot's jaws, are slightly parted" (Wendorf 102); the curvature of the page's left arm reverses that of the macaw's body; both page and macaw are turned toward Denbigh and direct their gaze toward him. Together, the bird and the servant form something like a frame for Denbigh's body, offsetting and encompassing it from above and below. If, for Van Dyck, there is no particular difference between a New World parrot and an Old World parrot, there also seems to be little or none between a parrot and a native guide.

Such habits of mind lead into one further innovation in sixteenth- and seventeenth-century parrot culture. During this period, the modern parrot joke begins to appear in printed jestbooks and other sources.

The Renaissance jestbook is the direct ancestor of present-day joke collections like *Alan King's Great Jewish Joke Book,* Garrison Keillor's *Pretty Good Joke Book,* and Judy Brown's *Joke Soup.* The Renaissance parrot joke, in turn, is the forerunner of a vast subgenre dedicated to such witticisms. My own impromptu Internet search for parrot jokes yielded about 52,800 hits in less than one second. Here, in all their glory, are some examples of the present-day phenomenon:

> One day a man went to an auction. While there, he bid on an exotic parrot. He really wanted this bird, so he got caught up in the bidding. He kept on bidding, but kept getting outbid, so he bid higher and higher and higher. Finally, after he bid way more than he intended, he won the bird—the fine bird was finally his! As he was paying for the parrot he said to the Auctioneer, "I sure hope this parrot can talk. I would hate to have paid this much for it, only to find out that he

can't talk!" "Don't worry," said the Auctioneer, "He can talk. Who do you think kept bidding against you?" ("Good Bird Jokes!")

A young man named John received a parrot as a gift. The parrot had a bad attitude and an even worse vocabulary. . . . John tried and tried to change the bird's attitude. . . . Nothing worked.

. . . Finally, in a moment of desperation, John put the bird in the refrigerator freezer. For a few minutes, John heard the bird squawk and kick and scream . . . then suddenly there was quiet. . . .

Fearing that he'd hurt the bird, John quickly opened the door to the freezer. The parrot calmly stepped out onto John's out-stretched arm and said, ". . . I am truly sorry, and I will do everything to correct my poor behavior."

John was astonished at the bird's change of attitude. As he was about to ask the parrot what had made such a dramatic change in his behavior, the bird continued, "May I ask what the chicken did?" ("Our Favorite Pirate or Parrot Jokes")

Why wouldn't the parrot talk to the Frenchman? Because he only spoke pigeon English. ("Joke Dictionary")

As luck would have it (or perhaps it's not luck at all), there exist Renaissance precursors for all three of these jokes. Let's take them in order.

The first example comes not from a jestbook but from Conrad Gesner's great zoological work, the *History of Animals* (1551–1558). It has to do with Henry VIII's pet parrot, whose exploits Gesner recounts as follows:

Recently a certain person told us a pleasant story of a parrot, which he said fell out of the palace of Henry VIII, at London in England, into the river Thames flowing nearby. It cried out, "A boat, a boat, for twenty pound!" which it had heard uttered very often, and which it had then memorized very easily, its voice accustomed to those who call the ferryman from the opposite bank by price (as if they were placed in some danger, or others even in jest). A certain ferryman, thus aroused, rowed out hastily and picked up the bird and returned it to the king (to whom he recognized it to belong) in hopes of just so much of a reward as the bird had promised. The king agreed that he would settle on whatever reward the bird named when again asked. The bird responded, "Give the knave a groat [four pence]." (2P1v; my translation)

This is the story to which John Taylor the Water Poet responded in his Epigram 31, and it's easy to see why this tale might annoy a boatman-turned-poet. While the parrot here is no medieval marvel, the boatman is clearly the butt of the joke. Underestimating the parrot's intelligence, he assumes that the bird can only name one sum of money, and when the bird proves otherwise, the boatman must endure a double insult: to be tricked out of a small fortune, and to be outwitted in the process by a parrot.

The present-day joke about the parrot at the auction gives us the same basic payoff. In both stories, a man and a parrot act as competitors, the man emerges as the loser, and his loss takes the form of a projected financial advantage that the bird unexpectedly chisels him out of. And so, despite their antagonism, the man and the bird ironically belong together. The parrot sets a standard of witlessness that throws the man's own greater imbecility into comic relief. No wonder Taylor felt compelled to even the score.

Indeed, the second contemporary joke—the one about the parrot in the freezer—gives us another version of the conflict between man and parrot, this time with the outcome reversed. As it happens, a parallel story survives in a volume entitled *A Banquet of Jests* (1640)—a collection of witticisms attributed to Archie Armstrong, court fool to James I and Charles I of England. This story involves a parrot who belongs to a wine merchant, from whom it has learned to call out the phrase "A groat a quart, a groat a quart" (Zall 163). Trouble comes when the merchant raises his prices but the parrot continues its own chatter unchanged, thereby prompting the merchant's customers to accuse him of false advertising. Incensed at this, the merchant hurls the parrot "in a great rage into the kennel [i.e., the gutter]—from whence she crawled forth, being nothing all over but dirt" (Zall 163). While the bird pulled itself out of the muck, "by chance, came by a Sow which had been wallowing in the mire and was in a most beastly pickle, which the Parrot spying, . . . said, 'Alas, poor Sow, hast thou cried wine for a groat a quart, too?'" (Zall 163).

As in the story about the parrot and the freezer, the joke here is on the bird. In both cases, it is the object of physical abuse. In both cases it earns this attention by talking too much. And in both cases, the punch line makes it just human enough to be ridiculous. The parrot in the modern story is smart enough to recognize a frozen chicken when it sees one, but not smart enough to understand why the chicken was frozen to begin with. The wine merchant's bird doesn't grasp the mechanics of inflation (perhaps understandably), and while it seems to comprehend the logic of cause and effect in the abstract, it misapplies that logic in the case of the bemucked sow. It takes its place among the numbskulls and nitwits who populate Renaissance jestbooks, and who serve as the object of the jestbooks' humor.

In the case of the third contemporary joke, the tables are turned yet again, this time in a way that involves racial difference. And this time John Taylor provides a parallel seventeenth-century tale in his jestbook *Wit and Mirth* (1630). Taylor's story is about a jackdaw, but the bird in question might as well be a parrot.

It seems that there was "A Wealthy *Monsieur* in *France* (hauing profound reuenues, and a shallow braine)," who for a great price purchased a jackdaw that was alleged to speak "*French, Italian, Spanish, Dutch*, and *Latin*" (*Works* 2Q2r). As it turns out, however, the French gentleman has bought a parrot in a poke: "Iack-Daw (after a moneth or fiue weekes time) neuer spake otherwise then his fathers speech *Kaw, Kaw*: whereat the Monsieur said, that the Knaue had cozened him of his money: but it is no great matter . . . : for, quoth he, though my Daw does not speak, yet I am ingood hope that he thinkes the more" (*Works* 2Q2r–v). Baiting the French is a venerable English pastime, of course, and Americans enjoy it to a certain degree as well. Here the impulse gets full play, and by the seventeenth century, talking birds provide a natural medium for it.

To be sure, parrots have been the subject of amusing stories almost from their first appearance in western society. As we've seen, John Trevisa described them in the fourteenth century as "y-ordeynede . . . for mannes mer[th]e." But starting in the Renaissance, they appear in printed joke collections as a conventional element of what we'd now call standup comedy. And they figure in jokes in a new way, corresponding to their own loss of mythic status during the Age of Exploration. No student of Freud will be surprised to discover that jokes can lend acceptable expression to violent impulses; however, from about 1500 forward, parrots increasingly appear on the receiving end of such violence. Whether tossed in the kennel, falling out of windows, getting their sides caned, or being threatened with a rope, the parrots of the Renaissance and Enlightenment occasion a newly brutal kind of laughter. It's a laughter the nineteenth century will take pains to correct.

# Chapter 4

# *Unhappy Bird!*

In Mark Twain's great parody of nineteenth-century sentimentalism, *The Adventures of Huckleberry Finn* (1885), Huck finds himself cast upon the mercies of a genteel Tennessee family named the Grangerfords. Their house is strewn with memorabilia of their dead fifteen-year-old daughter, Emmeline, including a number of her crayon drawings. Among these Huck encounters a picture of "a young lady . . . crying into a handkerchief [who] had a dead bird laying on its back in her other hand with its heels up, and underneath the picture it said 'I Shall Never Hear Thy Sweet Chirrup More Alas'" (157).

We don't learn the bird's species—who knows? perhaps it actually is a parrot—and this has clearly been of no interest to anyone, least of all Emmeline. What did interest her, unto obsession, was her own overwrought encounter with mortality, which she acted out vicariously through any corpse, actual or potential, real or imagined, that came her way. Now dead herself, she has bequeathed that obsession to her surviving relatives. Nor is it accidental that the Grangerfords, Twain's poster children for genteel melodrama and bourgeois sentimentality, should also be involved in a murderous blood-feud with a neighboring family. For all their lugubrious pieties, they remain casually ruthless, their civility simply cosmetic. The Grangerfords' possessions—hymnals and Bibles, *Pilgrim's Progress* and Henry Clay's speeches, and the like—may be designed to advertise their owners' character, but they don't, or if they do, it is in a way opposite to the one intended. Such objects become just more bric-a-brac in a house choked with it: "There was a clock on the middle of the mantel-piece. . . . Well, there was a big outlandish parrot on each side of the clock, made out of something like chalk, and painted up gaudy. By one of the parrots was a cat made of crockery, and a crockery dog by the other; and when you pressed down on them they squeaked, but didn't open their mouths nor look different nor interested" (155–156). Seeking a scene of sophistication, the Grangerfords have created tchotchke hell. This, of course, is one of the nineteenth century's great gifts to cultural history, and again it's no accident that Twain should give parrots a central place in this setting. For centuries now, parrots have been synonymous with empty pretension.

But the Grangerfords' parrots are no ordinary birds. Being figurines, they're not really birds at all, and they take their place among others of their kind. With its plaster-of-paris parrots, its squeaking crockery dog and cat, and Emmeline's chirrupless songbird, the Grangerfords' home is a museum of inanimate animals.

That's what makes it useful for a study of parrot culture in nineteenth-century Europe and America. Where the preceding three centuries see the development of a newly brutal and contemptuous attitude toward these birds, the nineteenth century reacts to this brutality and contempt in three major ways. First, it produces a cult of sentiment in which pets—including pet parrots—receive an unprecedented measure of emotional attention. But "pets" is an anagram for "pest," as anyone who has ever lived with an animal can testify. Obeying their own agendas, household animals don't always conform to our expectations of them, emotional or otherwise. So, second, there develops a marked preference for dead birds over the living variety. If nothing else, the dead ones don't annoy the neighbors and spoil the sofa cushions. Maintaining an emotional attachment to them becomes accordingly easier. And finally, if a dead animal is in some ways preferable to a living one, then an artificial animal may be best of all. In these three ways, this scene in *Huckleberry Finn* epitomizes the treatment of parrots in nineteenth-century Europe and America. And Emmeline Grangerford's dead songbird embodies the result of that treatment.

As to the conjuncture of high emotion and dead animals, consider the case of George Crabbe. His *Parish Register* (1807) extols the virtues of village life through a catalogue of baptisms, marriages, and burials, all pitched to elicit the greatest possible sympathy for the individuals involved. Among the burials, we encounter an "Antient Maiden" (Argument 9–10) named Catherine, who had suffered in her youth from a sexual fling with "A Captain . . . rich from *India*" (3.330), and had thereafter retired to quiet spinsterhood. She passed her remaining days in a picturesque cottage surrounded by trinkets and pets, but it is not entirely clear which of these categories her parrot belongs to:

> Her neat small Room, adorn'd with Maiden-taste,
> A clip't French-Puppey first of Favourites grac'd.

A Parrot next, but dead and stuff'd with Art;
(For Poll, when living, lost the Lady's Heart,
And then his Life; for he was heard to speak
Such frightful Words as tinge'd his Lady's Cheek,)
Unhappy Bird! Who had no power to prove,
Save by such speech, his Gratitude and Love. (3.352–359)

Here, as in *Huckleberry Finn*, we have a room furnished on the principle that clutter bespeaks gentility. Here, too, we have a prominent dead bird. Here, again, we have self-conscious delicacy fronting a smug callousness. Catherine's ears may be too tender to tolerate cursewords, but she has no qualms about executing her bird for fowl language. In fact, the bird's more useful dead than alive, because now it becomes a monument to its owner's sensitivity and depth of emotion. I shall never hear thy sweet chirrup more, alas.

Indeed, the only real difference between Crabbe's *Parish Register* and *Huckleberry Finn* may be that where Twain is jesting, Crabbe is in earnest. This is the distinction between irony and melodrama.

But if we seek the melodrama, we find it in pictures as well as verse. For instance, there is Joseph Wright of Derby's *Experiment on a Bird in the Air Pump* (1768; Figure 22), which to my mind provides a classic instance of Romantic and post-Romantic bad taste. It aims at provoking a horrific, exaggerated emotional response by shamelessly manipulating the reactions of both its characters and its viewers. It employs an expendable animal as a way of indirectly confronting the question of human mortality. And it invokes experimental science to give itself an air of spurious objectivity. I don't just hate this painting. I consider it an artistic atrocity of the first water.

At the picture's center lie a bird and a piece of scientific equipment. The equipment is a vacuum-pump—an apparatus developed by scientists in the late 1600s. Inside the pump's vacuum chamber lies the bird—a large, white cockatoo. The cockatoo may or may not already be dead from asphyxiation; in any case, it's not dancing a buck-and-wing. Surrounding its prostrate form appear the human figures who are the real focus of the tableau: a scientist intent on experimenting with animals, a father intent on traumatizing his young daughters, two daughters intent on their trauma, a pair of young lovers intent on each other, and so forth.

These characters sketch out a range of reactions to the death they are witnessing, and by extension to the possibility of their own death as well. The young

Figure 22. Joseph Wright of Derby, *An Experiment on a Bird in the Air Pump* (National Gallery, London)

girls display the pitiable horror of the defenseless and innocent. The lovers ignore the experiment and lose themselves instead in mutual narcissism. The father bends over his girls, expounding pious platitudes about how it's good for them to watch the torture and death of the family pet. The scientist, having transcended all such petty human concerns, peers with steely eyes into the void of mortality itself. He, the painting implies, is the best of us.

Wright is famous for his pictures of scientific subjects, and he drew this one from his own experience, in a perverse way. He had apparently attended the lectures of James Ferguson (1710–1776), a noted manufacturer of scientific equipment, and those lectures raise the possibility of an experiment just such as Wright depicts. But Ferguson himself firmly believes that "this experiment is too shocking to every spectator who has the least degree of humanity." In his eagerness to provoke an emotional reaction, Wright has not just ignored Ferguson's scruples. He has treated them as a dare. The result is a convincing photorealistic rendition of an experiment that would seldom have been conducted under any circumstances, and surely never in front of children. Still further, such an experiment would never have been performed on a rare and expensive cockatoo. From the standpoint of practical research, it makes no sense whatever; it only appears reasonable from the standpoint of a lurid artistic sensationalism. This, of course, is the perspective from which Wright operates. It produces a landmark instance of bad taste, and of bad faith.

Still, Wright's painting offers a brilliant example of the empirical method's increasing prominence in late eighteenth- and nineteenth-century treatments of the natural world. In the mid-1700s, for instance, the conventions of scientific bird illustration begin to emerge in Europe, reflecting an increased emphasis upon and confidence in objective observation. Unlike such artistic genres as portraiture and still-life, ornithological illustration aims to depict its subjects with perfect precision, in their native habitat, as an adjunct to scientific study. You could argue that in doing so, it encourages viewers to treat the realms of nature and culture as separate and unrelated. It certainly leads to a new anatomical precision in the visual portrayal of bird species.

But even as the new bird painters achieved unprecedented visual accuracy, they, like the Grangerfords in *Huckleberry Finn*, seem to have had unexpected trouble telling the difference between a living animal and a dead one. The earliest scientific bird-illustrators worked entirely from stuffed specimens called "skins," which were often of inferior quality. As the most famous of nineteenth-century bird illustrators, John James Audubon (1785–1851), complained,

> the persons *generally* employed for the purpose of mounting [animal specimens] possessed no further talents than that of filling the skins, until *plumply formed*, and adorning them with eyes and legs generally from their own fancy. Those persons, on inquiry, knew nothing of the anatomy of the subject before them; seldom the true *length* of the whole, or the *junction* either of the wings and legs with the body; nothing of their *gaits* and *allurements*; and not once in a hundred times was the bird in a natural position. (*Birds* 24)

As a result of these practices, early bird illustration could be a very imprecise art indeed. Consider, for instance, the *Cabinet of Natural Curiosities* of Albertus Seba (1665–1736), one of the first great illustrated natural history books of the eighteenth century. Seba, a Dutch apothecary, spent his lifetime amassing a private collection of biological specimens, and at the end of his life he arranged to have this collection documented in print with copperplate engravings. The resulting work, which appeared in four volumes between 1734 and 1765, became something of a landmark in the documentation of natural history. But it was by no means universally admired. By the early 1800s, scientists referred to Seba's illustrations as *"very unsuccessfully rendered,"* "gone badly wrong" in a way "which should never be cited elsewhere" (Musch, Willmann, and Rust 36). The volumes contain a limited number of bird illustrations, including a few of parrots, of which the most prominent is a lesser sulfur-crested cockatoo (*Cacatua sulphurea*; Figure 23). Although this may be a groundbreaking work from the standpoint of zoological history, from the standpoint of representational accuracy it's a disaster. The bird appears in a standard early side-view, perched on something approximating a bit of tree stump. Its posture is preternaturally stiff, as if it had just been shocked into life in Victor Frankenstein's laboratory. The bird's claws point one way and its body another, about thirty degrees to the right, while its head rotates back again in the direction of the claws. Moreover, the cockatoo's legs are placed much farther to the rear of the bird than the laws of physics would allow, with the result that it appears at once ramrod-stiff, strangely twisted, and disturbingly top-heavy. One expects it to keel over at any moment.

The worst thing about this illustration is the eyes. A parrot's eyes may be its most startling and fascinating physical feature, well able to challenge the skills of an accomplished draftsman. My own two Amazons provide a typical case in point; their irises are an iridescent orange-yellow, surrounding pupils of glossy jet that dilate and pixilate with disturbing mobility. In fact, there is no better way to tell a parrot's mood than to look into its eyes. The more wildly the irises flash, the more excited—and potentially violent—the bird. But Seba's cockatoo has eyes unlike anything that has ever graced, or disgraced, a living parrot. For one thing, they're divided unnaturally into three parts, with a gold rim, a kind of amber iris, and then the pupil. For another, the colors are all wrong—although at least they're at the warmer end of the spectrum. And as the final indignity, they are not properly aligned with the bird's beak, which angles left against the grain of their right-tending gaze. They're more buttons than eyes. If a dead thing were capable of self-consciousness, I would call this a self-consciously dead bird.

Unhappy with such work and the procedures that produced it, Audubon sought to distinguish himself from his forerunners. Complaining that "the dried skin of an exotic specimen . . . draws all attention whilst the *habits* of that same specimen are scarcely inquired after" (*Birds* 23), he insisted instead upon depicting "as much as possible *nature as it existed*" (*Birds* 22). To that end, he based his illustrations on painstaking personal observation of live birds in their natural

Figure 23.  Lesser sulfur-crested cockatoo, from Albertus Seba, *Cabinet of Natural Curiosities* (Tab. LIX, Koninklijke Bibliotheek, The Hague)

environment. And in the process, he announced that "I have never drawn from a stuffed specimen" (*Birds* 24).

But he didn't exactly draw from live specimens, either. As innovative as his methods were, Audubon still transformed his birds into inert matter in the process of sketching them. As he described his system of bird illustration, it evolved out of lengthy frustration with the technical problems of draftsmanship. One day, in a moment of something like enlightenment, Audubon went out before breakfast with his gun, and

> down with the first King Fisher I met! I picked the bird up and carried it home by the bill. I sent for the miller and made him fetch me a piece of soft board. When he returned he found me filing into sharp points pieces of my wires, and proud to show him the substance of my discovery, for a discovery I now had in my brains, I pierced the body of the fishing bird and fixed it on the board—another wire passing above his upper mandible was made to hold its head in a pretty fair attitude, smaller skewers fixing the feet according to my notion, and even common pins came to my assistance in the placing [of] the legs and feet. The last wire proved a delightful elevator to the bird's tail, and at last there stood before me the real manikin of a King Fisher! (*Birds* 17)

This became Audubon's signature method of work, and it improved upon that of his predecessors, in essence, by replacing one kind of dead bird with another. In doing this, Audubon also wedded his passion for ornithological drawing to an equal zeal for hunting, and the results were as macabre as the mannequins he made of his victims. Awkwardly for the man now regarded by many as "the patron saint of American wildlife conservation," Audubon spent his professional life "'in blood up to his elbows'" (Peterson x–xi), killing thousands of birds in his eagerness to depict them with objective precision.

In the process, Audubon only drew one species of parrot, but it happens to be an important one, and he is important to it. The species in question is the Carolina parakeet (*Conuropsis carolinensis*; Figure 24). Its story is famous among parrot fanciers and conservationists alike. The Carolina parakeet was the only member of the parrot family native to the United States. At its height, the species ranged from the Gulf of Mexico to the Great Lakes, and from the east coast to Colorado. Carolina parakeets flew in vast numbers throughout this area, often in flocks of two or three hundred birds. Audubon observed them closely in the 1820s and 1830s, but by then the species was already in decline. As he remarked in 1831, "Our Parakeets are very rapidly diminishing in number. . . . I should

Carolina Parrot.

PSITTACUS CAROLINENSIS. *Linn.*

Males 1. Females 2. Young 3.

*Cockle bur Xanthium strumarium.*

Figure 24. Carolina parakeets, from John James Audubon, *Ornithological Biography* (Library of Congress, Washington, D.C.)

think that along the Mississippi there is not now half the number that existed fifteen years ago" (*Ornithological Biography* 1:138). Within half a century of Audubon's death, the Carolina parakeet was functionally extinct. The last captive specimen died in the Cincinnati Zoo on February 21, 1918.

The principal reasons for this extinction are usually given as the destruction of the birds' habitat and persecution of the birds themselves. As to the former, Carolina parakeets preferred to nest in swamps and heavily forested valleys. Farming and other kinds of development ate away at these. And as farming increased in the eastern United States, persecution of the species also increased. Audubon described the reasons as follows:

> The Parrot . . . eats or destroys almost every kind of fruit indiscriminately, and on this account is always an unwelcome visitor to the planter, the farmer, or the gardener. The stacks of grain put up in the field are resorted to by flocks of these birds, which frequently cover them so entirely, that they present to the eye the same effect as if a brilliantly coloured carpet had been thrown over them. . . . They assail the Pear and Apple-trees . . . until the trees which were before so promising, are left completely stripped, like the ship water-logged and abandoned by its crew. . . . They visit the Mulberries, Pecan-nuts, Grapes, and even the seeds of the Dog-wood, before they are ripe, and on all commit similar depradations. (*Ornithological Biography* 1:136)

As one might expect, this behavior inspired harsh retaliation:

> The Parakeets are destroyed in great numbers, for whilst busily engaged in plucking off the fruits or tearing the grain from the stacks, the husbandman approaches them with perfect ease, and commits great slaughter among them. . . . The gun is kept at work; eight or ten, or even twenty, are killed at every discharge. The living birds, as if conscious of the death of their companions, sweep over their bodies, screaming as loud as ever, but still return to the stack to be shot at, until so few remain alive, that the farmer does not consider it worth his while to spend more of his ammunition. I have seen several hundreds destroyed in this manner in the course of a few hours, and have procured a basketful of these birds at a few shots, in order to make choice of good specimens for drawing the figures by which this species is represented. (*Ornithological Biography* 1:138)

Audubon fully understood that the Carolina parakeet was in decline, and that human persecution is part of the reason why. But far from seeking to conserve the species, he did his bit to edge it toward extinction. And his hunting of the birds may not even have been purely an adjunct to his artwork. He may have eaten them, too. At the very least, he observed that "their flesh is tolerable food, when they are young, on which account many of them are shot" (*Ornithological Biography* 1:139). Given Audubon's generally hands-on approach to ornithological matters, I'm inclined to hear in this the voice of direct experience.

Among the scientific bird illustrators of the nineteenth century, my personal hero is not Audubon but Edward Lear (1812–1888). Although Lear eventually made his reputation as the foremost nonsense-poet of his age, he began his career as an artist specializing not just in birds but in parrots. He achieved his only major professional success in this area with the publication between 1830 and 1832 of his first book, *Illustrations of the Family of Psittacidae, or Parrots.* Thereafter, his work as an illustrator was neglected by audiences and exploited by contemporaries like the entrepreneur John Gould, who in at least one case erased Lear's name from his own lithographic plate (Hyman 44). Unlike Audubon, who acquired a reputation he hadn't necessarily earned, Lear was denied the renown he deserved. Unlike Audubon again, Lear insisted on drawing his birds from life, working mostly from captive specimens in the London Zoological Gardens. While an assistant held the incensed animals, Lear would measure their bodily proportions with care; then the birds would be returned to their perches, harried but unharmed, and the sketching would begin.

As an illustrator, Lear was arguably just as innovative as Audubon. Not only did he help pioneer the practice of ornithological life-drawing, but he also experimented with a variety of nontraditional poses for his birds: shoulder views, unexpected angles, and specimens dangling upside down. Although he went on to depict other species, it is the parrots that reveal Lear at his best. The whimsy that distinguished him as a writer of limericks is already evident in these illustrations, and it speaks to the whimsical quality of the birds themselves. Lear and parrots were made for each other.

Consider, for instance, Lear's lithograph of the scarlet macaw (*Ara macao*; Figure 25). This is a classic instance of Lear's innovative postures; avoiding a standard side-on view, the macaw in question turns its back on the viewer as if oblivious to him. Instead of striking a pose, the bird seems preoccupied with one of the most popular of all parrot pastimes, feather-preening. There's a wisp of feather in its beak, and it has extended its left wing in a way at once perfectly natural yet ideal for displaying its primary feathers. But the best touch of all is the bird's gaze, which slyly, unexpectedly strays back to the viewer it seems at first to be ignoring. This is the parrot's equivalent of a nudge and a wink—a humorous

MACROCERCUS ARACANGA.

Red and Yellow Macaw.

Figure 25. Red and yellow macaw, from Edward Lear, *Illustrations of the Family of Psittacidae, or Parrots* (© The Natural History Museum, London)

PLYCTOLOPHUS ROSACEUS.

Salmon-crested Cockatoo. ½ Nat. Size.

Figure 26. Salmon-crested cockatoo, from Edward Lear, *Illustrations of the Family of Psittacidae, or Parrots* (© The Natural History Museum, London)

suggestion that the macaw remains very well aware of what it's ignoring, that its neglect of the audience may be both spontaneous and studied at the same time.

Again, Lear's image of the salmon-crested cockatoo (*Cacatua moluccensis*; Figure 26) makes for an exercise in playful self-awareness. Rightly or not, the curvature of their beaks seems to endow many parrots with an indelible smile, and this bird offers a perfect case in point. Add to this its standing crest—a sure sign of parrot excitement—and a claw half extended, as if in mockery of a handshake, and you have a bird that offers no pretense of neglecting the viewer but instead confronts him head-on with frank geniality. As superbly detailed as it is, this lithograph aspires to go beyond bird illustration to the status of portraiture. It's a remarkably intelligent and generous study of one living being by another.

But Lear's work provides the exception that proves the rule among nineteenth-century bird illustrators. Most seem either to depict dead birds or—like Audubon—to depict dead birds pretending to be living birds. This is so, in turn, because nineteenth-century ornithological painting gives visual expression to a broader fascination with dead animals. The illustrators themselves worked from stuffed specimens because stuffed specimens were the rage in late eighteenth- and nineteenth-century Europe.

This was the golden age of the gentleman collector. Words like "amateur" and "dilettante" were coined in the eighteenth century,[1] and private museums and *Wunderkammern* flourished. Along with everything from Roman coins and ancient manuscripts to fossils and seashells and minerals, birds became an object of the collectors' mania. Increasingly, this meant the acquisition of dead as opposed to living specimens, and this trend was further encouraged by improvements in the art of taxidermy. As a result, the earliest exercises in scientific bird illustration developed out of efforts to provide a visual catalogue of private collections like Albertus Seba's. At first, in other words, the ornithological illustrators really *were* trying to draw dead birds. The idea of trying to depict them alive came later.

The sheer extent of nineteenth-century collecting can take one aback. Indeed, the ornithological collections of the 1800s set lasting standards for such activity. At the outset of their book on the phenomenon, *The Bird Collectors*, Barbara and Richard Mearns point out the long-range consequences of this activity, noting that "in 1973 . . . there were about 4,200,000 birds in the major collections of Canada and the United States" and that by 1994 that number "had risen to 9,000,000" (12). Moreover, "for every bird preserved, many more have been wastefully killed by collectors, . . . so that the number of birds presently held in collections represents an incalculable, but presumably tiny percentage of those actually killed" (12–13). As the Mearnses point out, these vast assemblages of stuffed birds began to develop in earnest in the 1800s: "Whereas eighteenth-century collections of more than 3000 birds had been the exception, from the 1850s onwards private museums belonging to single individuals began to hold 5000, 10,000, 20,000, 30,000 and even 50,000 or 60,000 birds. At least two of them eventually exceeded 100,000 birds" (Mearns 80–81). The owners of these collections "belonged to every conceivable type of occupation, ranging from customs officials in China to one poor cabinet maker who ran away and joined the army" (Mearns 31), and the catalogue of their acquisitions makes for stupefying reading. Allan O. Hume collected 102,000 bird skins between 1862 and 1885; F. D. Godman and Osbert Salvin assembled 55,500 between 1850 and 1898; Adolphe Boucard acquired 43,000 between 1839 and 1904; Ercole Turati gathered 20,500 between 1844 and 1881; and on and on (Mearns 286–290).

The specimens in these collections are all dead, of course, but they're not *just* dead. They've been specially modified—preserved and stuffed and mounted—for the purpose of exhibition. As for the display, it aims to be both decorative and informative: to delight and to instruct, as Horace once said of poetry. In other words, the birds in these collections have been transformed into a kind of corpse-art.

Taxidermy provided the medium for this transformation, and, like the animal collecting that sustains it, taxidermy came into its own in the nineteenth century. The first stuffed birds to appear in Europe had arrived there 275 years earlier, in 1522, when the remains of Ferdinand Magellan's fleet straggled home to Spain after circumnavigating the globe. Among the expedition's cargo were some stuffed bird-of-paradise skins, a gift from the sultan of Batjan, that aroused great interest among contemporary naturalists (Stresemann 26). The earliest surviving European instructions for bird taxidermy appear shortly thereafter, in 1555, in the work of naturalist Pierre Belon (1518–1564). According to Belon, one should disembowel the bird through an anal incision, fill it with salt, and hang it by its feet to cure (8) before stuffing it. As for the stuffing, this could be anything from pepper to tobacco. But salt-cured birds succumbed to rot and to insect damage. It wasn't until 1770 that the French pharmacist Jean-Baptiste Becoeur developed an insect-proof preservative (Mearns 43). With this technology in place, dead animals became increasingly popular as objets d'art in the late eighteenth and nineteenth centuries.

And if dead birds possess artistic value, can bird effigies be far behind? There's nothing new about animal figurines and statuary, which are as old as the media in which they appear. But in the early 1700s, as the western trade with Asia expanded, Chinese and Japanese porcelains began to attract the attention and admiration of European collectors. Soon, European factories began to produce works influenced by these Asian models, and the heroic age of European porcelain sculpture was well under way by the 1750s.

From the first, parrots figured as popular subject-matter for the porcelain designers. The great porcelain houses of Meissen, Sèvres, and Wedgwood all produced ceramic parrot figures from the mid-1700s forward. But Meissen, in particular, made the parrot one of its signature motifs. The first great Meissen *Modellmeister*, Johann Joachim Kändler (1706–1775), felt a particular affinity for these birds. Between 1731 and 1745 he "is credited with modelling fifteen different varieties" (Cushion 21), including, in 1731, a delicate, brightly colored rose-ringed parakeet (Figure 27). The emphasis of this figure is on decoration, not on verisimilitude. The green glaze of the body is too bright for its subject-matter, and lacking in nuance. As for the bird itself, it "do[es] not look at the viewer, [it] represent[s]" (Menzhausen 19).

The gemlike luminosity of Kändler's designs proved popular at once, and it inspired imitations elsewhere. Between 1745 and 1754, for instance, the French porcelain factory at Vincennes—soon to move to Sèvres—produced a delicate parrot figurine, five and one-half inches tall and painted in green with highlights in yellow, blue, violet, and black (Figure 28). This is a French response to the artificial grace of Kändler's birds, and it, too, aims not to copy a living subject, but to reduce it to the status of a glittering object.

Work of this sort persists in eighteenth- and nineteenth-century porcelain design. At the end of the 1800s, for instance, when the Meissen factory sought to reinvigorate its reputation for porcelain sculpture, it hired the designers Erich Hosel (1869–1951) and Paul Walther (1876–1933) to reinterpret the old Rococo figurines in light of fin-de-siècle artistic principles. Walther, in particular, excelled at animal sculpture, and one result is a glittering pair of Jugendstil macaws that he produced in 1910 (Figure 29). In a way, the art of the 1890s and early 1900s makes a perfect counterpart to early Rococo Meissen. Both are about surface, both are about decoration, and both are interested in exploiting unusual

Figure 27. Rose-ringed parakeet modeled by Johann Joachim Kändler (Staatliche Kunstsammlungen, Porzellansammlung, Dresden)

materials and textures. Walther's macaws bring out this affinity. With their complementary blue and green plumage, their balanced poses, and their placement on an irregular white porcelain pedestal, they're more like a Lalique brooch than like anything you might see in a zoo or aviary.

Taxidermy, porcelain sculpture, paintings like Wright's, and poetry like Crabbe's: this sort of work illustrates an increasing trend in the late 1700s and 1800s toward the treatment of parrots as what we might call inert material. To this we might also add the steadily increasing popularity of bird feathers in women's haberdashery during the same period. In Britain, for instance, "the plumage industry was an important part of the national economy and it has been estimated that from 1870 to 1920 twenty thousand tons of ornamental plumage entered the country each year. The most popular species were herons and egrets . . . birds of paradise, cock o' the rocks, parrots, toucans, trogons, and hummingbirds" (Mearns 11). Here again, nineteenth-century parrot culture works toward the conjunction of art and death.

Figure 28. French porcelain parrot, artist unknown (Musée des Arts Décoratifs, Paris)

Yet perhaps the most outstanding instance of this association comes not in the visual arts but in literature. Gustave Flaubert's "A Simple Heart" (1877) has not only secured a reputation as one of the most complex and enduring works of nineteenth-century French literary realism; it has also inspired a major twentieth-century fictional response, Julian Barnes's *Flaubert's Parrot*, of which more later.

Written for Flaubert's friend George Sand, who had complained about the cynicism and gloom of his work (Lottman 285–86), "A Simple Heart" casts itself as a story of human faith and decency. It follows the life of a domestic servant, Félicité, who endures years of abuse and neglect from her superiors and yet remains pious, generous, and sweet-tempered to the end. The highlights of her tale are generally dismal. At eighteen, she is seduced by a young man who abandons her for a wealthy widow. She then enters the service of another widow, Madame Aubain, and her two children, to whom she grows deeply attached. Of the two children, the older, a boy, goes off to school and in time develops into a gambler and general ne'er-do-well. The younger, a girl of whom Félicité is especially fond, dies of pleurisy, and Félicité holds a grief-stricken vigil by her dead body. Félicité then becomes equally attached to a nephew who leaves France for the Caribbean

Figure 29. Porcelain macaws modeled by Paul
Walther (Staatliche Kunstsammlungen,
Porzellansammlung, Dresden)

and dies, after a long and heart-rending absence, under unexplained circumstances. During the time of this nephew's disappearance, Madame Aubain treats
Félicité with callous contempt. As Félicité grows older, she engages in good
works, eventually bonding with an old man who suffers from a cancerous tumor
on his arm. He, too, dies.

But Félicité forms the most important emotional connection of her life with
a parrot, not a human being. In 1824 a new subprefect arrives in her district:
"Baron de Larsonnière, a former consul in America, whose household included,
apart from his wife, his sister-in-law with three young ladies, already quite
grown-up. They could be seen on their lawn, dressed in loose smocks; they
owned a negro and a parrot" (26). The bird fascinates Félicité, and in time, when
Larsonnière is promoted to a prefecture, his wife, unable to bring the parrot along
to their new home, leaves it as a gift for Madame Aubain. Madame Aubain, in
turn, quickly tires of the bird and gives it to Félicité.

The parrot's name is Loulou. Hailing as it does from America, it reminds Félicité of her dead nephew. Flaubert describes her relationship with Loulou in idyllic terms:

> As if to entertain her he would reproduce the regular clicking of the spit turning, the fishmonger's shrill cry, the sawing of the carpenter who lived opposite; and when the doorbell rang, he would imitate Madame Aubain: "Félicité! The door! The door!"
>
> They would hold conversations, he repeating *ad nauseam* the three phrases of his repertory, and she answering with words which were equally disconnected but came from the heart. In her isolation Loulou was almost like a son, a lover to her. He would climb up her fingers, nibble her lips, cling to her bodice; and as she bent forward, wagging her head as nurses do, the wide wings of her bonnet and those of the bird quivered in unison. (31)

But Flaubert is not about to permit his heroine the consolations of lasting companionship, even with a bird. One frigid morning the parrot dies, apparently of a stroke. This final loss renders Félicité so inconsolable that Madame Aubain arranges to have Loulou stuffed, and in taxidermed form, at last, the bird becomes the old serving-woman's ideal companion.

Over the course of her tribulations, Félicité has grown understandably eccentric and religious. In her simplicity, she begins to identify the stuffed Loulou with the Holy Trinity:

> In church she always gazed at the Holy Spirit, and noticed that he looked something like the parrot. The likeness seemed still more evident in a popular print of our Lord's baptism. With his purple wings and emerald green body he was the very image of Loulou. . . . They became associated in her mind, so that the parrot became sanctified from this connexion with the Holy Spirit, which in turn became more lifelike and readily intelligible in her eyes. The Father could never have chosen to express himself through a dove, for those creatures cannot speak, but rather one of Loulou's ancestors. (34)

This association then leads into the tale's final and most notorious scene. For as Félicité lies on her deathbed, breathing her last, she thinks she sees the heavens open to reveal "a gigantic parrot hovering over her head" (40). With that, the story ends.

Among critical reactions to this tale, the best-known may well be Barnes's 1984 novel *Flaubert's Parrot*. Early in that work, Barnes remarks that "the control of tone is vital" to Flaubert's story:

Imagine the technical difficulty of writing a story in which a badly-stuffed bird with a ridiculous name ends up standing for one third of the Trinity, and in which the intention is neither satirical, sentimental, nor blasphemous. Imagine further telling such a story from the point of view of an ignorant old woman without making it sound derogatory or coy. But then the aim of *Un coeur simple* is quite elsewhere: the parrot is a perfect and controlled example of the Flaubertian grotesque. (17)

This, at least, is how Barnes views the matter. But whatever Flaubert's tale may have to do with the grotesque, it's fashioned from the stuff of nineteenth-century sentimental fiction. The story's bizarre combination of dead birds, dead people, grieving women, and religious belief is the very material we encounter in Huck Finn's visit with the Grangerfords, and again in Crabbe's *Parish Register*, and again in Wright's *Experiment on a Bird in the Air Pump*.

The reason for this seems clear enough to me. Called upon to write a story that runs counter to his personal instincts—a story about consolation rather than desolation—Flaubert draws instinctively upon the subject matter he despises. The result is a work that may indeed transcend both satire and sentiment, but it does so by forcing the two idioms into a kind of standoff. "A Simple Heart" is too pathetic, too sympathetic with Félicité's hardships, to qualify as satire, and yet too detached and mocking to pass as sentiment. Other readers of Flaubert, less well-known than Barnes but equally astute, have noted what cold comfort "A Simple Heart" offers both to its heroine and to its audience.[2] If the best recompense one can expect for a life of selfless devotion is a stuffed bird, then selflessness and devotion begin to seem as simple-minded as Félicité herself. Yet Félicité remains no mere object of ridicule. Her generosity is too profound, her heartache too genuine. In the end, "A Simple Heart" may succeed best as a work of sentiment that wants to be a work of satire, and that ends up as neither.

In any case, Félicité's attachment to Loulou begs to be read alongside the parallel attachments of other nineteenth-century sentimental heroines. Whatever else it does, Loulou's stuffed body provides the ultimate index of Félicité's capacity for love: the very thing that makes her more than an object of derision. When Emmeline Grangerford draws a weepy heroine with a dead songbird, she is working with the same general motif, and to the same general purpose.

It's only an additional irony that Flaubert himself, like Audubon before him (and, notionally, Emmeline Grangerford after him), was working from a dead model. In the course of researching "A Simple Heart," he borrowed a stuffed parrot from the Museum of Natural History in Rouen and kept it on his work-desk for inspiration.[3] As Flaubert remarks in a letter written to his niece Caroline on July 22, 1876, "I write in front of an Amazon [parrot] which sits on my table, its beak sideways to me, and observes me with its eyes of glass" (*Correspondance* 7:325; my translation). The image is a creepy one: Flaubert, the critic of human crassness, stupidity, and greed, drawing his inspiration from such an object. Despite his contempt for bourgeois behavior and sentimental writing, he ends up repeating the gestures of both, in his life as well as his art.

Still, in some ways Loulou reaches back to older images of the parrot. When the bird first appears in "A Simple Heart," in the company of "a negro" (26), and when the same "negro" conveys the bird to Madame Aubain as a present (28), Loulou recalls the Renaissance identification of parrots with ethnic servants. But more intriguing by far is the connection between Loulou and the Holy Spirit. In its turn, this recalls the Trinitarian associations of the Middle Ages.

I'm inclined to see this fact as more than coincidence. As it happens, only a few months before completing "A Simple Heart," Flaubert had finished its companion piece, "The Legend of Saint Julian," a tale with medieval setting whose protagonist begins life as a mighty hunter. Flaubert researched his fiction meticulously as a matter of course, and the process of researching "Saint Julian" brought him into contact with a good deal of medieval hunting- and beast-lore, as well as saints' lives and other religious literature. Any of these sources could have offered him material dealing with parrots and their medieval associations with the Trinity.[4]

The result, I think, is that Flaubert introduced such associations into "A Simple Heart," either by design or by instinct, to invest his tale with an element of the miraculous. At the very least, his physical description of Loulou takes on a markedly fanciful air, despite the fact that he had a stuffed bird staring him in the face while he wrote, and needed only describe it as he saw it in order to be realistic. In fact, Loulou is surprisingly unlike any actual Amazon parrot: "His body was green, his wingtips pink, the front of his head blue, his breast gold" (28). Flaubert, the master of realism, researched "A Simple Heart" with all of his customary thoroughness, even going so far as to obtain information concerning the habits and diseases of parrots. As he observes in a letter to a friend in July 1876, "I need to see some parrots and to learn as many details as possible concerning them" (*Correspondance* 7:319; my translation). Yet when it comes time to present Loulou to his readers, Flaubert departs from reportorial accuracy, creating a bird that is part Amazon (the body is green and the blue of the head corresponds to the facial coloration of a blue-fronted Amazon [*Amazona aestiva*]) and part unclassifiable (the pink wingtips and golden breast defy identification). Moreover, the "purple wings" of the Holy Spirit in Félicité's print of Christ's baptism (34) speak directly to the pink tips of Loulou's wings. Flaubert sacrifices anatomical accuracy at the moment his bird begins to resemble part of the Trinity. In the process, he also produces a parrot like those of the medieval bestiarists: miraculous and unrealistic in the same measure. In keeping with Félicité's emotional investment, these medieval associations endow the bird with an air of the marvelous.

Yet the very antiquity of such associations also renders them obsolete and inaccessible: hard to recognize as such, and harder still to take seriously. As a result, Félicité's attachment to Loulou seems both endearing and superstitious, the product of a naive spirit whose capacity for goodness has itself become a touching anachronism in the modern world. It's as if Flaubert had exhumed the miraculous parrots of a former age just to prove that they were dead, and then, having made his point, had laid them to rest again forever.

Still, amidst all this overwrought contemplation of dead parrots, a least one major nineteenth-century writer found them not quite dead enough, or at least not quite melancholy enough, for his purposes.

In *Graham's Magazine* for April 1846, Edgar Allan Poe offers some carefully sculpted insights into the composition of his lugubrious master-jingle, "The Raven" (1845). As to the origin of the poem's refrain, Poe explains that he wanted one word to reinforce the mournful quality of the entire production, and quickly chose "Nevermore." This choice being made, however, he next needed to invent a "sufficiently plausible reason for [the refrain's] continuous repetition" (165). It clearly wouldn't do, for instance, to have a human being say the word over and over. So Poe cast around for other expedients: "Here, then, immediately arose the idea of a non-reasoning creature capable of speech; and, very naturally, a parrot, in the first instance, suggested itself, but was superseded forthwith by a Raven, as equally capable of speech, and infinitely more in keeping with the intended tone" (165). Pretty boy, nevermore, pretty boy, nevermore, cracker, cracker, cracker: one can sense Poe's dilemma here. And the problem is rendered all the more pressing by Poe's own determination to screw sentiment to the breaking point. Assuming, as a general rule, that "Beauty of whatever kind . . .

invariably excites the sensitive soul to tears," he therefore concludes that "Melancholy is . . . the most legitimate of all poetical tones" (164). It's a view he shares with Emmeline Grangerford, among others. And, in a literary world devoted to the obsessive cultivation of one's personal misery, every hint of the risible must be rigorously suppressed.

Yet despite such attitudes and affectations, parrots don't stop being popular as live pets in the late eighteenth and nineteenth centuries. On the contrary, they grow increasingly available as such. Researching the for-sale and lost-and-found notices in French periodicals from the late 1700s, Louise Robbins notes that "beginning in the 1770s the ad columns usually included several pets per month. . . . At least 150 notices referring to lost parrots and parakeets appeared in the [biweekly] *Affiches* between 1778 and 1790. Considering that many people who lost parrots must not have listed them, and that most owners of parrots must not have lost them, that would seem to add up to a lot of parrots in Paris" (124). What holds true of Paris, in turn, holds for other cities as well.

Indeed, the growing middle-class popularity of pet parrots generates three landmark works of nineteenth-century French realist/impressionist painting: Gustave Courbet's *Woman with a Parrot* (1866; Figure 30), Edouard Manet's 1867 canvas of the same name (Figure 31), and Pierre-Auguste Renoir's like-titled work of 1871 (Figure 32). Although these paintings pursue very different aesthetic trajectories, the later ones clearly respond to the earlier (this is especially true of Manet's). In time-honored fashion, all three painters associate women with parrots, but they present this association as neither satirical nor aristocratic. Instead, at their hands it becomes a vehicle for intimate, everyday, domestic art.

In the case of Courbet, this intimacy takes a powerful erotic turn. Courbet's model sprawls naked on a bed in a dark, vaguely defined room, her gown discarded beside her. Against the surrounding gloom her pale body, stretched out upon a white sheet, radiates voluptuous warmth. The result is enormously sexy, but the sexiness isn't directed at the viewer; instead, the woman's body and attention are turned away, toward the pet parrot that hovers above her on her outstretched hand. And the entire design of the painting is calculated to give an unpremeditated air, as if one were gazing at a private and impromptu scene from which one was excluded. "The composition, for example, is strongly weighted toward the left" (Fried 203), with the empty space of the painting's right side occupied only by the parrot's equally empty perch. In short, the work's erotic

Figure 30. Gustave Courbet, *Woman with a Parrot* (Metropolitan Museum of Art, New York, H. O. Havemeyer Collection, Bequest of Mrs. H. O. Havemeyer, 1929 [29.100.57])

appeal derives largely from the care with which it has been staged to seem unstaged.

In response, Manet appears determined to emphasize the very self-consciousness of his domestic subject. She remains resolutely clothed and upright, staring back at the viewer with impenetrable composure. Her face is a mask, her hair pulled up in icy contrast to the glorious tresses of Courbet's nude. She fingers a monocle in her right hand—an implement of visual scrutiny that seems to mock the viewer's own voyeuristic impulses. And where Courbet presents his parrot as a kind of proxy lover, entirely given over to the intimate bond it enjoys with its mistress, Manet restores the bird to its perch. There it sits in its own space, wings folded sedately, as if challenging the viewer to discern anything other than appearances.

But if Courbet depicts an erotic world of private intimacy, and Manet presents a calculated vision of bourgeois self-possession, Renoir seems to combine the two impulses. His woman has a pre-impressionist solidity; her clothing is rich but restrained, and the room in which she stands is well lit and clearly realized, with all the appointments of a prosperous fin de siècle household. But the wom-

Figure 31. Edouard Manet, *Woman with a Parrot* (Metropolitan Museum of Art, New York, Gift of Erwin Davis, 1889 [89.21.3])

Figure 32. Pierre-Auguste Renoir, *Woman with a Parrot* (*La Femme à la perruche*), 1871 (Solomon R. Guggenheim Museum, New York, Thannhauser Collection, Gift, Justin K. Thannhauser, 1978)

an's attention is turned inward, toward the bird that perches on her hand and that figures as a substitute for the decorous middle-class society that the room exists to entertain. Made up for appearances, the woman and parrot nonetheless exist in intimate rapport with one another, illustrating the special bond that obtains between mistress and pet.

In their various ways, these three paintings illustrate the increasing popularity of parrots as pets of the affluent citizenry in nineteenth-century Europe. Such works attest to what we might call the bourgeoisification of the parrot. And they find an American literary counterpart in Kate Chopin's novel *The Awakening* (1899)—a work consumed by bourgeois life and its discontents.

Set in New Orleans, *The Awakening* traces the downfall of its heroine, Edna Pontellier, as she repudiates her unhappy marriage to a local merchant's clerk, conducts two extramarital affairs while seeking to live on her own, and finds the censure of polite society so damaging that she eventually commits suicide. Chopin's novel is filled with interiors like the one Renoir depicts in his *Woman with a Parrot*, decorated with "white muslin curtains" (68) and flowers and candelabras with "yellow silk shades" (143), and amidst these accoutrements of civilization there also appears "a green and yellow parrot, which [hangs] in a cage outside the door" of the Pontelliers' vacation cottage (43). The bird makes two appearances—first at the novel's beginning, where it calls out *"Allez-vous en! Allez-vous en! Sapristi!* That's all right!" (43), and later, when it gives vent to the same sentiments during a soporific piano recital given by twin fourteen-year-old girls: "He was the only being present who possessed sufficient candor to admit that he was not listening to these gracious performances for the first time that summer. Old Monsieur Farival, grandfather of the twins, grew indignant over the interruption and insisted upon having the bird removed and consigned to regions of darkness" (69). Caged and polyglot (it speaks "a little Spanish, and also a language which nobody understood" [43]), this bird parallels Edna in its impatience for bourgeois proprieties, and its consignment to "regions of darkness" prefigures her own fate.

Although parrots became ever more available to the European middle class in the late eighteenth and nineteenth centuries, they remained popular among the upper social ranks as well. In France, for instance, Louis XVI singled out a particular pet dealer for patronage as the "'governor, preceptor, and regent of the birds, parrots, monkeys, apes, and marmosets of his Majesty'" (Franklin 22:252). The mistress of Louis XV, Madame de Pompadour (1721–1764), had a favored parrot for whom she provided in her will (MacDonogh 57). The Marquise du Deffand (1697–1784), friend of Voltaire, Walpole, Benjamin Franklin, and many others, recorded that her contemporary Madame de Peyre, approaching her end, gave her two parrots to the duchesses of La Vallière and Aiguillon; "these women were her close friends," Deffand writes, "but the parrots will console them" (qtd. in Franklin 22:184). And such birds enjoyed certain consolations themselves. Ancien régime aristocrats kept their winged pets in cages of great luxury, some "adorned with imitation diamonds, others embellished with amber and ivory" (Franklin 22:182–183).

At roughly the same time, parrots were also becoming the preferred intimates of various unhappy aristocratic spouses. For instance, Elizabeth of Bavaria, empress of Austria (1837–1898) turned to her birds for consolation during her uncomfortable marriage to Franz Joseph I (MacDonogh 23). Alexandra of Denmark, princess of Wales from 1863 to 1901, had to tolerate a legendary amount of philandering from her husband, the future King Edward VII (Ashdown 181, 182, 185). In the process, she acquired a Moluccan cockatoo whose own emotional condition, as reflected in contemporary illustrations, could scarcely have been better than its mistress's; the bird was a morbid feather-plucker (Arthur G. Butler 30). Other royal partners, fond as they might be of their pets, refused to tolerate such neglect. Catherine the Great of Russia grew so disaffected with her husband, Peter III, that she conducted a variety of illicit affairs under his nose. When her suspicious consort attempted to restrict her movements, she declared indignantly, "I could not imagine why he wanted me to die of boredom in my room with no one but my dog and parrot for company" (qtd. in MacDonogh 30).

The owners of these birds took much joy from their pets and formed intense emotional bonds with them, as parrot-fanciers continue to do today. Yet even in the midst of such relationships, as Deffand's story of Madame de Peyre illustrates, the obsession with death could reappear. The French naturalist Georges-Louis Buffon (1707–1788) offers another case in point. Buffon kept an African gray, which he allowed to fly freely about his house, and he explained his attachment to this bird, and to parrots in general, as follows:

> In imitating our words, the parrot seems to take on something of our inclinations and habits: it loves and it hates; it has attachments, jealousies, preferences, caprices; it admires, applauds, and encourages itself; it becomes cheerful or mournful; it seems to be moved and touched by caresses; it gives affectionate kisses; in a house of mourning it learns to mourn; and, accustomed to repeating

the dear name of a deceased person, it reminds sensitive hearts of their pleasures and sorrows. (qtd. in Robbins 129)

At such moments, even the language of Enlightenment science reveals its deep association with sentiment. Therefore it seems only right that when Madame de Pompadour died, she arranged for her beloved parrot to pass into Buffon's keeping (MacDonogh 57). Such arrangements foreshadow the "royal cult of animal death" (MacDonogh 193) that arose in nineteenth-century Europe, especially in Victorian England, where deceased pets received burial with elaborate monuments, elegiac tributes, and much histrionic grief, all in imitation of Queen Victoria's mourning for her consort Albert.

Across the Atlantic, too, parrots grew ever more popular during the late eighteenth and nineteenth centuries. In fact, they were the first—and during the 1800s perhaps the most popular—of presidential pets. Martha Washington owned one and took it with her to the first presidential residence, in New York City, and thence to Philadelphia as well. In September 1794, her granddaughter, Eleanor Custis, who was spending the summer with her, wrote to a friend that "I spent ten days very agreeably . . . teaching our pretty green pet to sing Pauvre Madelon. You may guess what kind it was. A master peice of thorough Base (in music spelt Bass, but I thought Base would give you a better idea of his harmonious voice)" (18). As Nelly's pun might intimate, such bravura musical performances seem not to have endeared the bird to George. On the hard journey back from Philadelphia to Mount Vernon by wagon, his term as president expired, Washington wrote to his secretary, who had remained behind in Philadelphia: "On one side I am called upon to remember the Parrot, on the other to remember the dog. For my own part I should not pine if both were forgot" (1:25).

Three presidents later, parrots were in the White House under James Madison, whose wife Dolly owned a blue and gold macaw. This bird was her "great treasure" (Anthony 243), perhaps because its gorgeous plumage alleviated the gloom of her Quaker upbringing. As First Lady, she encouraged schoolchildren to gather and watch through a window while she fed the bird, and when the British burned Washington in 1814, she had it conveyed for safety to Octagon House, the temporary residence of the French Minister to the United States. In 1837, now a widow approaching her seventieth birthday, she still had the parrot with her, and its antics were still a subject of conversation (Anthony 335).

When Andrew Jackson arrived at the White House in 1829, he did not bring his parrot with him. The bird, a gift he had given to his wife Rachel, remained behind at the Hermitage in Tennessee. Yet even so, it serves as the central character in the most famous of presidential parrot anecdotes: the apocryphal tale that it had to be ejected from Jackson's interment in 1845 because, true to its erstwhile owner's character, it insisted on screaming obscenities over the ex-president's body (Truman 85). Here again one detects an odd association between parrots and the funereal.

After Jackson, presidents Grant, McKinley, Theodore Roosevelt, and Coolidge populated the White House with parrots of various species. Grant's was an ill-tempered bird given to the family by Mexican minister Matias Romero (perhaps as payback for the Mexican War) and quickly pawned off on friends (Kelly 34). McKinley's double yellow-headed Amazon, named Washington Post, grew famous for accosting any and all women with the cry, "Oh, look at all the pretty girls!" (Truman 15). Roosevelt kept a massive hyacinth macaw named Eli, which lived in the White House greenhouse (Roosevelt 33). In a letter to Joel Chandler Harris, Roosevelt confessed to viewing the bird "with dark suspicion" and described it as having "a bill that I think could bite through boiler plate" (35). The Coolidge parrot, of indeterminate species, belonged to the president's wife Grace (Kelly 62).

Indeed, the 1800s marked a temporary zenith of the parrot's popularity as a household animal. In the early twentieth century, when these birds came to be associated with various kinds of disease—especially psittacosis, or parrot fever—their demand as pets dropped dramatically, and, for better or worse, it has recovered only over the past few decades. In keeping with this trend, the birds' early popularity with presidential families reached its height under Theodore Roosevelt and has since declined to nothing.

The ill-tempered parrot of Grant's administration in fact belonged to his son Jesse; likewise, Roosevelt's hyacinth macaw, Eli, belonged to *his* son, Teddy. These cases attest to the enduring fascination parrots have exerted for children. And less than twenty years before Roosevelt entered the White House, there appeared in Britain a work of children's literature that would capitalize upon this same fascination while permanently altering the parrot's cultural associations in the process. That work was Robert Louis Stevenson's *Treasure Island* (1883), an adventure tale written primarily for boys like Teddy Roosevelt, Jr., which incidentally established the greatest psittacine cliche of the past hundred and fifty years: the link between parrots and pirates.

This fact becomes all the more intriguing given that *Treasure Island* itself was not unique either in form or in subject matter. It was preceded by a wide range of pirate novels, both British and American, which appeared with increasing frequency from the late 1700s onward. The nine or ten of these I've skimmed through all conform to the same general pattern: popular, bodice-busting melodramas that involve pirates, threatened innocence, and exotic locales. None of those I've read through mention parrots at all. Nor do parrots serve as a regular fixture of the theatrical pirate melodramas on the Anglo-American stage at roughly the same time, which culminate in that parrotless masterpiece, *The Pirates of Penzance* (1879).

Yet *Treasure Island* also draws its subject-matter from a broad body of nonfictional pirate literature, much of it already in circulation by the early 1700s, which had itself helped create a ready audience for the later pirate novels and plays. Of these works, the most influential were John Esquemeling's *Buccaneers of America* (1684) and *A General History of the Pyrates* (1724), often attributed to Defoe.[5] The work by Esquemeling, a surgeon who sailed with Henry Morgan, remains the single most important printed source for pirate lore, and it left a clear imprint upon Stevenson's novel. Moreover, as it happens, both Esquemeling and Defoe mention parrots in their histories, but rarely, and not at all in the way one might expect. These references occur entirely in the context of geographical descriptions, and never in connection with the pirates whose careers are being documented. Amidst a discussion of the birds of Hispaniola, for instance, Esquemeling remarks, "It is already known to everybody that the parrots which we have in Europe are transported to us from these parts of the world. Whence may be inferred that, seeing such a number of these talkative birds are preserved among us, notwithstanding the diversity of climates, much greater multitudes are to be found where the air and temperament is natural to them" (42–43).

Likewise, Defoe mentions parrots during an account of the islands of São Tomé and Del Principe. In describing trade with the inhabitants of the former, he notes that "with Money you give . . . half a Dollar for a Dozen of Paraquets" (1:179). As for Del Principe, Defoe describes it as "a pleasant Intermixture of Hill and Valley; the Hills spread with Palms, Coco-Nuts, and Cotton-Trees, with numbers of Monkeys and Parrots among them" (1:183). Esquemeling and Defoe keep parrots very much in the background of their narratives. And rightly so: the pirates they describe led squalid, makeshift lives, with little occasion for—or interest in—pet-keeping of any kind. The association between pirates and parrots that we now take for granted is in fact an artistic embellishment, traceable to Stevenson.

Stevenson's own thoughts on the parrot in *Treasure Island* have nothing to do with the pirate tradition as such. Writing about the novel's composition some years after the fact, he attributes his inspiration for Long John Silver's bird to Defoe, but not to Defoe's *General History of the Pyrates*: "No doubt the parrot once belonged to Robinson Crusoe. No doubt the skeleton is conveyed from Poe. I think little of these, they are trifles and details; and no man can hope to have a monopoly of skeletons or make a corner in talking birds" (xii). Stevenson himself doesn't see the device of the parrot as intrinsic to pirate-lore, and he dismisses it as a trivial feature of his story. Yet this particular detail of *Treasure Island* may well be the book's most lasting legacy to modern culture.

As a literary device, Long John Silver's parrot embodies all that is most attractive and threatening about the pirates of *Treasure Island*, but it actually takes up very little space in the novel. The bird first appears after young Jim Hawkins takes ship aboard the *Hispaniola* in search of buried treasure. There, he enters an exotic world of risk and adventure, a world over which Long John Silver, parrot on his shoulder, presides. The bird makes it presence felt in early scenes of ship-life where Hawkins bonds with the old pirate:

> "Come away, Hawkins," he would say; "come and have a yarn with John. Nobody more welcome than yourself, my son. Sit you down and hear the news. Here's Cap'n Flint—I calls my parrot Cap'n Flint, after the famous buccaneer—here's Cap'n Flint predicting success to our v'yage. Wasn't you, cap'n?"
> And the parrot would say, with great rapidity, "Pieces of eight! Pieces of eight! Pieces of eight!" till you wondered that it was not out of breath, or till John threw his handkerchief over the cage. (59–60)

The bird's refrain, like its name, lends it both allure and menace. Small wonder that Hawkins falls in love with its owner. A user-friendly reincarnation of Captain Flint, Silver's parrot renders piracy attractive, and Silver invites Hawkins to participate in the pirates' exploits vicariously through the bird:

> "Now, that bird," he would say, "is, may be, two hundred years old, Hawkins—they lives for ever mostly; and if anybody's seen more wickedness, it must be the devil himself. She's sailed with England, the great Cap'n England, the pirate. She's been at Madagascar, and at Malabar, and Surinam, and Providence,

and Portobello. She was at the fishing up of the wrecked plate ships. It's there she learned 'Pieces of eight,' and little wonder; three hundred and fifty thousand of 'em, Hawkins! She was at the boarding of the Viceroy of the Indies out of Goa, she was; and to look at her you would think she was a babby. But you smelt powder—didn't you, cap'n?"

"Stand by to go about," the parrot would scream.

"Ah, she's a handsome craft, she is," the cook would say, and giver her sugar from his pocket, and then the bird would peck at the bars and swear straight on, passing belief for wickedness. "There," John would add, "you can't touch pitch and not be mucked, lad. Here's this poor old innocent bird o' mine swearing blue fire, and none the wiser, you may to that. She would swear the same, in a manner of speaking, before chaplain." And John would touch his forelock with a solemn way he had, that made me think he was the best of men. (60)

As it attests to the corrupting influence of bad company, the bird offers a tacit warning to Hawkins. But Silver's energy and appeal make it easy to overlook such signs. As a result, critics like to view *Treasure Island* as an exercise in

> the "sentimental education" theme of a boy growing to maturity and learning new values. . . . Yet it is typical of Stevenson's ambivalence that the process of reaching maturity should be viewed with jaundiced eyes; at the end of *Treasure Island* Jim Hawkins, with the treasure in his grasp, is set for a life of boring and inglorious retirement; only with and through Long John Silver has he truly lived, so that the rejection of Silver . . . entails the rejection of what is best in the hero's nature. (McLynn 199)

Stevenson's animal emblem for that part of the self—exotic, adventurous, animated, colorful, morally ambiguous and vaguely threatening—is Captain Flint the parrot.

Given Hollywood's traditional fondness for the comforting and saccharine, it should be no surprise that when America's film industry took up *Treasure Island* in 1934 (for the fourth time; the first three efforts were all silent), the project's director sought to suppress just this aspect of Stevenson's book. The director in question, Victor Fleming, was a man of no mean gifts; later in his career he filmed *Gone with the Wind* and *The Wizard of Oz*. In adapting *Treasure Island* for the screen, Fleming lent special emphasis to the relationship between Jim Hawkins (played by Jackie Cooper with half-witted naivete) and Long John Silver (Wallace Beery, whose combination of bone-headed duplicity and superficial good nature foreshadow the character Ernest Borgnine played in *McHale's Navy*). When it comes to their farewell, Fleming reworks his material at length.

In fact, Stevenson's novel doesn't give Silver and Hawkins a farewell scene at all, and makes absolutely no effort to account for the fate of Silver's bird. Captain Flint receives its last mention at the climax of the novel, when Silver, Hawkins, and the only five pirates still remaining under Silver's command set out at length to dig for the treasure they've been seeking. As Hawkins narrates, "Silver had two guns slung about him—one before and one behind—besides the great cutlass at his waist, and a pistol in each pocket of his square-tailed coat. To complete his strange appearance, Captain Flint sat perched upon his shoulder and gabbling odds and ends of purposeless sea-talk" (187). After that, there's no mention of the parrot at all in the ensuing action and denouement. It might as well never have existed; indeed, once Hawkins begins to harden his heart against Silver, the parrot gradually disappears altogether. As for Silver himself, he makes his exit while a prisoner aboard the *Hispaniola*, returning to England to stand trial for his crimes. One evening, Hawkins relates, a sympathetic crew member frees Silver from custody and gives him a bag of money "to help him on his further wanderings. I think we were all pleased to be so cheaply quit of him" (205). Hawkins's final comment here signals his rejection of Silver and all he stands for. Like his bird, the old pirate slips ingloriously into the mists of Stevenson's tale, without so much as a goodbye.

But Fleming completely rewrites Stevenson's ending to make Hawkins responsible for Silver's escape. As Silver, parrot on shoulder, lies amidship in durance vile, Hawkins comes to visit him, and Silver describes the horrors of death by hanging in such detail that Hawkins cannot bear it. Seizing a handy key, he unlocks Silver's cell and leads him above deck, where the two conduct a final conversation. When Silver, who has surreptitiously stuffed his pockets with gold, lets drop a bag of his ill-gotten gains, Jim picks it up and offers to return it to him. Silver high-mindedly refuses and climbs into one of the ship's boats. He then turns back to Jim for a last farewell:

> Silver: Well, matey . . . [removing the parrot from his shoulder and placing it on Jim's] here. Feed her good. And put her . . . you put her down below decks when any women are around.
> Hawkins [starting to cry]: I will. I promise I will.
> Silver: Oh, belay that. Don't do that. Our courses will cross again some time. [Fights back a sniffle himself.]

Silver consoles Jim by suggesting a possible return trip to Treasure Island, with Hawkins in command of a ship seeking the bar silver that remains there, and with himself aboard as mate. And with that, he rows off into the distance.

Figure 33. Long John Silver (played by Wallace Beery), Jim Hawkins (Jackie Cooper), and a feathered friend in Victor Fleming's production of *Treasure Island* (Metro Goldwyn Mayer)

Although Silver is now gone, his bird remains with Hawkins, a marker of the enduring affection that binds the old pirate and the young boy together (Figure 33). The shadow of death that hangs over Stevenson's book is dispelled in favor of a future reunion and a pet in the here and now. And if we recall Silver's own claim, in Stevenson's novel, that parrots "lives for ever mostly," then Fleming's rewrite of the end to *Treasure Island* can be read as a rejection of death in the literal sense as well. Where the nineteenth century offers us a lugubrious parade of feathered corpses in the name of high seriousness and refined emotion, the twentieth gives us something else: the parrot as eternal party animal, always there, always game, reassuringly amusing. Death doesn't disappear from this intellectual environment; if anything, it becomes more ubiquitous than ever. But in the process, it also becomes a joke.

# Chapter 5

# Dead Parrot Sketch

In the twentieth century and beyond, dead parrots are everywhere, and often they're considered funny, or at least surreal. But why should dead parrots suddenly become such a regular object of hilarity? For one thing, this response offers a welcome reversal of the nineteenth-century solemnity—a posture that certainly invites ridicule. Then again, western society in the twentieth century developed as a culture of abundance and redundancy, saturated with goods of every shape and description, a world in which life itself becomes subject to mechanical reproduction via film and video and television. In such a world, death may seem hard to take seriously, and one way to make light of it is to displace it onto a succession of talking birds. So the parrots that appear in this chapter often seem like figures from a Roadrunner cartoon; annihilated repeatedly for the viewer's pleasure but none the wiser for the experience, they keep coming back for more of the same.

Still, behind the parade of plentiful, reliable gratification there remains the possibility that modernity is using itself up, exhausting its resources, ignoring its own irresponsible levity and bad faith. This anxiety emerges in recent environmental concerns, and in the looming specter of mass extinction that casts its shadow upon the nonstop party of modern and postmodern culture in the west. My final chapter will address these matters.

George Bernard Shaw is wrongly credited with a remark that helps define the twentieth-century literary use of parrots: "Parrots are amusing and never die. You wish they did."[1] In its brevity, this quip works both as a flippant one-liner and as a patent truism. From the former standpoint, it's an exercise in form. If, for argument's sake, we take its attribution seriously, one doesn't get the sense that the vegetarian Shaw really wants to kill parrots; he simply considers them annoying and finds it funny to express his annoyance as a kind of rhetorical death wish. But at the same time, the line works as a serious corrective to overwrought

Victorian sensibilities: it embraces violence and death matter-of-factly, even joyously, as if daring the reader to object to such basic features of our lot. From this standpoint the really outstanding annoyance would seem to be not parrots but mortality itself, and our reaction to it. Shorn of its emotional enormity, it becomes something that just happens, and it doesn't bear making too much of.

Twentieth-century writers work many variations on this theme, invoking psittacine mortality as a way to make light of death in general. Evelyn Waugh's *The Loved One* (1948) provides a typical case in point. Waugh's novel is all about death, both animal and human, and it elides the two through its principal settings: a Los Angeles pet cemetery called the Happier Hunting Ground, where the English expatriate Dennis Barlow makes his living, and Whispering Glades, the posh funeral home where Barlow's nemesis and rival in romance, Mr. Joyboy, holds forth as head undertaker. The self-indulgent excess of the pet cemetery finds a perfect counterpart in the atrocious vulgarity of Whispering Glades, a kind of mortician's Disney World with resting-plots organized around copies of great European statuary.

As his novel develops, Waugh forces these establishments to collide through parallel funerals. On one hand, there is the lamentable demise of Mr. Joyboy's mother's parrot, a singularly charm-free beast named Sambo. When Joyboy brings the novel's love interest, Aimee Thanatogenos, home for supper on their first date, Mrs. Joyboy remarks, "If I hadn't Sambo to love me I might as well be dead" (114). In Waugh's novel death is easily enough arranged, but as things transpire, it is the bird, not Mrs. Joyboy, who shuffles off its mortal coil. This curious circumstance places Dennis Barlow, pet undertaker and Joyboy's rival for Aimee, in the awkward position of conducting a funeral on behalf of his sexual competitor.

The resulting obsequies prove embarrassing in various ways, causing Aimee, one of the few mourners present, to sever her ties with Dennis. When Dennis presses her to marry him, she replies simply, "I'd rather die" (137). And in the end that's just what she does, slipping by night into Mr. Joyboy's embalming-room at Whispering Glades and committing suicide by lethal injection. So Waugh's novel leaves one with dueling deaths—those of the parrot and Aimee—in dueling funeral homes—the Happier Hunting Ground and Whispering Glades—presided over by dueling suitors—Dennis Barlow and Mr. Joyboy. In the end the confrontation between Barlow and Joyboy—England and America—overshadows the others. At heart, Waugh's novel is pure anti-American satire, and this explains the parallel it develops between Sambo the parrot and Aimee the girl. The parrot's name cheerfully recalls the ugliest features of American racial bigotry, while the girl's evokes the vulgarities of American mass-marketed religion (in addition to her "born dead" surname, which mocks the born-again-ness of American Christianity, she's named after Aimee Simple McPherson [90]). Like Sambo, Aimee is a creature of imitation, living as she has been trained to do, acquiring incoherent bits and pieces of learning to which she gives vent at unexpected moments in inappropriate ways. Sincere in her mindlessness and mindless in her sincerity, she's both tragic and ridiculous: a typical denizen of southern California, where everything is a cheesy copy of something else, with funeral plots organized around marble knock-offs of Rodin and pet cemeteries arising in imitation of human resting-grounds. In such a world, the deaths of Aimee and Sambo become somehow coincidental: minor manifestations of a much more dire phenomenon. This larger issue—one might call it the death of civilization or the demise of culture in America—is the real subject of the book.

In effect, Waugh uses his parrot both as an instrument of racial discrimination—in the Renaissance manner—and as a parody of nineteenth-century earnestness. Other writers endow their birds with greater sympathy.

Consider, for instance, Julian Barnes's tour de force, *Flaubert's Parrot* (1984). The tale of a dead wife and her surviving husband, the retired doctor Geoffrey Braithwaite, it dwells on one's relation to the past. Braithwaite's wife, Ellen, was repeatedly unfaithful, then she attempted suicide, and the effort left her on life support, which Braithwaite terminated. As a result, the doctor is haunted by not one but two ghosts: that of Ellen, for whose death he feels responsible in ways he can't quite express, and that of Gustave Flaubert, the tortured novelist, who unaccountably fascinates him, and whose voice he seems to confront in the figure of Félicité's parrot from "A Simple Heart." As Braithwaite himself complains, "I feel I understand [Ellen] less than a foreign writer dead for a hundred years" (168). His obsession with Flaubert (and Flaubert's parrot) compensates for the failure of his relationship with his wife.

But in another way, the obsession with Flaubert also helps to explain the doctor's own predicament. As Braithwaite ponders the novelist's sources for "A Simple Heart," he pauses over a news story Flaubert had clipped from the June 20, 1863, issue of *L'opinion nationale*:

In Gerouville, near Arlon, there lived a man who owned a magnificent parrot. . . .
As a young man, he had been the victim of an ill-starred passion; the experience

had made him misanthropic, and now he lived alone with his parrot. He had taught the bird to pronounce the name of his lost love . . . a hundred times a day. . . .

Solitude enflamed the imagination of Henri K——, and gradually the parrot began to take on a rare significance in his mind. For him it became a kind of holy bird: he would handle it with deep respect. . . . One day, however, people noticed that Henri K—— was looking gloomier than usual, and there was a strange, wild light in his eye. The parrot had died.

Henri K—— continued to live alone, now completely so. . . . Gradually he began to believe that he himself had turned into a parrot. As if in imitation of the dead bird, he would squawk out the name he loved to hear; he would try walking like a parrot, perching on things, and extending his arms as if he had wings to beat.

Sometimes, he would lose his temper and start breaking the furniture; and his family decided to send him to the *maison de santé* at Gheel. (57–58)

This tale's transference of affection provides the ground not only for "A Simple Heart" but for Barnes's novel as well. Braithwaite takes the position of Henri K——, bereft of his human love, compensating for her absence through a phantasmatic attachment to a dead author who is in turn replaced by a stuffed parrot. This sequence takes us from life (Henri K——'s psychosis) to art (Flaubert's "A Simple Heart") back to life (Geoffrey Braithwaite's obsession), which last is itself given artistic figuration via Barnes's novel. Beneath this chain of transference lie two relationships—Braithwaite's with his wife, and Braithwaite's with Flaubert—that somehow remain equally imaginary. After all, the obsession with Flaubert has developed entirely in the writer's absence, whereas Braithwaite's marriage is distinguished by the absence of any satisfactory emotional connection. In a sense, they're both a big misunderstanding.

Finally, this sense of misunderstanding comes home to roost with the bird—or more accurately, birds—at the book's center. Barnes's novel starts by noting that there are in fact two stuffed Amazon parrots reputed to be the one that stood on Flaubert's desk as he wrote "A Simple Heart": one on display at the Flaubert Museum, Hôtel-Dieu, in Rouen, and the other at the Flaubert Pavilion in Croisset. As Braithwaite wonders in response to this fact, "How do you compare two parrots, one already idealised by memory and metaphor, the other a squawking intruder?" (21). The problem is only exacerbated by the explanation he finally receives: the curators of both Flaubert collections, knowing that the writer had borrowed his stuffed bird from the Museum of Natural History at

Rouen, had both applied to that museum for the specimen in question. In both cases, the museum's officials were most obliging: "'You want a parrot? they said. Then we go to the section of the birds. They opened the door, and they saw in from of them . . . fifty parrots. *Une cinquantaine de perroquets!*'" (187). Given the number of birds in the museum's collection, and given the understandable failure to record the precise specimen that Flaubert borrowed, any one of fifty candidates could equally stand for the bird in question. Truth, relatedness, life . . . all become an arbitrary textual exercise, a proliferation of dead parrots, all claiming with equal authority to be the real thing.

Again, consider Mr. Green, the parrot in Robert Olen Butler's eponymous short story (1992) about a Vietnamese emigrée living in Versailles, Louisiana, in 1989. Mr. Green has traveled with the story's narrator from Saigon, which she left at the end of the Vietnam War. The bird was given to her by her grandfather at his death in 1972. It speaks with his voice, uttering phrases like "Hello, kind sir" (*Good Scent* 17) and "Not possible" (21)—language rendered doubly creepy by the fact that the narrator's grandfather, as a Buddhist, believed in ancestor-worship and also believed that his children, by converting to Catholicism, had condemned the spirits of their ancestors "to wander for eternity in loneliness" (18).

Under the circumstances, it only makes sense that the relationship between Mr. Green and the narrator should grow vexed. As the bird resorts to antisocial behavior, plucking its feathers and eventually attacking the narrator, it calls attention to the younger generation's abandonment of old family ways, and the older generation's repudiation of its offspring. But family conflict favors youth, and this case is no exception. When Butler's story reaches its final confrontation, there's no doubt who will emerge the winner: "I quickly reached to Mr. Green and grasped him at his chest, lifted him and caught him with my other hand before he could struggle. His wings were pinned and he was bigger in my hands than I had ever imagined. But a Vietnamese woman is experienced in these things and Mr. Green did not have a chance even to make a sound as I laid him on his side, pinned him with my knee, slid my hands up and wrung his neck" (*Good Scent* 28). With this gesture, the narrator turns her back on a heritage that has already grown foreign and hostile; she disowns her past as it has disowned her. As in *The Loved One*, the parrot here embodies something like the death of culture. "Mr. Green" is the story of its narrator's assimilation into the American world, and the price she must pay to be assimilated.

As a literary historian, I write mostly about authors who have been dead for centuries. Seldom do I analyze the work of my contemporaries, and never before have I had the pleasure of discussing a writer with whom I interact on a daily basis. But Bob Butler is an esteemed colleague of mine at Florida State University, where he holds forth, enviably, as our resident Pulitzer Prize winner. "Mr. Green" forms part of his prize-winning collection of short fiction, *A Good Scent from a Strange Mountain*, but since Bob himself is a former parrot owner, "Mr. Green" by no means exhausts his interest in psittacine fiction. In a later collection of stories, *Tabloid Dreams* (1996), Butler revisits the genre with a tale entitled "'Jealous Husband Returns in Form of Parrot,'" a work whose tabloid-style title states its premise while also introducing the note of surreal humor that distinguishes it from "Mr. Green." "'Jealous Husband'" is a classic instance of the dead parrot as cartoon character, a seriocomic revenant whose demise has been greatly exaggerated.

In his former life as a man, Butler's narrator died by falling from a tree while attempting to catch his wife in an act of infidelity. Now reincarnated as a yellow-naped Amazon, he is placed in his former wife's custody by a sadistic twist of poetic justice. After purchasing the bird/man at a local pet store, his wife carries him home to his own former living room, where he must observe her new lovers as they repair to or return from the bedroom.

This arrangement generates predictable discomfort, but also some unexpected comedy. Fueled by jealousy, the narrator attacks his rawhide chew toys with maniacal vigor. He attempts to fly through the sliding glass patio door, only to be cold-cocked by the effort. And when the narrator's wife cleaves unto "a guy with a thick Georgia truck-stop accent and pale white skin" (*Dreams* 76), the bird/narrator finally finds an ideal use for his limited vocabulary: "This guy with his cowboy belt buckle and his rattlesnake boots and his pasty face and his twanging words of love trailed after my wife, through the den, past my cage, and I said, 'Cracker.' He even flipped his back a little at this in surprise. He'd been called that before to his face, I realized. . . . 'Cracker,' I said. 'Hello, cracker'" (*Dreams* 78).

Still, such moral victories don't really compensate for the narrator's perdurable distress. In overall design, "'Jealous Husband'" is a lot like "Mr. Green." Both tales are about relations between the sexes; both are about failures of masculine authority; both are about the transition from past to future and the loss it entails; both are about reincarnation. But more important, both give voice to a sense of helplessness and a longing for transcendence that can eventuate only in death. The final confrontation of "Mr. Green" is as much a mercy killing as a murder; likewise, "'Jealous Husband'" ends in an act of suicide that serves both as an expression of despair and as a gesture of deliverance.

The latter story first appeared in the *New Yorker*, and oddly enough, the editors of that august magazine have shown great fondness for parrot-theme fiction and nonfiction over the past two decades. Another case in point is Michael Knight's short story "Birdland" (1998), which reverses the literary figure of the dead parrot so as to present us with living birds, like Butler's Mr. Green, that embody dead human voices. Set among the rustic inhabitants of Elbow, Alabama, Knight's tale focuses on that hamlet's seasonal visitors: a flock of African gray parrots that winter in Alabama before returning each spring to their home in Pawtucket, Rhode Island, and a woman ornithologist known only as the Blonde, who has come to Elbow to study the parrots. The parrots, imported to Rhode Island by an eccentric millionaire named Elgin Archibald, who released them in a fit of dementia, just before his death in 1907, embody the principles of vagrancy and recurrence. Like the black citizens of Elbow, they originated in Africa; like the Blonde, they're visitors who have settled, for reasons not wholly clear, in small-town Alabama. During their winter sojourns in Elbow, they've acquired the outraged vocabulary of the local Crimson Tide football fans: "The parrots perch in pecan trees beyond the open window and listen to us rant. At night, with the river curving silently, they mimic us in the dark. '*Catch the ball,*' they caw in Mayor Dillard's desperate tones. '*Catch the ball, you stupid nigger.*' Mayor Dillard is an unrepentant racist, and I can only wonder what the citizens of Pawtucket, Rhode Island, must think when the birds leave us in the spring" (82).

In fact, if Knight's parrots are about recurrence, they embody a recurrence more chronological than geographical. "Birdland" is full of the past: Elgin Archibald's personal history, the legacy of southern racism, Alabama's attachment to the gridiron exploits of the late Bear Bryant. The Blonde, when first confronted by the bigotry of Elbow's citizens, responds with a jeremiad "welcoming us to the 'twentieth fucking century'" (84); elsewhere, the story's narrator declares that she "holds all history against me" (86). In a sense, thus, Elbow's parrots represent the comically inescapable weight of the past. History is death, with feathers.

Three quarters of a century earlier, Princess Marthe Bibesco had also given psittacine form to the past and its recurrences, but Bibesco's treatment of these matters proved far less comic than Knight's. An acquaintance of Proust and Claudel, among others, the Romanian-born Bibesco was one of the outstanding women writers of her day, and her masterpiece, *The Green Parrot* (1924), became the first twentieth-century French novel accepted by the Literary Guild. It's a claustrophobic, despairing story whose narrator, the daughter of aristocratic Russians who emigrated to Biarritz prior to World War I, grows up in a villa in perpetual mourning for her elder brother, Sasha, who had died of diphtheria at the age of eight. Into her childhood a green parrot briefly appears and alleviates the gloom of her surroundings, but it is snatched away from her, and from that time forward the narrator deliberately divorces herself from all emotional attachments. Standing in for a corpse, the parrot in its turn becomes the functional equivalent of one, and its loss confirms the heroine's unhealthy fixation upon death.

As the novel proceeds through its various horrific turns of plot, the narrator remains enduringly disengaged and indifferent. And when, at tale's end, a friend learns her story and reaches out to her by actually presenting her with a green parrot, it functions only as an emblem of loss. She gives the bird to her former governess, declaring that "it isn't my nature to be consoled. . . . I love my bird, but he comes to me too late, by a trick of destiny. His name is Nevermore. . . . Immoderate souls like mine . . . must choose between death and the cloister; we can find no refuge except in God" (241–242). Even a living bird has to all intents and purposes ceased to be alive, for the heroine herself is effectively dead to the world.

I especially admire the name Bibesco gives to her green parrot: Nevermore. Edgar Allan Poe is to French literature what Jerry Lewis is to French television: the improbable American who has somehow developed into a national obsession. There is no evidence that Bibesco knew the obscure magazine article in which Poe declared that he first considered making his raven a parrot (and which I discussed earlier). For what it's worth, I very much doubt that she had read the piece. But deliberately or not, Bibesco acted out her own version of Poe's original instinct, producing an articulate parrot (in fact it knows not one but three languages) whose name allies it with the lugubrious talking bird of Poe's most famous poem. Nevermore is a living bird that nonetheless remains dead to Bibesco's protagonist; it gestures toward an earlier green parrot that was once alive to the protagonist and that stood, in its turn, in place of a dead sibling; and at the same time Nevermore alludes to yet another parrot, killed off by its creator in the process of literary composition and replaced by a raven, that stands in place of yet another dead loved one. This chain of association is too good not to be true.

So in story after story, twentieth-century writers give us parrots that die (*The Loved One*), that replace dead people (*The Green Parrot*), that recall dead people ("Birdland," "Mr. Green"), that are inhabited by dead people ("'Jealous Husband'"), or that spontaneously divide into multiple dead parrots that in turn replace and recall dead people (*Flaubert's Parrot*). This pattern reaches its apotheosis in the eighth episode of *Monty Python's Flying Circus* (1969), where the comedy troupe introduced its notorious dead parrot sketch. The premise of the sketch is simple enough: a man returns to a pet store because the shopkeeper has sold him a dead parrot. Now the customer demands satisfaction, only to discover that the shopkeeper, like many a novelist before and after him, can't seem to tell a dead bird from a live one. As John Cleese remonstrates to Michael Palin, "This parrot is no more. It has ceased to be. It's expired and gone to meet its maker. This is a late parrot. It's a stiff. Bereft of life, it rests in peace. If you hadn't nailed it to the perch, it would be pushing up the daisies. It's rung down the curtain and joined the choir invisible. This is an ex-parrot." Monty Python's dead parrot works purely as a surrealistic exercise in form; symbolizing nothing but itself, it ridicules the very idea of what we might call parrot symbolism.

But parrot symbolism nonetheless remains an abiding resource for twentieth-century novelists. It looms especially large in postcolonial writing, where the dead parrot motif recurs again and again in both comic and horrific forms.

For a case of the latter, consider Coco in Jean Rhys's *Wide Sargasso Sea* (1966). Rhys's last and most famous novel rewrites the story of Charlotte Brontë's *Jane Eyre* from the point of view of Bertha Mason, first wife to the hero Rochester and confined, presumably by reason of her insanity, to the attic of Rochester's country house. Bertha Mason triggers the climax of Brontë's novel by setting Rochester's house on fire and plunging to her death, in flames, from the attic.

*Wide Sargasso Sea*, in contrast, supplies the backstory to Brontë's work, delineating the events that lead up to Bertha's marriage and imprisonment in Rochester's home. Rhys gives her heroine the original name of Antoinette (which Rochester eventually replaces), along with a background absent from *Jane Eyre*; she is born in Jamaica, the Creole daughter of a West Indian planter and his second wife, Annette. Antoinette's father dies early in her childhood, leaving

Antoinette and her mother in their rotting mansion, Coulibri Estate, without male protection and surrounded by contemptuous, intimidating ex-slaves. Eventually, Annette marries again, this time to a wealthy Englishman named Mr. Mason.

Antoinette's childhood at Coulibri comes to a painful end in the first great set-piece of Rhys's novel. Following the Emancipation Act of 1833, the estate is encompassed by a population of embittered, newly freed blacks who despise Annette and her children as "white niggers" (42)—neither full-blooded English nor people of color. One night, a belligerent mob of these former slaves gathers outside the mansion and begins to riot, hurling curses and then stones at the people inside. The worst then happens as the rioters set fire to the house, forcing Antoinette and the rest of the family to run for freedom. As they dash for their carriage, the crowd closes in on them, but just as bloodshed seems inevitable, the mob falls silent:

> Our parrot was called Coco, a green parrot. He didn't talk very well, he could say *Qui est là? Qui est là?* and answer himself *Che Coco, Che Coco.* After Mr. Mason clipped his wings he grew very bad tempered. . . .
> I opened my eyes, everybody was looking up and pointing at Coco on the *glacis* railing with his feathers alight. He made an effort to fly down but his clipped wings failed him and he fell screeching. He was all on fire.
> I began to cry. . . . I heard someone say something about bad luck and remembered that it was very unlucky to kill a parrot or even to see a parrot die. They began to go then, quickly silently, and those that were left drew aside and watched us as we trailed across the grass. (41–43)

On one level, Coco's death assumes a redemptive character, standing in for the threatened murder of its human owners and making their escape possible. Once more, parrot replaces person. While doing so, Coco also introduces the themes of magic and prognostication, voodoo and obeah; killing a parrot, we learn, is unlucky, and in response to this belief the rioting mob falls mute and docile. But if there's an ill omen in Coco's incineration, it seems to apply first and foremost to Antoinette, for Coco anticipates her own eventual death with eerie precision. To this extent, the bird functions not just as foreshadowing and framing device; it's also a literary echo of the very event it predicts.

Again, Derek Walcott's play *Pantomime* (1979) revisits *Robinson Crusoe* so as to make Defoe's parrot an emblem of colonial bigotry. Harry Trewe, the white, English owner of a Trinidadian hotel, proposes to Jackson Phillip, his black, West

Indian assistant, that they perform a dramatic adaptation of Defoe's novel for the hotel's guests in order to improve business. As Harry introduces the idea, Jackson redirects it to the subject of the hotel's resident macaw:

> Harry: I kept thinking about this panto I co-authored, man. *Robinson Crusoe*. . . . I can bring it all down to your level, with just two characters. Crusoe, Man Friday, maybe even the parrot, if that horny old bugger will remember his lines . . .
>
> Jackson: Since we on the subject, Mr. Trewe, I am compelled to report that parrot again. . . .
>
> Harry: (*imitating parrot*) Heinegger, Heinegger. (*In his own voice*) Correct?
>
> Jackson: Wait, wait! I know your explanation: that a old German called Herr Heinegger used to own this place, and that when that macquereau of a macaw kept cracking: "Heinegger, Heinegger," he remembering the Nazi and not heckling me, but it playing a little havoc with me nerves. This is my fifth report. I am marking them down. Language is ideas, Mr. Trewe. And I think that this pre-colonial parrot have the wrong idea.
>
> Harry: It's his accent, Jackson. He's a Creole parrot. What can I do?
>
> Jackson: Well, I am not saying not to give the bird a fair trial, but I see nothing wrong in taking him out of the cage at dawn, blindfolding the bitch, giving him a last cigarette if he want it, lining him up against the garden wall, and perforating his arse by firing squad. (99–100)

As Crusoe's parrot gives voice to "pre-colonial" racism, Jackson reserves the bird for a comic punishment not very different from that suffered by Rhys's Coco. It's just an additional touch that the macaw, like Coco's owners, is supposedly "Creole."

More recently, Barbara Kingsolver's novel *The Poisonwood Bible* (1999) once again brings dead parrots into the realm of postcolonial fiction in a manner more terrifying than amusing. Kingsolver's protagonists, a mother and her four daughters, are haled into a remote Congolese village by their husband/father, a brutal and arrogant Baptist missionary. When they arrive, they take over the recently vacated digs of the preceding minister, who has left them, among other things, an African gray parrot named Methuselah. Methuselah speaks, but in ways that promise trouble: the previous missionary has taught it to say "Piss off," and worse still, the new reverend's wife inadvertently teaches it to say "Damn" as she struggles with her baking in the Congolese climate. Inevitably, the bird curses once too often, and the minister pitches the bird out of his house into the latrine, where it lingers, its wings atrophied from years in a cage, begging for food from more sympathetic members of the family. Eventually, as life becomes more and more menacing for the missionary household, one of the daughters discovers the inevitable: "Following the trail I found first the red and then the gray: clusters of long wing feathers still attached to gristle and skin, splayed like fingers. Downy pale breast feathers in tufted mounds. Methuselah" (185). Methuselah's name refers to the bird's longevity, but in this case it's also ironic. The parrot is the first creature to die in Kingsolver's missionary household, and its death presages other, human deaths to follow. As Kingsolver's characters explore their own peculiar heart of darkness, Methuselah points to the horror that awaits them.

In contrast, the works of Gabriel García Márquez explore a peculiar subset of the dead parrot motif: what one might call the boiled parrot variation. This comic-surrealist device first appears in *One Hundred Years of Solitude* (1967). As that novel's epic account of the village of Macondo comes to an end, the town plunges into a state of feverish decadence. Aureliano Buendia, last scion of Macondo's first family, bonds with four bookish friends; and in the process he realizes that "literature [is] the best plaything . . . ever . . . invented to make fun of people" (357). He and his companions, "holed up in written reality" (357), frequent a "small imaginary brothel" (358) where life seems wholly consumed by fiction. To test this proposition, Aureliano and his friends indulge certain "extravagances . . . just as when Germàn tried to burn the house down to show that it did not exist, and as when Alfonso wrung the neck of the parrot and threw it into the pot where the chicken stew was beginning to boil" (358). The dead bird here attests to Aureliano's growing suspicion that the world itself is a textual creation.

But like any good fiction, the bordello's parrot dies only to return in later work. This revival occurs early in *Love in the Time of Cholera* (1985), where a version of the same bird kills Dr. Juvenal Urbino, husband of the novel's heroine, Fermina Daza. Urbino's parrot has "been a local attraction for years" (9), and like its forerunner in *One Hundred Years of Solitude*, it's an emblem of language out of control. Despite having "learned to speak French like an academician," as well as "the Latin accompaniment to the Mass and certain selected passages from the Gospel according to St. Matthew," the parrot nonetheless "d[oes] not speak when . . . asked but only when . . . least expected" (20).

As for its nakedness, that is the result of a domestic accident. Its wings clipped, the parrot was at first permitted to wander at will throughout the Urbino household: "But one day he began to do acrobatic tricks on the beams in the kitchen and fell into the pot of stew with a sailor's shout of every man for himself, and with such good luck that the cook managed to scoop him out with the ladle, scalded and deplumed but still alive. From then on he was kept in [a] cage" (24). Urbino's death occurs when the bird breaks confinement and lures him onto a ladder, from which he suffers a fatal fall; so the pattern of *One Hundred Years of Solitude* is reversed. Instead of giving us a man who kills a parrot and places it in a pot of stew, *Love in the Time of Cholera* produces a parrot that emerges from a pot of stew in order to kill a man. The parallelism is too perfect to ignore; as figures of language's ability to constitute reality, the two parrots themselves engage in a typical pattern of literary balance and antithesis.

But not every literary parrot of the twentieth century has a near-death experience. In Joseph Conrad's *Nostromo* (1904), for instance, the bird of the moment is altogether too alive, exemplifying all that is wrong with democracy. It lives within the palatial home of the English imperialist Charles Gould and his wife, in Sulaco, capital of the fictional South American nation of Costaguana:

> Barefooted servants passed to and fro, issuing from dark, low doorways below; two laundry girls with baskets of washed linen; the baker with the tray of bread made for the day; Leonarda—her own *camerista*—bearing high up, swung from her hand raised above her raven black head, a bunch of starched underskirts. . . .
> A big green parrot, brilliant like an emerald in a cage that flashed like gold, screamed out ferociously, "*Viva Costaguana!*" then called twice mellifluously, "Leonarda! Leonarda!" in imitation of Mrs. Gould's voice, and suddenly took refuge in immobility and silence. (68–69)

Here the bird provides a kind of bridge between the servants and their employers. Caged and inferior, it holds forth alongside the domestics and speaks to the chief of them in Mrs. Gould's own voice. Yet it also calls out popular patriotic slogans, suggesting the mindlessness of political rhetoric and parties. *Vox populi, vox psittaci*: the voice of the people is the voice of a parrot. Conrad's bird conveys this typically Conradian sentiment with added irony, for the slogan it screams, literally translated, means "Long live the birdshit coast!"

In Virginia Woolf's *To the Lighthouse* (1927), a parrot appears once more as an emblem of intellectual vacuity, but in Woolf's case the mindlessness in question derives not from populist politics but from bourgeois pretension. Woolf's protagonists, Mrs. and Mr. Ramsay, preside over a gathering of family and friends at their summer home on the coast of Scotland. Among those to resort to the house is one Minta Doyle, a sprite of a young woman whom Mrs. Ramsey hopes to see engaged to another houseguest, Paul Rayley. Amidst the great interior monologue that comprises Part 1 of Woolf's book, Mrs. Ramsay ponders young Minta and the unlikely surroundings from which she has emerged into adulthood:

> [Mrs. Ramsay] was responsible to Minta's parents. . . . Dear, dear, Mrs. Ramsay said to herself, how did they produce this incongruous daughter? . . . How did she exist in that portentous atmosphere where the maid was always removing in a dust-pan the sand that the parrot had scattered, and conversation was almost entirely reduced to the exploits—interesting perhaps, but limited after all—of that bird? Naturally, one had asked her to lunch, tea, dinner, finally to stay with them up at Finlay, which had resulted in some friction with . . . her mother, and more calling, and more conversation, and more sand, and really at the end of it, she had told enough lies about parrots to last her a lifetime. (56–57)

Here the unfortunate parrot stands for the limitations and meaningless proprieties of a privileged life. You could say that Woolf's bird is to the world of entitlement what Conrad's is to the world of revolution. The sand that it scatters provides a genteel counterpart to the guano of "Viva Costaguana!"

Then again, Colette's *Ripening Seed* (1923) includes a parrot that reworks the bird's traditional association with women and with language. Colette's novel is a coming-of-age story about two teenagers, Philippe and Vinca, spending the summer with their families on the coast of Brittany. The novel ends with the couple's transformation from friends to lovers, but before Philippe can consummate their relationship, he must be awakened sexually by an older woman. The seductress, a neighboring vacationer named Mme. Dalleray, first entices Philippe into her villa with an offer of orangeade, then overwhelms him with her commanding presence:

> "Don't drink it all at once," said the voice of Madame Dalleray. "Totote, you were crazy to put ice in it. It was cold enough from the cellar." . . .
> Philippe shut his eyes and, with a tightening of the throat, took two sips but tasted nothing, not even the acidity of the oranges. On opening his eyes by then accustomed, he dimly discerned the red and white upholstery. . . . A female he had not before noticed was leaving the room, carrying a tinkling tray. A red and blue macaw, on a perch, spread one of its wings with the snap of a fan, to display pink underfeathers, the hue of livid flesh.
> "How handsome he is!" Phil said in a hoarse voice.
> "All the more handsome for being a non-talker," said Mme Dalleray. (44)

This bird's flesh-colored underfeathers correspond to no discernible species of macaw, but that's unimportant. What matters is that they correspond to Philippe. As the boy sips his orangeade, he finds himself increasingly befuddled and intimidated by his host, who reduces him at last to something like the status of her inarticulate pet:

> The Lady-in-white smiled, to add to the atmosphere of nightmarish luxury, of startling uncertainty, of equivocal rape, so that Philippe was left without a stitch of composure. . . .
>
> "Are you not feeling well, Monsieur Phil? No? . . . But, on such a hot day, I couldn't agree with you more—far better to stay still and not talk. So let's not talk."
>
> "I never said that." (44–45)

Clearly, Mme. Dalleray is no more interested in Philippe's conversational skills than in those of her parrot.

At moments like these from *Nostromo*, *To the Lighthouse*, and *Ripening Seed*, twentieth-century writers seem to abandon the dead parrot motif for other concerns. Yet even here, you could argue that death remains a pervasive *figurative* presence, implicit in the mindlessness of Costaguanan politics, the soullessness of privileged London life, or the voicelessness to which a teenaged boy is reduced by a sexually dominant older woman.

And incredibly, the dead parrot motif abounds in twentieth-century visual art as well. Take, for instance, Joan Miró's *Poetic Object* (1936; Figure 34), a bizarre jumble of odds and ends including a celluloid fish, a cork ball hanging by a string, a derby hat, a printed map, a hollowed-out hunk of wood, a stocking, shoe, and garter suspended by another piece of string, and, surmounting the entire improbable assemblage, a stuffed yellow-crowned Amazon parrot on a wooden perch.

This sculpture dates from Miró's surrealist period, and it exemplifies the creative illogic of surrealism. Like other such objects drawn from this stage of the artist's career, it "seem[s] to have been made casually, effortlessly, without constraint, and seemingly without control," as an exercise in "strangeness for its own sake" (Dupin 462). The work's power derives from its utter randomness; it collects the most banal and inauspicious of articles, juxtaposes them with no detectable method, and generates something arresting and unpredictable in the process. The overall effect is of an object created out of odds and ends by someone completely unfamiliar with the world as we know it: perhaps a visitor from another galaxy or from another time. Detached from their functional context,

Figure 34. Joan Miró, *Poetic Object* (© 2003
Successió Miró/Artists Rights Society [ARS, New
York, ADAGP, Paris])

maps and hats and stockings reassemble in new configurations that seem imbued
with creative energy.

Yet in this particular case, there is in fact a certain amount of logical relation
between some parts of the sculpture. The unit of shoe, stocking, and garter forms
an intelligible sequence, as does the pairing of parrot and perch. And these, in
turn, represent pieces or remnants of living beings. This fact gains an ominous
quality in light of the work's date, for in 1936, as political tensions gave way to
civil war in Spain, Miró emigrated to France for personal safety. The jumble of
body parts and dead animals in *Poetic Object* seems appropriate to a world in the
process of losing its sense of balance. And if a severed leg and a stuffed bird suggest the imminent threat of death and dismemberment, they also become relics
of a social order passing out of existence: fragments shored against the ruins of a
lost world.

On the other side of the Spanish-speaking Atlantic, at almost the same time that Miró produced his *Poetic Object*, Frida Kahlo was at work on a haunting series of self-portraits that feature her with one or more of her numerous pet parrots. Kahlo, horribly wounded in a streetcar accident during her youth, spent her adulthood in great pain, unable to give birth, and, partly as a result, she developed strong emotional attachments to a wide range of animals, including various monkeys, dogs, cats, doves, a deer, an eagle, and an assortment of parrots, many of which beasts appear in her paintings almost "as a substitute for children" (Herrera 148). Among the parrots was one that held forth on the patio of the house Kahlo shared with Diego Rivera, where it would attack innocent passersby, drink beer and tequila, and call out, " '*No me pasa la cruda!*' (I can't get over this hangover)" (Herrera 307). But her favorite parrot, and for some time her favorite pet, was a double yellow-headed Amazon named Bonito, who loved to eat butter, and whom Frida and Diego would lure through a variety of dinner-table obstacles in search of this treat. In 1941, the year of her father's death, Kahlo painted the most powerful of her parrot-portraits, the *Self-Portrait with Bonito*, depicting herself in the company of this beloved bird (Figure 35).

For this painting, Kahlo appears not in the brightly colored Mexican embroidery of which she was so fond, but instead "in a simple dark blouse that suggests mourning—for her father, for the victims of war, and perhaps also for the death of Bonito, who perches on her shoulder" (Herrera 312). On the personal level, the picture takes shape as the lament of a woman now both childless and fatherless, with Bonito's sunny head marking the absence of human connections; however, the painting is also a *memento mori*, a salute to the dead from those still living, if only for the moment. And this preoccupation with death marks the painting's historical context just as clearly as it does the context of Miró's *Poetic Object*; where the earlier sculpture alludes to the advent of civil war in Spain, the later portrait glances at the looming threat of international fascism in 1941. It's an elegy at once personal and political, intimate and global.

The background of *Self-Portrait with Bonito* is alive, but not in ways that generate much gaiety. Kahlo and her pet appear against the dark foliage of a tropical shrub whose leaves are crawling with caterpillars and scarred by their depradations. Kahlo herself is linked to this backdrop by a spider web that reaches out from the bush to anchor itself in her hair. Within this web, one of the caterpillars writhes in a death-agony. The overall theme here is clear enough; as Shakespeare's Gertrude puts it, "All that lives must die,/ Passing through nature to eternity." It's a message also echoed in another portrait from 1941, *Me and My*

Figure 35.  Frida Kahlo, *Self-Portrait with Bonito* (© 2003 Banco de México Diego Rivera & Frida Kahlo Museums Trust. Av. Cinco de Mayo No. 2, Col. Centro, Del. Cuauhtémoc 06059, México, D.F.)

*Parrots* (Figure 36). Here again, Kahlo's attire is simple, the background plain and dark, the overall atmosphere of the work brooding and severe. Kahlo herself almost seems to be a corpse here; her arms folded in repose, her face expressionless, her eyes looking past the viewer, out into nothingness. Even the cigarette dangling from her right hand seems to be dead, devoid of ember and smoke. The artist's parrots perch on her shoulders and in her lap as if they were taking their places on an inanimate object: a bush or a tree or an outcropping of rock. Their bright colors make Kahlo seem deader than ever. The scene is only redeemed by the half-embrace with which she holds the two center birds to her breast, hanging onto them tenuously, as if they represented life itself.

By contrast, David Hockney's etching *My Mother with a Parrot* (1974) seems gentle and reassuring. In it the artist's mother appears twice, as does the bird: once on the bottom half of the plate, in black and white, where the parrot seems almost to be perching on Hockney's mother's shoulder; and once in color, at the top of the plate. Here the parrot has grown and the mother has shrunk. The former, all pale blue with orange wings, perches on nothing; the latter rests her head against a vestigial pillow. The image is one of repose, but with broader implications, and these become obvious if we note that during the early 1970s Hockney had read Flaubert with great enthusiasm and had begun to experiment with illustrations for "A Simple Heart" (Hockney 288). *My Mother with a Parrot* asks to be read against this preoccupation, as a visual reprise of Flaubert's tale.

Twenty-five years earlier, in 1949, the reclusive Joseph Cornell displayed twenty-six of his signature box-constructions in a show entitled *Aviary*. In these and related works, parrots figure as a kind of alter ego for the artist himself: intelligent, vocal yet silenced by the medium in which they appear, isolated and incarcerated. These qualities, in turn, suggest a broader sense of victimization rendered manifest in *Habitat Group for a Shooting Gallery* (1943; Figure 37). Here, in a work described as "an emotional response to World War II" (Waldman 90), Cornell has placed engravings of two cockatoos and two macaws behind a pane of glass that has been shattered as by a bullet. Feathers litter the bottom of the box, and against a white background, Cornell has thrown splotches of red, yellow, and blue paint, echoing the gay colors of the parrots themselves. It's as if bits of the birds were splattered on the walls of their container.

Similarly, the later work entitled *Isabelle (Dien Bien Phu)* (1954; Figure 38) marks a horrified response to the events that ended the French colonial presence in Indochina. A single engraved cockatoo dominates this composition, again be-

Figure 36. Frida Kahlo, *Me and My Parrots* (© 2003 Banco de México Diego Rivera & Frida Kahlo Museums Trust. Av. Cinco de Mayo No. 2, Col. Centro, Del. Cuauhtémoc 06059, México, D.F.)

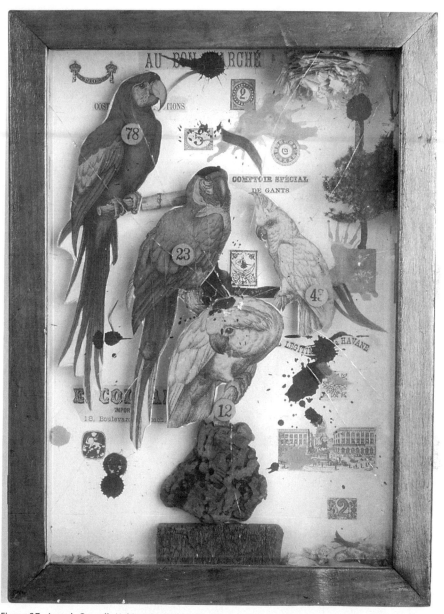

Figure 37. Joseph Cornell, *Habitat Group for a Shooting Gallery* (Purchased with funds from the Nathan Emory Coffin Collection of the Des Moines Art Center, 1975.27. Photo by Michael Tropea, Chicago)

Figure 38. Joseph Cornell, *Isabelle (Dien Bien Phu)* (The Saint Louis Art Museum, 181:1986)

hind shattered glass. Outside the box, on its back, Cornell has pasted a newspaper article describing the fall of Isabelle, a southern spur of the French defenses at Dien Bien Phu that had been cut off from the main fortress during months of siege. Again, paint spatters the interior of the box like so much blood; a single nail lies on the bottom of the box. And the glass of the box has been broken in a pattern that radiates out perfectly from the cockatoo's one visible eye. The bird's beak is parted, as if in an effort to scream. Such work is balanced nicely by a piece like *Deserted Perch* (1949), whose box, emptied of its tenant, functions as an emblem both of death and of deliverance.

Finally, one should mention the contemporary work of Walton Ford, which applies the dead parrot motif to postmodern dilemmas in a way that clearly recalls the achievements of previous artists. Ford's extraordinary pictures of animals combine the hallucinatory feel of surrealism with the precision draftsmanship of the nineteenth-century ornithological illustrators. The result is a visually irresistible, technically breathtaking commentary upon the baneful effects of global capitalism and environmental degradation. In *Au Revoir Zaire* (1999; Figure 39), for instance, Ford presents two African gray parrots copulating on a branch. The female reaches its head forward, toward a berry that acts as the bait of an elaborate noose like those often used to capture parrots in the wild. The narrative here is obvious, doubly so given the work's ironic title; the birds will be taken from their homeland to become items of exchange in the machinery of international consumerism. The noose threatens death at the very moment that the copulating birds seek to perpetuate life.

Or again, Ford's *Sensations of an Infant Heart* (1999; Figure 40) speaks to the twenty-first century's environmental concerns by recalling the practices that have led to them. In an interview, Ford described the subject of the painting: "*Sensations of an Infant Heart* is about Audubon's earliest memory. His mother kept a menagerie in their house, and she had a monkey that strangled Audubon's favorite parrot when he was a tiny child. . . . He went hysterical when it happened, because he loved the parrot, and that gave rise to his love for birds. But later, he's like the monkey, a killer of birds himself. He never painted an image of this, so I just had to" (Ford 66). True to this account, Ford has painted a picture in which love and death are almost indistinguishable. At first blush, his monkey and parrot seem almost to be playing with one another, rather than engaging in a life-or-death struggle. The monkey gazes at the viewer with unnerving calm.

Figure 39. Walton Ford, *Au Revoir Zaire* (courtesy Paul Kasmin Gallery, New York)

One might like it to manifest some sense of shame, but it does nothing of the sort.

But in painting, as in literature, not every parrot of the twentieth century proves to be a dead one. For instance, consider Max Beckmann's 1936 portrait entitled *Quappi with a Parrot* (Figure 41). A study of his second wife and frequent model, Mathilde von Kaulbach, this work typifies Beckmann's post-expressionist use of bright colors and flat surfaces to achieve a chilly, unnerving objectivity. The pet parrot that perches on Quappi's arm, all green save for its yellow head, merges with the green background of Quappi's dress. Quappi herself looks down at the bird with an inscrutable absorption; the bird, for its part, seems to be looking away toward the viewer. The result is a new and startling variation on the

Figure 40.  Walton Ford, *Sensations of an Infant Heart* (courtesy of Paul Kasmin Gallery and the Artist)

Figure 41. Max Beckmann, *Quappi with a Parrot* (© 2003 Artists Rights Society (ARS), New York/VG-Bild-Kunst, Bonn)

intimate portraits of women and parrots attempted seventy years earlier by the likes of Courbet, Manet, and Renoir: a scene that depicts neither staged intimacy nor poised self-possession, but a kind of isolated composure, of which Quappi's bird is at once a part and apart.

But to return for a moment to literature, this time to popular fiction. Given the nature of things, it was perhaps inevitable that psittacine homicide would sooner or later invade the realm of the crime novel, but surely it would be a bizarre coincidence to find the resulting work echoed in actual judicial practice. However, that's just what happens.

In 1939, Erle Stanley Gardner published *The Case of the Perjured Parrot*, one in his long and popular series of Perry Mason mysteries. True to its title, the novel engineers two murders and culminates in a trial whose star witness is a bird. And as we'll see, the idea of a parrot taking the stand in a court of law proves less far-fetched than it might seem.

The plot of Gardner's novel is typically intricate, inviting the reader to share in the deductive challenges confronting its hero. Mason serves as attorney for a man named Charles Sabin, whose father, the millionaire Fremont Sabin, has been found shot to death in his vacation cabin in the mountains of southern California. (Given his father's wealth, Charles is a prime suspect in the ensuing investigation.) As it happens, the elder Sabin had brought his pet parrot to the mountains with him, and its squawks eventually attracted the attention of passersby, who entered the cabin and discovered the corpse.

As Gardner's complicated tale unfolds, we learn that the parrot in Sabin's cabin is an impostor, since Sabin's original bird, Casanova, spoke politely and lacked a toe on its right foot, whereas the bird in the cabin "is given to profanity" (13) and possesses all eight of its God-given claws. Next we discover that the real Casanova has somehow come into the keeping of a woman named Helen Monteith, and that it has learned to cry out the words "Put down that gun, Helen! Don't shoot! *Squawk. Squawk.* My God, you've shot me!" (46). We then watch while Mason, who has custody of the impostor bird, breaks into Helen Monteith's home and substitutes the fake parrot for the real Casanova. This gives rise to some humor as Mason's friend, the detective Paul Drake, counsels him, "If anything goes wrong, don't get pigheaded and keep trying to make the switch. . . . For God's sake, drop that parrot and make a run for it" (92).

Here the story begins to focus upon Helen Monteith, who was apparently conducting a secret romance with the dead Sabin, and who is of course implicated in his murder by Casanova's newly acquired line of chatter. As soon as she can, Helen eludes surveillance and returns to her home, where the authorities apprehend her just as she has finished decapitating the impostor bird with a butcher knife. This leads to an interlude in which Mason observes that "The murder of a parrot . . . is somewhat similar to the murder of a human being; that is, a person must look for a motive. Having found a motive, there must then be opportunity" (105). Given the nature of the dead parrot motif, we should not be surprised to find that the murder of Sabin's impostor bird parallels the murder of Sabin himself. And the parallel makes Helen Monteith appear responsible for both.

Helen does not emerge as the malefactor at the novel's end, however, and Perry Mason never seriously suspects her as such. As usual in Gardner's novels, the climax comes in the courtroom, amidst a coroner's inquest. There, Mason's hapless nemesis, the district attorney Raymond Sprague, questions Helen aggressively, and Mason counters by asking her to identify the lifeless body of the parrot she killed. When it becomes evident that the bird is not Casanova, Mason then produces the real Casanova and asks Helen to confirm its identity. As the bird runs through its vocal repertoire, it suddenly appears to metamorphose from evidence into witness:

> The parrot, tucking its head slightly to one side, said in a low, throaty voice, "Come in and sit down, won't you? Come in and sit down, take that chair . . . *Squawk . . . Squawk* . . . Put down that gun, Helen . . . don't shoot . . . *Squawk* . . . My God, you've shot me." . . .
>
> "*That's* Casanova!" Helen Monteith exclaimed.
>
> The district attorney said dramatically, "I want the words of this parrot in the record. The parrot is accusing the witness. I want the record to show it." (155)

The humor of this moment is punctured by the sudden news that a key member of the inquest's audience has bolted. Richard Waid, former secretary to Fremont Sabin, surprised to find that Casanova is still alive, has turned tail, thus revealing his own involvement in the murder. Of course, no one who knows parrots would expect Casanova to learn a line like "Put down that gun, Helen . . . don't shoot . . . *Squawk* . . . My God, you've shot me," in a single sitting; the bird had obviously been coached to implicate someone other than the actual murderer. Since the only people with sufficient access to the parrot to coach it would have been Sabin himself and his secretary, it becomes clear that the secretary is responsible for the heinous deed. One is left wondering why he would seek to deflect suspicion by an act—coaching a parrot to say incriminating things—that would so openly advertise his own perfidy.

So the tale ends unexpectedly well for Helen. We discover that Helen has actually *not* been intimate with the dead Fremont Sabin, but has instead married the dead man's brother, who looks like him and has been kept out of sight throughout the preceding story. As Helen rejoins her husband at novel's end, we're left with a double pattern of doubling: Casanova has been impersonated by the dead impostor bird just as Fremont Sabin's brother has been confused with the dead man. In both cases, the resulting perplexities are resolved by an act of murder, so that at last only one man and one bird remain standing.

Gardner delights in the complexities of his plot (of which my summary is a very spare version). He takes great pleasure in exploiting the parallels—between bird and bird, man and man, and man and bird—at the heart of his tale. But even Gardner might have been astonished by one such parallel: the one that develops between his novel and actual courtroom practice.

As valuable property, parrots have of course long been the subject of litigation. For instance, in the 1991 case of *Latham v. Wal-Mart Stores, Inc.*, the Court of Appeals of Missouri's Eastern District heard arguments concerning liability in the matter of a parrot sold by Wal-Mart in 1987 to a certain James and Roberta Latham. The bird had psittacosis; worse still, James Latham contracted the ailment. So the Lathams filed suit in 1988 against Wal-Mart, the manager of the Wal-Mart branch from which they had bought the bird, and the suppliers of the bird, arguing that they, the Lathams, should receive "damages for mental anguish, permanent impairment of all bodily functions and loss of consortium" because "the parrot constituted an unreasonably dangerous and defective product" (*Latham v. Wal-Mart Stores* 12).

In this case, the Missouri Court of Appeals sided with Wal-Mart, citing Illinois legal doctrine that "living creatures . . . are by their nature in a constant process of internal development and growth and they are also participants in a constant interaction with the environment around them as part of their development. Thus, living creatures have no fixed nature and cannot be products as a matter of law" (28). So if a parrot is not a product, and if it is a living creature, is it capable of giving legal testimony?

Even Perry Mason denies this, in the strict sense. As Gardner's coroner declares at the climax of *The Case of the Perjured Parrot*, "A parrot can't be a witness, but the bird *did* say something. What those words were can be put in the record for what they're worth" (156). Technically, the parrots in Gardner's novel—both the live one and the dead one—are evidence, not witnesses. But, as the Missouri Court of Appeals acknowledges, a living creature is not an inert object. And from the practical point of view, a living, *talking* creature tends to look a lot more like a witness than like ordinary evidence. Hence the title of Gardner's novel; no parrot—or person, for that matter—can commit perjury without first having been sworn in as a witness. Casanova may not be a witness in the purest legal sense of the word, but for all intents and purposes, that is the role the bird assumes.

And in the twenty-first century, we have the case of Cora the parrot to prove that Casanova's legacy survives. In January 2002, Cora and its owner were summoned to court in Düsseldorf by outraged neighbors who claimed that the bird's incessant squawking was a nuisance and sought to have it evicted. The presiding judge in the case, the Honorable Dirk Kruse, ordered the parrot to take the stand on its own behalf, and the ensuing events came fairly close to pandemonium. Cora, an African gray, introduced itself to the judge and immediately burst into "a cackling laugh" ("Judges Hear Evidence from Nuisance Parrot"). After an expert witness testified that the shrieking of a parrot could penetrate walls, the bird replied, "Ja, ja," and when the jurors left the courtroom to deliberate, Cora wolf-whistled after them.

Given this performance, Judge Kruse felt justified in ordering Cora's owner to pay a hundred-euro fine and move to a new address. But Cora got the last word. After the verdict, as the principals were leaving the courthouse, "the cheeky bird gave a loud, shrill whistle down the waiting journalists' microphones" ("Judges Hear Evidence from Nuisance Parrot"). So much for the majesty of the law.

# Chapter 6

# *Extinction and Beyond*

Charlie Bird is a skilled metalsmith, in his early fifties, who lives in Southern California and produces exquisite objets d'art—brooches, pendants, miniature sculptures—from fine silver and twenty-four karat gold and enamel and precious stones. In addition, he's a falconer, a self-trained field biologist of great breadth and experience, a certified scuba diver, and a highly skilled mountain climber. He's also a convicted parrot smuggler.

I got to know Charlie (not his real name) through a mutual friend and gallery director who recently prepared a show of his work. She has been acquainted with him for years, and when he came to Tallahassee for his opening, she arranged for us to spend some time together.

Charlie is friendly, engaging, talented, curious, knowledgeable, and in depressingly good shape. He's also a little too energetic, a bit alarming, like one of those characters from a Broadway musical who are always threatening to burst into song. If he were a dog, one would have great trouble keeping him on the porch.

Perhaps that's why he got involved in parrot smuggling. Certainly he was lured by the adventure it promised, and the money and travel doubtless provided further incentive. While attending graduate school in upstate New York (an MFA program in metalwork), he met the man who would introduce him to the business: a fellow—I'll call him Big Bird—who was regularly surrounded by large numbers of parrot chicks, all various kinds of cockatoo. Given Charlie's formidable climbing skills and zoological knowledge, he made an ideal recruit to Big's operation, and so Charlie ended up making a series of trips to Australia between 1991 and 1993 for the purpose of smuggling. On the final trip, as he prepared to return to the United States, the Australian authorities arrested him at his departure gate. They'd been watching him and other members of the ring for some time.

Big's operation was distinctive in that it didn't actually smuggle wild-caught birds. Such birds make inferior pets: they've already imprinted on other birds, they're past the age at which they acquire language easily, and they have acquired a range of survival-specific behaviors that don't show to best advantage in a formal living room. Also, they're big and cantankerous and noisy and therefore hard to smuggle. So Big didn't bother with them; he went after their eggs instead. That's where Charlie came in.

Upon his arrival in Australia, Charlie would rent a car and drive to the general area where he did his collecting—either north of Melbourne or outside of Perth. He'd take a room in a hotel, and he'd hike out into the country and look for parrots. When he spotted a nest, he'd go to work. The nests were often high in tall trees, in holes in the tree trunks, and this is where Charlie's climbing skills proved essential. He'd scale up the tree in question until he reached the operative hole, and then he'd extract the eggs and climb back down carefully, so as not to damage the eggs in the process. Sometimes the nest would be hidden very deep in a tree trunk, out of arm's reach, so Charlie carried a special piece of equipment for such occasions: a long pole with a net at the end. As the nests were dark, he'd attach a flashlight to the pole with a little duct tape. Then he'd simply stretch the contraption down into the bowels of the tree, scoop up the eggs he found there, and be on his way.

But of course eggs are eggs, which means they need to be kept warm and safe. Since it doesn't do to go through customs with incubation equipment, Charlie devised an alternative, consisting of the regulator from an incubator, a modified oven grill, a hair dryer, and a few other odds and ends. During his days in the field, the accumulating stock of eggs would remain in his hotel room, where he maintained them at a steady temperature of 98.6 degrees Fahrenheit. He candled them regularly to track the development of the embryos.

The crowning difficulty of this smuggling operation—like any other—remained the obvious one: how to get the goods back home without detection. Again, the Bird gang rose to this challenge with elan. Exploiting the elasticity of ace bandages, Charlie improvised a skin-tight vest with pockets for up to forty-eight eggs. He wore this next to his stomach, underneath his shirt, so that his body heat would keep the eggs warm during the lengthy flight from Melbourne to Los Angeles, where his contact would be waiting. As for the flight itself, it could be exquisitely uncomfortable. Not only would it involve all the usual annoyances of trans-Pacific travel—the sleeplessness, the burning eyes, the aching back—all coupled with the natural misgivings of someone in the process of committing a felony; also, inevitably, some of the eggs would start to hatch, and the tiny cockatoo chicks within would begin the long, laborious process of breaking through their shells. When this happened, Charlie said, most of his fellow-smugglers would head for the restroom, remove the chicks in question, and flush them down the toilet. But Charlie insists that he never did this himself, preferring instead to keep the chicks alive and take his chances with them at customs.

As Charlie told his story, I found myself growing more and more uneasy. Not only did the details of the business seem both fascinating and repellent, in more or less equal measure; Charlie himself just wasn't what I expected of a parrot smuggler. For one thing, he's highly intelligent and immensely talented. His metalwork has won awards and appeared in shows from coast to coast and around the world. He produces single pieces on commission for as much as $30,000 and more. He doesn't need to smuggle parrots for living, and as far as I can tell, he never did. For another thing, he clearly loves the birds, and nature in general. His artwork reflects this passion, consisting as it does of exquisite renditions of natural forms: baby snakes emerging from their eggs, pitcher plants, tropical reef fish, tiny birds, all crafted in fine silver and enamelwork with the precision of someone who knows his subject matter intimately. How, I found myself wondering, could someone this skilled and sensitive get into such a sordid business?

In one sense, the question's a stupid one. If we learn anything from the process of growing up, surely it is that everyone misbehaves sooner or later. And if we learn anything else, surely it is that life resists the terms of a naive moral reductionism. I'm disturbed by Charlie's story and have no desire to justify parrot-smuggling, much less to romanticize it. However, neither can I pretend that my own behavior has been beyond reproach. Charlie doesn't seem at all concerned about the unsavory side of his career in smuggling. If anything, he sees himself as more sinned against than sinning. And as self-serving as this view of matters may be, he does have a point. Charlie admits that he was arrested and briefly imprisoned in Australia for smuggling protected bird species. But he notes that even as the Australian government was punishing him, it was also permitting massive persecution of the very same birds.

In July 1998, Mike Elliott, leader of the Australian Democrats and member of Australia's legislative council, addressed this issue by moving that the Australian Parliament "examine and report on the interaction of native animals with agricultural activities and, in particular, current proposals and/or approvals to shoot native bird species" (Elliott). In speaking to this matter, Elliott noted that "the need for destruction permits for killing protected species" had recently been relaxed, and that this relaxation, largely in response to lobbying by the national farmer's federation, potentially threatened the survival of rare subspecies of the crimson rosella (*Platycercus elegans*). But the persecution was by no means limited to rosellas. As Elliott continued, "There have been, just in the past twelve months, a number of quite high profile cases of culls," including wholesale slaughter of Australia's ubiquitous galahs (*Eolophus roseicapillus*). In Elliott's words, "It is not long ago that we saw the culling of galahs in Port Lincoln; they were being shot with shotguns and many were falling wounded to the ground and being clubbed to death." In 1999 Australian Conservation and Land Management Minister Marie Tehan approved the use of agricultural chemicals to poison large numbers of cockatoos, galahs, and corellas. Critics of this decision pointed out that "Australian wildlife faced agonizing deaths under the plan" and that "other bird life, including eagles and hawks, could be poisoned." Under the terms of this new initiative, "Accidental kills of non-target species [would] be excused" ("Poison Plan").

As it happens, the species to be killed under these programs include the very ones Charlie used to carry through customs. And even if we recognize that Charlie has his own ax to grind, it's hard not to agree that something is wrong with a legal system that imprisons one man for smuggling birds while allowing others to poison, or shoot, or club to death thousands of the same birds. The matter becomes even more vexed in light of current problems in parrot-human relations worldwide.

Parrot populations are currently in decline throughout the world. Of the approximately 350 species in the order *Psittaciformes*, the International Union for Conservation of Nature and Natural Resources has one hundred on its 2002 Red List of Threatened Species. These include many of the kinds of parrot—military macaw, Moluccan cockatoo, hyacinth macaw—most prized by collectors and pet owners (IUCN). Other species—the Carolina parakeet, for instance, and the Cuban macaw (*Ara tricolor*)—are already extinct, while still others, such as Spix's macaw (*Cyanopsitta spixii*), may well become extinct within the next half century. No other order of bird contains so many endangered species, nor is so high a proportion of any other bird group endangered.

The reasons for this trend are obvious enough. Most prominent among them is the ongoing destruction of the birds' native habitat. Most parrots live in tropical rain forests, where they have adapted specifically to life in the canopy. But the destruction of these forests has become a high-profile environmental issue over the past two decades. In 1989, it was estimated that rain forests were being clear-cut globally at the rate of 142,200 square kilometers per year (Myers 30), and if anything, that figure has increased. One consequence of this destruction, in turn, is that species of life indigenous to the rain forests (which covered only 2 percent of the globe to begin with) have become particularly endangered. Parrots are prominent among them.

In addition, persecution by farmers has taken a serious toll on parrot populations around the world. For one famous example, we have Audubon's eyewitness description of the mass hunting that helped eradicate the Carolina parakeet in the nineteenth century (see Chapter 4). Although some contemporary readers think it exaggerated, they offer little by way of corrective evidence. And the ongoing culls of parrot species in Australia suggest that the scope of such killing can indeed be impressive.

Then again, parrots also fall prey to the pet industry, in both legitimate and illegitimate ways, with the result that these birds must endure a double threat: while farmers try to hunt them out of existence on one hand, trappers take the few remaining birds on the other. Again, the extent of this latter activity can be breathtaking. According to ornithologist Joanna Burger, "more than 4.2 million parrots were legally exported" by the international pet trade "in a recent five-year span" (72). The activity is big business; as Burger goes on to note, "in the early 1990s, the United States legally imported at least 250,000 parrots a year . . . worth in excess of $300 million. About four fifths of these birds were taken from the wild" (72). And of course, such figures don't begin to account for the birds taken illegally by smugglers like Charlie.

These trends lead to bizarre consequences. For one thing, while there are fewer parrots in the wild now than at any time in recorded history, there are more parrots than ever before in captivity. Likewise, as wild parrots have grown ever more scarce, parrot culture—the subject of this book—has grown increasingly extensive and varied.

On that score, the increasing presence of parrots in human society has produced a marked affection for the birds, an abiding sense of emotional attachment. And this bond, in turn, has led to a peculiar literary development: the growth of what we might call the psittacine pet memoir. Pets have become an expanded presence in twentieth-century personal narrative, and not all of them have been parrots. (One thinks, for instance, of *Millie's Book*, the canine autobiography supposedly ghostwritten by Barbara Bush in 1990.) But parrots have been among them, in ways that increasingly connect the birds with their human owners. One early, if incidental, example is Thor Heyerdahl's *Kon-Tiki* (1950), the account of Heyerdahl's journey from Peru to Polynesia on a raft modeled upon those of the South American Indians. When Heyerdahl and his companions set out to sea on April 28, 1947, to test the theory that Polynesia was populated by raft-borne immigrants from South America, they found themselves accompanied by an unexpected crew-mate, "a green parrot . . . a farewell present from a friendly soul in Lima" (95). Not wholly welcome at first, the bird gradually won the affection of its human comrades. When it became seriously ill after eating the *Kon-Tiki*'s radio antenna, the radio operators Torstein and Knut nursed it back to health and became its "chosen friends" (191). Thereafter, the parrot "would never sleep anywhere but in the radio corner" (191). While it spoke Spanish at first, it gradually assimilated the crew's own language: "Bengt declared it took to talking Spanish with a Norwegian accent long before it began to imitate Torstein's favorite ejaculations in full-blooded Norwegian" (191).

As this process of bonding continued, Heyerdahl and his companions eventually "reckoned ourselves as seven on board—six of us and the green parrot" (190); the bird had earned itself an unexpected place in a band of unsentimental Norwegian adventurers. So what happened next was bound to come as shock: "We enjoyed the parrot's humor and brilliant colors for two months, till a big sea came on board from astern while it was on its way down the stay from the masthead. When we discovered that the parrot had gone overboard, it was too late" (191). As Heyerdahl observes with typical detachment, "The loss of the parrot had a depressing effect on our spirits . . . ; we knew that exactly the same thing would happen to ourselves if we fell overboard on a solitary night watch" (191). As it turned out, the parrot would become the *Kon-Tiki* expedition's only casualty—a fact one could perhaps predict, given some awareness of the dead parrot motif. Once again, life imitates art.

As endearing as it proved to be, Heyerdahl's parrot remains a curiosity in a story about other things. But three years after *Kon-Tiki* was published, when Paul Bowles published the memoir "All Parrots Speak" in his essay collection *Their Heads Are Green and Their Hands Are Blue* (1953), parrots move to the center of the story. Bowles is scarcely more sentimental than Heyerdahl, but like Heyerdahl, he admits to an affection for his feathered pets. Still, as if to compensate for this potentially embarrassing fondness, Bowles presents his various birds (and he has quite a few, one after another) as objects of humorous contempt. One such parrot he describes as having "a voice that could have shouted orders in a foundry" and a vocabulary whose "few recognizable words . . . owed their intelligibility solely to chance" (164). He remarks of another one that "whoever was in hearing [of it] quickly departed, in sheer self-protection" (169). He saves his highest compliment for Seth, the African gray that resided with him while he wrote "All Parrots Speak": "Seth . . . is the greatest virtuoso performer I have ever had. But then, African Greys are all geniuses beside Amazons; it is unfair to compare them" (169). For the record, and on behalf of Amazons everywhere, I deeply resent this slur; if anything, African grays are as famous for insanity as for intelligence. But on the whole Bowles's narrative, poised as it is between the maudlin and the hard-boiled, is more charming than objectionable.

In recent years, and perhaps in response to the growing environmental crisis surrounding parrots in general, such memoirs seem to have grown more emotionally engaged. In 1990, for instance, Jane and Michael Stern's lengthy essay "Parrots" became part of a string of parrot-related fiction and nonfiction pieces in the *New Yorker*. The Sterns' article is by no means confined to personal narrative; it includes much fascinating historical material as well, and its central subject is the obvious one: that "in the forests and savannas where they come from [parrots] are disappearing" (55). The Sterns present this loss not merely as environmental or biological or material, but also as emotional and spiritual, and this view leads directly into autobiography: "Our own pet parrot, Lewis, a yellow-naped Amazon, treats us as his flock, and the rooms in our house . . . as a grove of trees. When he is in one room and we are in other rooms, he frequently initiates a calling game by shouting out 'Jane!' or 'Michael!' We call back 'What, bird?' . . . Calling from room to room of a yellow Colonial house in Connecticut is the closest he will ever get to the natural parrot behavior of tree-to-tree communication in the forest" (56). The image of this parrot without a forest complements the larger image of forests—and a world—without parrots. It gives the latter loss a human face.

If anything, this gesture acquires broader scope in Joanna Burger's book *The Parrot Who Owns Me*. Here Burger, a prominent ornithologist and field biologist, sets aside her scholar's mantle in order to tell the story of her relationship with a red-lored Amazon named Tiko. As the tale progresses, the lives of Burger and her parrot become more closely intertwined; Burger alternates between descriptions of Tiko's home life and her own experiences as an avian researcher in the field, learning about birds and experiencing firsthand the growing environmental pressures that are beginning to affect them in the twenty-first century. As the bird enters human space, so the woman enters bird space. The result is a marvelously accessible and informative look at the contemporary ecology of bird life. But it's also a story whose subject becomes increasingly—and I think deliberately—unclear: is Burger writing about herself or about her parrot? Or is it really possible to distinguish between the two? As Burger herself remarks of their relationship, "It was a moot question whether I had trained [Tiko] or he had trained me" (122). One hears this refrain a lot from contemporary parrot owners, and—as the title of Burger's book makes clear—it ultimately calls into question the very concept of ownership itself.

The trend toward personal engagement with parrots may even be said to affect scientific research. Over the past twenty-five years, the animal behaviorist Irene Pepperberg has been conducting a long-term study of language acquisition in African grays, with extraordinary results. Her star pupil, Alex, has become a bonafide psittacine superstar, appearing in documentary films and on television, doing interviews for the print media, and occasioning much discussion within learned circles. Alex has also lent his name to a nonprofit organization established and supervised by Pepperberg, the Alex Foundation, "dedicated"—in the words of the foundation's website—"to psittacine intelligence and communication research."

Alex's skills are indeed extraordinary, and well documented. He knows how to distinguish between the colors, materials, and shapes of different objects, and he can communicate these distinctions in English. He has coined new words by combining words already in his vocabulary. He can give voice to personal preferences—for food, toys, and so on—and express dissatisfaction when they are ignored. He has taught himself complete sentences such as "I am going to go away," and has learned how to apply them meaningfully in consistent circumstances—as, for instance, when he wants to be left alone by his handlers. Pepperberg believes that Alex may eventually be able to read. Here's a sample of Alex's conversation, transcribed from a taped training session with Pepperberg:

> Alex: Wanna nut.
> Irene: Yeah, you're a good boy. You can have a nut. . . . Do you want anything
> else, Alex? Hmmm?

A: Wanna nut.

I: Want another one? How about a different kind? What kind of nut is this? (She holds out a walnut.)

A: Walnut. . . .

(Takes walnut, drops it immediately.)

I: You don't like walnuts? Do you want anything else? . . .

A: Want cork. (205)

Alex's intelligence is such that the bird has even become a fictional character, figuring in Margaret Atwood's novel *Oryx and Crake* (2003). Atwood's hero, Jimmy, grows up in a futuristic dystopia whose ecology has been ruinously impaired by massive corporate programs in genetic engineering. The hero spends his youth in a residential compound from which ordinary pets, which might carry genetic aberrations, are rigorously excluded, and this lack of pets emphasizes his loneliness. In high school he becomes enamored of "old instructional CD-ROMs," and among the figures in these, "Alex the parrot [is] his favorite." Jimmy sees in Alex a figure like himself: intelligent, isolated, out of his depth in a frightening world: "He liked the part where Alex invented a new word—*corknut* for almond—and best of all, the part where Alex got fed up . . . and said, *I'm going away now. No Alex, you come back here.* . . . But Alex was out the door. Five stars for Alex" (54). The bird's successful escape from his trainers provides Jimmy with an ideal to which he can only aspire in fantasy. In the end, Atwood's novel is not about Alex but about Jimmy, not about parrots but about another endangered species entirely.

As Atwood recognizes at least intuitively, one consequence of Pepperberg's research with Alex is to narrow the conceptual gap between parrots and people. Pepperberg herself maintains that parrots are the mental equals of most primates (322), and this idea alone goes far to humanize them. Moreover, the potential applications of her research extend far into the realm of human brain function; for instance, the techniques she has developed to teach Alex language may prove valuable in the education of learning-disabled children. Pepperberg takes care not to overstate the findings of her research, and they certainly can't be described as autobiographical writing. But they just as certainly reflect an increased inclination to consider parrots as conscious, autonomous individuals, with minds and wills and voices of their own.

This book is a story about parrots, but it's also a story about stories about parrots, and one of those is the story of the book's own composition. Oscar Wilde once said that criticism is the purest form of autobiography, and I offer no exception to his rule.

I became aware of parrots in my late adolescence. When I was twelve my father, whose health was poor, retired, and we moved from the suburbs of Washington, D.C., to the west side of El Paso, Texas. I, for one, was unhappy with the move. El Paso was heaven for cowboys, drug dealers, and metallurgical engineers, but it didn't have much to offer a weedy teenager with an interest in French Symbolist poetry. As a result I threw more than the necessary number of tantrums, but at length I made the best I could of things there, and the best thing about El Paso was undoubtedly Ciudad Juárez, the great old Mexican city right across the Rio Grande.

As one might expect, parrots were plentiful in Mexican markets during the 1970s, and they remain so today. I first got to know about them in my late teens, while attending the University of Texas at El Paso, where I fell into the company of a lad who had grown up in Guadalajara. Although his family had moved across the border, he still kept a couple of Mexican Amazons. Intelligent, colorful, vocal, and exotic, they fascinated me, and at length I decided I must have one for myself.

I bought my first bird from a shop in Juárez's old Mercado: a great, grimy, chaotic building right in the heart of the downtown area, next to the old town hall. The shop itself was a tiny thing, wedged into a corner of the building along with leatherwork dealers and silversmiths and shoe salesmen and greengrocers and menudo stands. It held one small window, too dirty to see through, and a single wooden chair for the proprietor, and enough bare concrete floor space for maybe three people, and stacks of wire cages containing different kinds of birds. One cage held half a dozen doves; another housed a brace of chickens; there were starlings in a third. In one corner sat a little cage with a pair of half-moon conures in it. These are small and rather drab parrots, more or less entirely green, but the two in this cage sported brilliant yellow heads because, to increase their saleability, the dealer had partially immersed them in hydrogen peroxide. An ignorant customer, thinking the yellow heads natural, would buy the birds and discover his error a few weeks later as the feathers molted back to their original green.

But the birds I wanted were in yet another cage. When it comes to parrots, you can never be sure just what the shops in Juárez will have to offer. I've seen them retail half a dozen species of Amazon at different times, together—on rare occasions—with a couple of species of macaw. On this particular day, the dealer in question had a group of terrified lilac-crowned Amazons, all huddled together in a rectangular cage not large enough to house one in comfort. When I approached them, they hissed and screeched in desperation. I gave the proprietor of the shop fifteen dollars, and he opened the birdcage and wrestled one of the parrots out. This didn't make for a pretty scene; the bird, recently wild-caught, with its wings just clipped, struggled for all it was worth, and it managed to land a nasty peck on the shopkeeper's right hand. But the man hung on anyway, and finally managed to force the squirming ball of beak and feathers into a mesh shopping bag.

I took my newly acquired treasure back to where I had parked my car, and I placed the bird, bag and all, in the car's glove compartment. Within this dark space the parrot fell completely silent, and within half an hour I had driven across the Santa Fe Street Bridge and reentered the United States. Growing up on the border one learns not to take customs officials too seriously. Even if they had found my feathered contraband, the offense would have been too petty to merit their attention. So I became a parrot owner and, like Charlie, a parrot smuggler at the same time.

It was years before I really thought about the environmental consequences of what I had done. And maybe they weren't worth much thought. After all, smuggling one parrot across the border is nobody's idea of the crime of the century. But if one agrees with Eldridge Cleaver that you're either a part of the solution or a part of the problem, there's no doubt that my little venture had made me the latter. And by a more severe standard, you could argue that I continue to be a part of the problem today, because even the perfectly legal, Florida-bred, hand-raised birds I currently own have been produced by extracting other birds from the wild. In any absolute sense, one cannot own parrots without compromising certain moral and ecological principles. I've had girlfriends point this out to me with great satisfaction.

Still, the parrots abide. We've grown together over the years, and while I know I could live without them, I wouldn't want to. As for them, at this point I doubt they could survive very well without me. Neither one would last a week in the wild. Of the two birds I currently own, the elder, a red-lored Amazon named Lazarillo, has been with me for twenty years; the younger, a double yellow-headed Amazon named Persefina, is eight years old. Neither one has acquired the skills necessary to secure food and avoid predation under natural circumstances. Both are accustomed to intimate interaction with me, so much so that Lazarillo is markedly jealous of Persefina. Between us, the birds and I have formed a distinct family group with its own history, customs, and patterns of interaction. We're stuck with each other—from my viewpoint, at least, happily so.

In our symbiosis, my parrots and I embody a broad historical tendency for parrot populations to become ever more closely connected to human populations. This trend appears variously in the growth of the modern pet industry, the depletion of the birds' natural habitat, the development of a global economy based on different kinds of parrot entertainment, and the establishment of feral parrot colonies in cities around the world. These broader trends, one could say, lend a public face to private relationships.

Consider, for instance, the growth of parrot-themed entertainment parks over the past seventy-five years or so. These have opened throughout the world, developing into an oddly successful subset of the amusement-park trade that offers many people their first experience of parrots at close quarters. Such facilities, half aviary and half carnival, exploit the traditional appeal of the birds as pets, objects of admiration, and articulate performers. But at the same time, these parks have also become a major resource in the effort to educate people about endangered species, to keep endangered parrots species alive in captivity, and in some cases to reintroduce them to the wild.

In Europe, the biggest institution of this sort is Loro Parque (the name means "Parrot Park"), located on the island of Tenerife in the Canaries. At this point Loro Parque is by no means all about parrots; among other things, it boasts displays of tigers, jaguars, chimpanzees, porpoises, penguins, alligators, tortoises, and sharks, together with a traditional Thai village, an orchidarium, a porcelain museum, and so forth. But historically, parrots have been its central distinction. It started off in the early seventies as a small hotel that offered a parrot collection and show as added attractions. Today, Loro Parque maintains the world's largest population of these birds in captivity.

Most of Loro Parque's parrot population remains hidden from the public. While the theme park itself generates commercial revenue, the breeding center and other facilities of Loro Parque Fundación, the conservation wing of the business, operate separately, a few miles south of the main site. There the foundation houses about 330 of the roughly 350 parrot species known to exist, and in 2001 it bred about 1,150 specimens of 168 different species. One aim of this breeding program is to establish a genetic reserve of parrot species endangered in the wild;

the birds are left to rear their own young, and they flock together in a way that permits them to choose partners freely. The beauty and intelligence of parrots make them an ideal high-profile poster species for broader conservation efforts, and to increase this visibility Loro Parque also hosts an international parrot convention every four years. The fifth meeting occurred in September 2002, when, among other things, the convention's delegates voted overwhelmingly to support a last-ditch effort to breed the world's rarest bird, Spix's macaw (*Cyanopsitta spixii*), by placing all captive specimens under the ownership of the Brazilian government.

For years now, the fate of Spix's macaw has hung by a thread, occasioning much despair among ornithologists and parrot fanciers. Once indigenous to northeastern Brazil, this large blue parrot was declared extinct in the wild in 2000; the species' death-throes and the efforts taken to save it have been detailed by conservationist Tony Juniper in his book *Spix's Macaw: The Race to Save the World's Rarest Bird*. Spix's macaw is a classic case of a species destroyed by habitat loss; adapted to the arid savanna and gallery woodland of northeast Brazil, it suffered immensely as its limited preserves of nesting area dwindled. Then, in a development typical of the final phase of a species' extinction, trappers moved in to take the last remaining wild birds, whose market value had skyrocketed as their numbers had diminished.

In captivity, however, the number of Spix's macaws has begun to rebound. When emergency conservation efforts began in the late 1980s, only seventeen such birds were known to exist in zoos and private collections (Juniper 176). By 2003, that number has grown to almost seventy. Still, the increase is not all due to successful captive breeding. Some of these specimens have been traced to owners who secretly conveyed them out of Brazil when they still existed there in the wild. Moreover, the captive breeding program itself has been poisoned by the fact that a handful of wealthy private owners control most of the remaining birds, making breeding decisions according to personal expediency rather than genetic calculation. As a result, the captive population of Spix's macaws has already become dangerously inbred, "swamped with offspring from the same few parents" (Juniper 226).

Indeed, the politics of this species' preservation have had a great deal to do with the rights and influence—and scruples, or lack thereof—of wealthy private bird collectors, most of whom refuse, despite any nonbinding international agreements to the contrary, to return their birds to the Brazilian government's ownership. These owners have been described as men "who got to where they are because of the way they operate," as "driven men" for whom "compromise and consensus does not always sit comfortably" (Juniper 228–229). Ridiculously privileged, with egos to match, they form a kind of exclusive avicultural club whose governing principles are profit and vanity. As for Loro Parque, it continues to maintain a breeding pair of Spix's macaws, which it houses on behalf of the Brazilian government. And the Loro Parque Fundación has led research aimed at eventually reintroducing the Spix's macaw to its native habitat, funding "nearly all of the fieldwork" directed at this goal during the 1990s (Juniper 229). Obviously enough, a commercial venture that profits from maintaining live parrots has something to gain from the birds' continued well-being in the wild. Such institutions may offer one of the best available means for saving endangered bird species.

Another such attraction, Jurong Bird Park, exists on the island of Singapore. If Loro Parque boasts the world's largest captive parrot collection, Jurong lays claim to the world's largest walk-in aviary, itself disposed around the world's largest enclosed waterfall, with an extraordinary variety of birds congregating in its waters and the surrounding foliage. The park itself is vast—a monorail conveys you from point to point with silent efficiency—and one of its star exhibits is the so-called Parrot Paradise, built in 1996 to celebrate the park's twenty-fifth anniversary. Consolidating a variety of prior exhibits, Parrot Paradise contains five hundred-odd specimens of more than one hundred parrot species. In addition, Jurong, like Loro Parque, operates an extensive captive breeding program for endangered bird species, including a variety of parrots: the umbrella cockatoo, hyacinth macaw, military macaw, scarlet macaw, palm cockatoo, and many others.

The North American equivalent to these parks is neither as large as is Jurong nor host to as extensive a collection of parrots as is Loro Parque, but it is the oldest of the three attractions. First opened to the public on December 20, 1936 (Gittner 21), Parrot Jungle (now renamed Parrot Jungle and Gardens) in Miami has operated continuously for almost seventy years, becoming, in the process, one of Florida's signature tourist meccas. For most of its history, the park has remained open on its original site: a twenty-acre property in South Miami that was well off the beaten track when the founder of Parrot Jungle, the Austrian immigrant Franz Scherr, acquired it. Over the years, however, urban sprawl engulfed the site, so that by the 1990s Parrot Jungle found itself surrounded by private residences and entangled in litigation with wealthy homeowners who disliked the noise and crowds associated with a major theme park. As a result, the entire operation completed an immense relocation project in the spring of 2003. That June, Parrot Jungle reopened on seventeen acres of Watson Island, between downtown Miami and South Beach, across the water from Miami's cruise port.

One casualty of this relocation is the distinctive flock of free-flying parrots that until recently has been one of the park's defining features. Franz Scherr had originally envisioned a tourist site in which parrots flew free and yet also would interact with the visitors, and to some extent this is what Parrot Jungle has always been. Yet over the years, the park's free-flying parrots have done less and less well, and for predictable enough reasons. As Parrot Jungle's historian, Cory Gittner, explains, "The phenomenon of that rainbow squadron gleefully swooping out of the park each morning and then squawking home each night was possible only if the birds had a place to go. Even as late as the 1980s, there were still enough park land, treetops, and undeveloped natural habitat to sustain the fruit- and nut-munching free flyers. But by the dawn of the new millennium, the concrete, asphalt, and rooftops of South Dade had approached totality. Free flyers had few places left to roam in their daily travels" (137). Coupled with this difficulty were legal complications. Since the opening of Parrot Jungle, Dade County has passed ordinances to prevent bird owners from letting their animals fly free; however, the original Parrot Jungle site had been grandfathered (grandfeathered?) into immunity from such laws. With the move to Watson Island, the park loses this exemption. So even if the birds themselves could still find hospitable territory to visit during the day, the park's management would no longer be entitled to release them in search of it.

This change in Parrot Jungle's operations can be seen as both a little sad and a lot ironic. Like its sister parks in Europe and Asia, Parrot Jungle has devoted considerable resources over the years to the preservation and captive breeding of parrot species. In 1982, for instance, Parrot Jungle bred the first Lear's macaw (*Anodorhynchus leari*) to be hatched in captivity (Gittner 108); this macaw, like Spix's, is nearly extinct. Likewise, Parrot Jungle and its sister institutions have spent much time, money, and effort developing their educational mission, which aims to introduce the public to parrots and related exotic animals, teach people about the precarious state of these creatures in the wild, and inspire a broad commitment to their nurturance and preservation. But now the park's own land and birds have been challenged by litigious neighbors, local regulations, and aggressive urban development. Sartre once said that hell is other people, but from the psittacine point of view, he might have done well to drop the adjective.

Certainly people have done a world of harm to these birds over the centuries, most of all in the past few decades, nor is the harm in question confined to incidental damage inflicted in pursuit of other ends. Even as pets and companions, parrots have come in for an extraordinary amount of abuse.

You could argue that this is so because, at heart, parrots are just too intelligent for their human owners. The chimpanzees of the bird world, they're without question far smarter than any dog or cat, and intelligence of this sort breeds complexity. Parrots can be clever and entertaining and endearing, but like most of the really bright people I've known, they're also temperamental and demanding and self-centered. While they offer extraordinary companionship to their owners, they also expect extraordinary companionship in return. By contrast, many human beings are not even equal to the responsibilities of owning a dog.

Moreover, parrots are essentially wild animals. As Bonnie Doane and Thomas Qualkenbush point out in their book on psittacine behavior, "parrots today are at best only three or four generations away from 35 to 38 million years of wild inheritance" (1). Although their intelligence allows them to adapt to human society with amazing speed, their instincts are adapted to a very different kind of life, in which human beings figure—to the extent that they figure at all—not as master but as potential threat. This fact has far-reaching consequences for the behavior of captive birds; as Doane and Qualkenbush summarize, "our parrots . . . relate to us because they wish to, not because it has been bred into them. A good relationship with a parrot will always be one of mutual agreement, never of the owner and the owned" (4).

Since parrots are now more available to human society, and simultaneously more threatened in the wild, than ever before, they are also now on the cusp of becoming domesticated animals, in the sense that dogs and cats and horses are domesticated. Over the next few centuries, if parrots survive at all, they will probably be bred in captivity, and in ways that select for the traits human society finds most attractive. So they may well become easier to live with and care for in the future. But for now, they can be loud, testy, headstrong, flighty, destructive, defiant, jealous, suspicious, remorseless, selfish, devious, implacable, quarrelsome, bloody-minded, bloody-beaked ministers of God's vengeance. When one of our birds is on a particularly bad tear, I will look at my wife, Linda, or Linda will look at me, and one of us will say to the other, in a tone of deepest sorrow and resignation, "Honey, we are afflicted." There's a sense in which having parrots is not much different from having yaws.

This is so, in turn, because parrots will simply not accept being treated as anything other than equals. All the difficulties one experiences in dealing with one's spouse or parents or siblings or children or colleagues will reassert themselves, in one guise or another, within the parrot-owner relationship. Unfortunately, many prospective pet owners don't reckon on, or relish, dealing with such challenges. As a result, irresponsible owners have abused and neglected their parrots to an unconscionable degree.

As Jane and Michael Stern have pointed out (61–62), the television detective-drama *Baretta* served as an unintended catalyst for much of this abuse. Running between 1975 and 1978, the show centered upon a detective (played by actor Robert Blake) who, when not busy bringing murderers to justice, spent his leisure time with a pet sulfur-crested cockatoo named Fred. By predictable association, *Baretta*'s popularity begat Fred's, and cockatoo purchases soared nationwide during the late seventies. But of course the television show was about fighting crime, not about pet ownership; it presented a most unrealistic image of the parrot-owner relationship (which is not to say that its depiction of police work was appreciably better). Still worse, as the Sterns observe, Fred's popularity "couldn't have happened to a less appropriate species" (62). Cockatoos are immensely loyal and loving birds, but they're also the most emotionally needy of all parrots, and that is saying a lot. You can't just give them a bowl of water and a banana and leave them alone. They insist upon constant affection, including head-scratches and beak-rubs and games and cooing and baby-talk and group squawking and general togetherness. And if you ignore them, they go to pieces. They will screech endlessly. They will rip furniture to shreds. I've seen a Moluccan cockatoo, given its own bedroom, chew a man-sized hole in the drywall. And when these expedients fail to get the desired attention, they will go really crazy.

It's perhaps a semi-amusing aside to note that in recent years Fred the cockatoo has enjoyed a brief, if equivocal, return to the limelight, in connection with the misfortunes of the actor who had played Baretta twenty-five years earlier. On May 4, 2001, Robert Blake accompanied his wife, Bonnie Lee Bakely, to an Italian restaurant in southern California. Shortly after the couple left the restaurant, Bakely was shot to death in a nearby parking lot, and as of this writing, Blake stands accused of her murder. The affair has fascinated scandalmongers throughout the United States. And one purveyor of online satire, *The Galactic Inquizitor*, has run a purported interview with Blake's erstwhile colleague Fred the cockatoo, conducted by a lean and hungry-looking cat named Mr. Fluffy. The interview cheerfully concludes with Mr. Fluffy devouring his source, and perhaps that will be the end of Baretta's parrot's public life. But in the meantime, Fred has commanded audience attention for over a quarter century, and in the process the bird (or birds: five cockatoos were used on the set of *Baretta*) has encouraged numberless idiots to throw down their money on similar pets. Other people have been left to clean up the consequences.

Two such people are John and Mary Bradford, founders and proprietors of the Tropics Exotic Bird Refuge in Kannapolis, North Carolina. Kannapolis is a dreary and depressed bedroom community, located about twenty miles northeast of Charlotte and consisting mostly of small frame houses and mobile homes with bits of automobile strewn in their front yards. The town's signature celebrity is the late Dale Earnhardt, who lent his name to a major local thoroughfare.

The Bradfords were living here in 1989 when Mary, who had been fascinated by parrots for some time, acquired her first bird. It was an Amazon, a gift from her son and his fiancee. But the Bradfords' interest in abused birds began in earnest two years later, when they acquired a blind blue and gold macaw named Georgie. Georgie had belonged for about five years to an invalid who had made no provision for his pet's maintenance in the event of his death. For some years thereafter, the macaw had been handed from one reluctant relative to another, until the family discovered the Bradfords. Mary, delighted at the prospect of acquiring a second parrot for free, offered to give Georgie a home.

When I visited the Bradfords, they brought Georgie out to perch on my hand for a bit. One of the bird's eyes is clouded, but the cause of her blindness is unclear. Somewhere in the process of being shunted from home to home, she not only lost her sight but broke both of her wings as well. Her former owners said nothing of this to the Bradfords, who discovered the problem with Georgie's wings when the surgical pins used to repair them began to cause scabbing and bleeding on delicate joints. It's possible that the bird's blindness and broken wings might have resulted from a single incident of headlong flight into a sliding door or window, but no one will ever know for sure.

Georgie is a heartbreakingly sweet bird, and all too typical of the parrots

John and Mary care for. At present, the Bradfords look after about 360 of them, and as you might imagine, this has entailed major changes to the couple's lifestyle. Over the past twelve years they have refinanced their home and property four times to pay for upgrades to the bird-care facilities. Their house itself, a modest affair of 900 square feet, is crawling with various psittaciformes, many of them in cages, others flying freely. Silence there is an endangered species.

Given the emotional instability of cockatoos in general, it should come as no surprise that the Bradfords play host to many of these neurotic birds. Mary ushered me into one room, built as an addition to their house and jammed full of parrot cages, in which most of the inmates were Moluccans with feather-plucking problems. The Moluccan, or salmon-crested cockatoo (*Cacatua moluccensis*) is an unforgettable bird and regrettably popular as a pet. At over fifty centimeters, it's one of the largest of all cockatoos, virtually a match for the huge macaws of Central and South America. Its feathers are an extraordinary rosy white, surmounted by a vivid salmon crest and a large, onyx-black beak. The species is native to four small islands in the southern Moluccas, where it is nearing extinction.

As a pet, the Moluccan cockatoo displays all the qualities that make cockatoos in general a most high-maintenance kind of companion, and if anything, in the case of the Moluccan, these qualities are writ especially large. These birds are intelligent and immensely sensitive. When distraught or bereft, they can make a sound such as Nina Hagen might produce in concert with The Breeders if the entire ensemble had eaten bad potato salad. Given sufficient time, their beaks could reduce a Steinway concert grand to a pile of easily digestible morsels. Like all parrots, they live to chew.

Worse still, if deprived of affection and attention, and if punished, in addition, for the screeching and biting that are its natural responses to this deprivation, a Moluccan cockatoo can go spectacularly, heart-rendingly crazy. Feather-plucking is the classic form of this insanity: bit by bit, the bird will pull its feathers out, starting often with the breast, sometimes with the tail or flight feathers, and working meticulously until every accessible shaft has been pruned away. Once they are gone, they will never grow back.

At its worst, this behavior can be life-threatening. At its best, it's tear-inducing yet also—at least to some people, although not to me—horrifically comical. Imagine a row of big, caged parrots, their salmon crests intact and quivering with excitement, the rest of their bodies stripped down to a uniform black skin, all

Figure 42. Mary Bradford, co-founder of the Tropics Bird Refuge in Kannapolis, North Carolina, posing with her favorite Moluccan cockatoo, Orco (photo by Bruce Thomas Boehrer)

squawking and dancing about in agitation like some macabre chorus line; that was one of the sights to greet me in the Bradfords' home. Their favorite Moluccan, a nearly naked inmate of ten years named Orco (Figure 42), earned them $10,000 on *America's Funniest Home Videos*.

At heart, feather-plucking is a form of obsessive-compulsive disorder, a kind of psittacine anorexia. As such, it's a testimony to the amazing intelligence and—for want of a better word—humanity of the birds that succumb to it. It's no accident that African grays, reputedly the brightest of all parrot species, are notorious pluckers. As with anorexia, feather-plucking seems to involve some sort of mental trauma that leads to a radically revised notion of personal appearance. Feather-pluckers, like anorexics, are militants of the body, perfectionists whose idealism has run terribly amuck, so that they see their feathers as physical blemishes. In extreme cases, a plucked bird will still preen itself and seek to eliminate imperfections on its naked body. This behavior, in turn, can lead to severe self-mutilation, particularly chest-biting. The Bradfords told me of one such Moluccan that resided with them for two years, during which time they tried in vain to cure him of his disorder. They even had a kevlar jacket designed for the bird, and he underwent eight surgical procedures and one pigskin graft. Every time his wounds were almost healed, he'd start tearing his flesh again. Eventually he died.

If you take such stories and multiply them by 360, the effect can be oppressive for any human being with a heart. After interviewing the Bradfords for one morning, I left their establishment with relief, happy to get away from the scene of so much psittacine distress. But the Bradfords themselves don't have it so easy. They don't get to walk away from their charges, and their operation is bedeviled with financial woes. As the nation's economy has contracted, the private donations that keep them in business have dwindled to a trickle. Of the buildings they've constructed to house their birds, the biggest and newest has developed serious structural problems. And they don't have anyone willing to continue their work after them. Given the longevity of parrots, this last is an ever-pressing concern.

Such perennial problems have taken their toll on the Bradfords—particularly Mary, whose delight in parrots led her, twelve years ago, to begin taking in the damaged and deranged of psittacine society. Nowadays, her conversation is suffused with bitterness. "Humanity," she declares, "has been totally irresponsible in its treatment of animals." She despises parrot breeders, who she sees as sacrificing the birds' well-being for mass-produced profit. She detests pet-store owners. She distrusts animal psychologists and claims they refuse to cure psychotic pets completely for fear of losing clients. She's suspicious of veterinarians. As for parrot owners, she has no use for them, either. As she remarks, "We do not believe in birds in captivity, period. We do not believe in breeding birds in captivity, period. Not even endangered species." For her, as for some others as well, the survival of parrot species has become a zero-sum game; either it's to be accomplished on the parrots' terms, or it shouldn't be accomplished at all. It's as if the feather-plucking severity of Mary's guests had somehow left its mark on her as well.

But irrespective of Mary Bradford's wishes, parrots have become an inbred part of human society at the outset of the twenty-first century. The developed world swarms with them, in homes and pet stores and zoos and parks and hotels. Breeding facilities abound. My younger bird, the double yellow-head Persefina, hails from a breeder ninety miles west of Tallahassee who runs a spotless and picturesque operation on twenty acres of north Florida countryside. He's by no means unique to the area. And then there are the innumerable meetings of parrot enthusiasts. Every August, my hometown hosts the North Florida Bird Fair, sponsored by the local bird-fanciers' association and cousin german to countless such fairs throughout the world. In it, parrot breeders congregate with cage builders and toy merchants and seed salespeople and so on and so forth, ad infinitum, for a three-day orgy of all things avian. Linda and I almost never miss it, although we regret the exposure of nestling birds to large crowds that such gatherings entail. Sooner or later a mature bird always seems to break free of confinement, leading its owners on a merry chase throughout the exhibition hall and causing the doorkeepers to suspend admissions until it is retrieved. This causes much rejoicing.

Then again, consider the profusion of parrot accessories and gewgaws and bric-a-brac that seems to be a natural byproduct of the march of western civilization. Through the sheer prodigality with which our society pours forth such items, parrots have installed themselves in the fabric of our daily life. Indeed, as parrot species have declined in their native regions, they've reemerged as birds of the city and suburbs. If they were once an emblem of western culture's encounter with the exotic, they now attest to how fully the Other has been absorbed and domesticated.

And in the process of becoming familiar, parrots have sometimes grown more familiar than anyone ever expected or intended. One irony of western culture's appropriation of these birds is that captive parrots have escaped around the world, establishing hardy and insolent colonies in places where they were once foreign curiosities. In a kind of karmic response to the destruction of their native habitat, feral parrots have gone global with a vengeance.

The first time I saw such a bird was in Hong Kong, in 1996. I was on vacation and had spent the day at the local zoo, where with some surprise I encountered a display on the local feral parrot population. As the exhibit explained, birds are exceptionally popular pets in Hong Kong, where space is too limited to sustain a large population of dogs and cats. Moreover, Hong Kong is in relatively easy reach of Australia, New Guinea, and Indonesia, where numerous attractive species of cockatoo are to be had. Perhaps inevitably, certain of those birds, imported as pets, have fled their owners, and now they live and reproduce on their own in the city, where they've become a notable pest. Hong Kong boasts limited green space; cockatoos have an almost limitless capacity to turn vegetation into match-wood.

As I left the zoo I wandered aimlessly across a plaza surrounded by government buildings. Pausing, I looked up into the naked branches of a large, exotic-looking tree, and there I saw it: a single bird, high up, its kind at first indistinct. But it was a startling white color, and as I gazed at it a bit longer I realized that here was a sulfur-crested cockatoo, on its own in a once-foreign land, holding forth with all the confidence of ownership. The tree it perched on, although a good forty feet tall, was completely leafless. Somehow this seemed appropriate.

Across the United States, similar colonies of expatriate parrots have established themselves in astonishing diversity. They are most common in Florida and California but appear as far north as Seattle on the west coast and Bridgeport on the east. Among the greater psittaciformes, Temple City, California, hosts a flock of about two thousand red-crowned Amazons (*Amazona dufresniae*), along with a second flock of about four hundred lilac-crowned Amazons (*Amazona finschi*); the enclave from West Palm Beach to Miami is home for another four hundred red-crowned Amazons; about one hundred orange-winged Amazons live in Fort Lauderdale and Miami; and a flock of one hundred chestnut-fronted macaws (*Ara severa*) holds forth in the same area. Naples, Florida, is home to one hundred rose-ringed parakeets—one of the original species of Indian parrot that Alexander's troops brought home to Greece over 2,300 years ago (LaFay 1).

In general, however, those parrots that go on the lam successfully tend to be of less expensive, less showy, less delicate species. The Nanday conure (*Nandayus nenday*), for instance, has prospered in exile. A smallish, drab bird originally from Paraguay, it has established itself widely in South Florida and elsewhere. Peach-faced lovebirds have taken up in the hundreds north of Phoenix and Scottsdale, Arizona. San Francisco's Telegraph Hill is home to a small but popular flock of red-masked conures (Eaton).

But the most successful of such colonists has to be the monk, or Quaker, parakeet (*Myiopsitta monachus*). A native of Argentina, central Bolivia, and southern Brazil, it has put down roots in a wide variety of unexpected places, from Puerto Rico (Forshaw 442) to Chicago's Hyde Park to Flatbush, Brooklyn, where it has become a kind of neighborhood mascot. The fence around a local playground is decorated with a running motif of welded monk parakeets (Figure 43), and wildlife activists have rallied to the birds' defense when they were recently threatened with persecution by the city power authority.

Figure 43. A playground fence in Flatbush, Brooklyn, New York, adorned with a running motif that depicts the local monk parakeets

Monks are unique among parrots in that, rather than roosting in tree trunks, they construct elaborate communal nests out of twigs, some housing a hundred birds or more and weighing over a ton. In Flatbush, as in their new urban environments generally, the birds have discovered that power poles provide an ideal site for the construction of such nests and this discovery, in turn, has led power companies to regard them as a nuisance. As Adam Gopnik put it in a *New Yorker* piece on the parrots, "Con Ed . . . sees them as rats with wings in drag" (45). Early in 2003, when the New York power provider floated a plan to capture the parrots and remove their nests, public reaction forced officials to rethink their options (Flaim).

Monk parakeets have done especially well in South Florida, where the feral population is estimated to exceed ten thousand, distributed throughout all the major urban areas. Like other naturalized parrots, the monks cluster in cities and suburbs, where food is plentiful. Contrary to common expectation, they can withstand quite severe cold, and it is the food supply, more than anything else, that limits their geographical range. As a new fixture of America's urban landscape, they take their place alongside a wide range of other introduced species—

the pigeon, the starling, the house sparrow—but the authorities seem to view naturalized parrots with particular suspicion, perhaps because of their novelty. Still, like it or not, they seem to have established themselves as permanent residents.

To find out more about South Florida's monk parakeets, I recently traveled to Sarasota, where I visited Pelican Man's Bird Sanctuary. This is a privately managed wildlife rescue operation founded in the early 1980s by Dale Shields, a bird-lover with a particular interest in Florida's brown pelicans. Shields died in January 2003, less than three months before my visit, but he left detailed instructions for the continued operation of his preserve. When I arrived, I was escorted around the premises by Kevin Barton, a gentle-mannered four-year veteran of the program.

Pelican Man is located next to the Mote Marine Laboratory Aquarium, in a ridiculously prosperous neighborhood on Saint Armand's Key. It takes in all injured wildlife that come its way—there were squirrels and iguanas and a raccoon in residence when I visited—but it specializes in caring for birds. Mourning doves are its most common visitors. Two species of parrot—Nandays and monks—show up on a regular basis, but not in great numbers. Barton estimated that they treat between and five and twenty monks per year. Some of them have been singed by power lines—an occupational hazard for birds that nest on electrical poles. But the monks of South Florida also find exotic palm trees to offer an attractive nesting place, and when yard crews do their seasonal pruning they sometimes injure birds in the process. Since the monks are not an indigenous species, Pelican Man is prohibited by law from releasing them back into the wild after treatment; instead, they must be adopted out to human owners.

On the day I visited, Barton had one feral monk in the long, open outbuilding that functions as his MASH unit. It sat quietly in a small wire cage, first in a row of cages that contained doves and anhingas and owls and pelicans and storks and an osprey, among other things. This parrot's term of treatment was coming to an end. In fact, it looked perfectly healthy, but when it had arrived, five days earlier, it had been unable to stand or raise its head. These are typical symptoms of head trauma, possibly caused by mid-flight collision with a window or some similar object. In this bird's case, bed rest—or would it be perch-rest?—had been a sufficient restorative.

Sitting calmly, this single parrot looked meek enough, and yet it takes a lot of determination for such a species to make its way as a newcomer amidst other established bird populations. Adam Gopnik has depicted the monk parakeets of Flatbush as quintessential New Yorkers, tenacious and "pushy" (46) and "aggressive" (45), rumored "to have killed a house sparrow in Pittsburgh" (45). As for Kevin Barton, he does not wholly disagree. As he told me, "I've treated a lot of birds here in the past four years. They can all put a hurting on you, and they're never happy to be here. But none of them bite harder than the monk parakeets. Pound for pound, they're even worse than the eagles."

Dozing on the floor of its hospital cage, the monk before me was a study in serenity, its body the usual monk green, with butternut-gray breast feathers fluffed up comfortably. As I watched, its eyelids flickered open for a moment and then gradually closed once more.

When I left Pelican Man, Kevin Barton suggested I spend some time at Sarasota's marina, where I could observe the monk population in its own element. So I drove back to the mainland and parked my car and had lunch at the marina and then walked around it in the direction of the adjacent Bayfront Park. I hadn't gone a hundred feet before I heard a suspiciously familiar racket emanate from the palm trees.

You know the sound of one parrot squawking. I'd describe it as the noise one might expect from a sexually aroused power tool. But what of the sound of two parrots squawking? or three? or an entire flock or gaggle or murder or exaltation or whatever it is one calls the imposing collectivity of such birds when they congregate together in large numbers? With parrots, as with the Russian army, quantity possesses a quality all its own.

However you describe it, the sound was inescapable. It immobilized mothers with baby carriages; it made young couples strolling hand in hand stop and gaze into the treetops in consternation. And the worst thing about it was that you couldn't see what was making it.

I eavesdropped upon my fellow park-strollers, and none of them seemed to associate that piercing metallic chatter with parrots. After all, why should they? One usually thinks of Sarasota as the land of overprivileged retirees, not of fugitive hookbills. And unlike the retirees, with their yachts and condominiums and gold jewelry and Lincoln Town Cars, the fugitives were invisible.

I stood under one particularly raucous palm, my head craned upward and my hand to my forehead to shield my eyes from the sun, for a good ten minutes without observing a thing. Like most parrots, monks are ideally colored to blend with their surroundings; they were made to be heard and not seen. But finally a pair hurtled from the cover of the palm fronds and out across the bay, their wings flapping furiously, their green feathers glowing brightly against the blue water.

I spent that entire afternoon and the next morning staring at palm trees, making a spectacle of myself to passersby but gradually, in the process, learning to identify the monks and their nests. They're seldom solitary, preferring to move about in pairs, and they had built several nests in adjacent palm trees, in effect creating a kind of parrot village in the midst of the park. They kept up an endless chatter as they hopped about the fronds outside their nests, occasionally stepping inside, or coming back out to preen each other, or leaping off in sudden flight.

Also amidst the park was an Irish pub with a large outdoor deck built right upon the water, shaded by a banyan tree and surrounded by palms. When I came upon it, the place was packed, and a guitarist on the deck was singing Jimmy Buffett tunes to entertain the crowd. As "Margaritaville" predictably metamorphosed into "Sarasotaville," the surrounding palms came alive with a familiar competing chatter.

Although I respect Jimmy Buffett's abilities as a businessman and entertainer, I'm afraid I've never been terribly fond of his music. Still, one can't live in Florida for sixteen years without coming to appreciate the sheer energy of Buffett's musical followers, who call themselves Parrot Heads and trail him from show to show with a loyalty of which only confirmed fans are capable. At Sarasota's marina, finally, in the heart of Buffett country, I found myself facing a rare critical conundrum: real parrots responding to Parrot Head music with native parrot wood-notes. The parrot heads were literal here, and it's not clear whether they were applauding or heckling.

As the music continued, I edged toward the palms surrounding the deck. The birds refused to shut up, and I soon found myself once more with my hand to my forehead, gazing into the trees to find the small green authors of all this pandemonium. A man and woman noticed me and came to stand nearby. "Listen," the woman said to the man. "Those are the local thrushes."

A small green head with a curved beak peeked out of a shady place among the palm fronds. Soon it was joined by another head, then two matching bodies.

I watched the two creatures squawk and cluck and preen and dance about, as much at home as I think they could be anywhere. These, I thought, are America's most recent immigrants, brought to western shores at last by two millennia of western fascination and persecution, enamorment and exploitation. I have no idea where they'll go from here.

# *Epilogue*

When I bought my younger bird, Persefina, in June 1995, she was about ten weeks old. Her body was virtually featherless, and she fit into the palm of my hand. I fed her formula through an eyedropper, at first four times a day, then three, then two, and then I weaned her on millet and other kinds of seed. But before she could take solid food, she would gobble the formula greedily, until her crop—the pouch, located in her throat, where her food collects before proceeding to her stomach—grew nearly as large as her entire body. Then, too weak to stand up, she would fall asleep in my hand as I cradled her against my stomach.

I spoke to her a lot in her infancy. Double yellow-headed Amazons are renowned talkers, and Persefina has proven true to form. She's eight years old at this point, with a privileged swagger redeemed by her general sweetness of temper, and her vocal repertoire ranges from the usual "Hello!" and "Good girl!" to "Hey, bird girl!" and "Hey, old girl!" (This latter my general salutation to my other parrot, Lazarillo) and her own name, "Persefina!" which she crows out in four sustained syllables of which the third ascends a couple of octaves above middle C, and thence to murkier and more complex utterances such as "Wanna go to birdy jail?"—a disciplinary question I like to pose whenever she misbehaves, and which she has cheekily taken to throwing back at me. She also sings operatic vocalises at great length and with great vigor. Don't ask me where she learned them; I'm hopelessly opera-impaired, with musical tastes that run more to Camper Van Beethoven than to Bizet. But she sings opera anyway, in great swooping intervals belted out with a vibrato you could drive a truck through.

One of her lines gives me greater joy than any other, a joy redoubled by the fact that I never deliberately tried to teach it to her. The line is "I love you"—which I repeated to her often during feedings and was startled and delighted to hear in return one day when she was still months rather than years old. Nowadays she often says it with a sense of irony, as for instance after she has wrestled an especially choice morsel off of my dinner plate, or when she is enduring an unwanted bath. It's as if the bird knew that my fondness for this line is a function of my own narcissism, that I like it because of what it seems to say about *me*: to wit, that I'm the kind of guy who's at home with his feelings, nurturing and affectionate to small dependent creatures, unafraid of intimacy—all in all, a prime specimen of enlightened western masculinity.

But I'm not the first person for whom a parrot has served as a mirror of the self, nor am I the first person for whom that mirroring effect has acquired an ironic dimension.

Between 1799 and 1805, the explorer and polymath Alexander von Humboldt traced the course of the Orinoco River as part of his extended travels in South America. In the process, he came to the first of the great cataracts that rendered the upper stretches of that river inaccessible by boat: the cataract of Atures, home to a Jesuit mission of the same name, both of which, in turn, derived their name from the tribe of Atures Indians that had formerly dwelt at the mission. By Humboldt's time that mission was in sad shape; whereas it had formerly housed more than three hundred Indians, its population had dwindled to barely fifty. As for its original inhabitants, the Atures, they were gone forever, having vanished, almost without a trace, within the past half century. Some nearby burial grounds still attested to their former presence; otherwise, Humboldt has only this to say about them:

> The warlike Atures, pursued by the Carribbees, escaped to the rocks that rise in the middle of the Great Cataracts; and there that nation, heretofore so numerous, became gradually extinct, as well as it's [*sic*] language. The last families of the Atures still existed in 1767, in the time of the missionary Gili. At the period of our voyage an old parrot was shown at Maypures, of which the inhabitants related, and the fact is worthy of observation, that "they did not understand what it said, because it spoke the language of the Atures." (5:620)

This dry comment makes the hair stand up on the back of my neck. The parrot's language, which originally marked the presence of a human being and of a relationship between that person and the bird, has by Humboldt's day ironically come to mark the absence of both. What's more, this absence has been generalized from an individual to a racial calamity: the loss of an entire tribe. And finally, and perhaps most ironically of all, this loss of the "extinct" Atures prefigures the threatened twenty-first-century loss of the race of parrots that has provided Humboldt with the last little trace of the Indians' otherwise-vanished tongue. Birds mirror people mirror birds, in life and in death, from past to present to future.

But of course extinction isn't just a collective phenomenon. It has a personal dimension too, concomitant with the death of single individuals, and as I grow older I find myself contemplating this fact ever more lugubriously. As a result, Persefina's "I love you" has come to sound more and more to my ear like an intimation of mortality. After all, a month after Persefina celebrates her eighth birthday, I'll celebrate my forty-seventh. Accidents aside, it's just a matter of time before she becomes for me what Humboldt's parrot was for the Atures: a marker of loss, the last echo of my dead voice.

And what will this mean for Persefina herself? In researching this book, I've had plenty of opportunity to see what can happen to parrots that have lost their primary human companion. The picture is often a painful one to behold. Like people—indeed, perhaps even more than people—parrots form lasting, exclusive emotional bonds. In the wild they generally mate for life, and in captivity they cleave unto their human partner with a determination as fierce as it is endearing. No one else matters quite as much. So I worry about Persefina without me. Who will look after her, and how well? How will she respond? It's best, I think, to make provision for such matters. But how solid can such provision ever be?

This last question bears repeating in a broader context, too. For will we nill we, humanity as a race must henceforth make provision for Persefina and her cousins everywhere, in captivity and in the wild, if they are to survive at all. The welfare of these birds, like that of the natural world in general, lies in our hands. For want of a better, we are their caretaker.

If nothing else, this book should show how deeply parrots are involved in the story of western society, and of human culture in general. They have been our companions for millennia, offering solace and amusement, inspiring wonder and curiosity, taking their own peculiar place in some of our greatest artistic and literary achievements. I hope they will continue to do so for millennia to come. But that depends on us.

# Notes

*Prologue:* **Circa 40 Million B.C.**

1. See Harrison for the original scientific description of *Palaeopsittacus georgei*. For more recent findings of Eocene-epoch parrot bones in England and Germany, see Mayr and Daniels. Thomas Stidham has proposed that a fossilized lower mandible dating from the upper Cretaceous period (roughly 65 million years ago) could have belonged to an early parrot, and this would make the birds' lineage still more ancient (Stidham). Stidham's hypothesis, however, has not yet been fully accepted by other scientists.

*Chapter 1.* **Invasion of the Parrots**

1. Numerous eyewitness accounts of Alexander's campaigns were produced by his followers, but all have been lost. The standard surviving classical biographies of Alexander, apart from that by Arrian, are those of Quintus Curtius (A.D. 31–41) and Plutarch (A.D. 100–125). For a discussion of the lost early histories of Alexander, see Bosworth 295–300, Baynham 69–74. Of those early accounts, that of Nearchus was particularly influential, and apparently—as Arrian's remark about parrots suggests—it dwelt at length upon the Greeks' experience in India.

2. As Andrew Dalby remarks, the most popular parrot to be brought to the classical Mediterranean from India (a term used loosely by classical writers) was the rose-ringed or "Indian ring-necked parakeet" (*Psittacula krameri*) (193), for a description of which see Forshaw 326–328. This species is well-documented (albeit sometimes with extra-anatomical embellishments) in Roman visual art; see Toynbee 247–249, Keller 2:46–47. Keller also notes that "a very few pictures show the straight tail by which the southern Indian and Ceylonese *Psittacus* or *Palaeornis Alexandri* can be recognized" (47, my translation); however, Keller's biological taxonomy is off here. *Psittacula* (not *Psittacus*) *alexandri*, the moustached parakeet (for which see Forshaw 342–343) does not range south of the Himalayas or west

of Burma; it is also visually distinctive in ways not accounted for in Roman painting and other visual arts. Keller clearly means to refer to the Alexandrine parakeet, *Psittacula eupatria*, whose common name he has confused with the
moustached parakeet's Latin name. For a description of *Psittacula eupatria*, see
Forshaw 324–325. As noted further on in this chapter, Ktesias of Cnidus seems to
describe the blossom-headed parakeet (*Psittacula roseata*; see Ktesias 1.3, Forshaw
335); but then, he is not writing of an imported bird per se. As Toynbee notes
(249), there is a partly blue parrot in a Pompeiian mosaic depicting a cat watching
two parrots and a dove (see Figure 2). This may perhaps be the blue mutation of
*Psittacula krameri* familiar to pet-owners today, or it may simply be a case of artistic license. Other Roman illustrations of parrots display such license, in one case
going so far as to give the bird in question horns.

3. The conversational ability of parrots—particularly African grays—has become the subject of extensive recent research by Irene Pepperberg, which I dis-
cuss in the final chapter of this book (see Pepperberg). As for parrot musical
performances, they are fairly commonplace in contemporary theme parks and
other comparable settings; operatic parrots have appeared, for instance, on
Johnny Carson's *Tonight Show*, and in the PBS "Nature" documentary *Parrots:
Look Who's Talking*.

4. For an overview of ancient educational practices, see Bonner 143–145,
who remarks that "throughout antiquity, from the time of Socrates to that of St.
Augustine and beyond, across the whole Mediterranean world, from Egypt to
Bordeaux and from Carthage to Antioch, corporal punishment was a constant
feature of school life" (143). The principal instruments for such punishment, he
notes, were "the ferule (*ferula*), which corresponded roughly with the cane," "the
*scutica*, or whip," and "the rods (*virgae*), formed of a bundle of pliant withies"
(143). The iron rod Pliny identifies with parrot-training bears more than a coincidental resemblance to such implements.

5. For discussion of this illustration and others like it, see Toynbee 249.

*Chapter 2.* **Mysteries and Marvels**

1. Beryl Rowland has speculated that this notion arose because medieval
writers had confused the parrot with the West African turaco, "which has a crimson pigment in its feathers that is indeed soluble in water" (122).

2. For this identification, see Mayer 392–394. Jacques de Vitry, in turn,
seems to have influenced Thomas of Cantimpré's work quite deeply. *The Walden-*

*sian Physiologus* seems to be a late (fifteenth-century) copy of a translation into Old Occitan of Jacques' original (and now lost) Latin.

3. For further examples of this parrot-motif in Italian fabrics of the twelfth to fourteenth centuries, see Devoti, figures 7, 10, 11, 14, 34, and 39.

### Chapter 3. **Return of the Parrots**

1. "Popinjay," according to the *OED* (sb. "Popinjay") derives from cognate terms in Arabic and medieval Greek. Thus a word associated with the parrot's identity as an eastern bird drops out of usage at the same time that parrots themselves are increasingly associated with the New World rather than the Old.

2. The Wing Catalogue of Early English Books published between 1641 and 1700 identifies this as a translation/adaptation of work by the great Spanish satirist Francisco de Quevedo (1580–1645; Wing Q193). In my search of Quevedo's work, I have failed to locate the original.

3. The *OED* explains this name as a familiar form of "Mary" (equivalent to "Moll"), and gives its earliest recorded use as 1630, a quarter-century after *Volpone*, when it appears in Epigram 31 by Jonson's admirer, John Taylor the Water Poet (*OED* sb. 3 "Poll"). For the text of Taylor's poem, see the ensuing discussion.

### Chapter 4. **Unhappy Bird!**

1. The *OED* gives initial usages of "amateur" in 1784 and "dilettante" in 1733–34 (sb. "Amateur" 1, sb. "Dilettante" 1). For the relationship of these words to the cult of the gentleman collector, see Garber 12–18.

2. Enid Starkie, for instance, remarks that while "*Un coeur simple* is generally taken as a realistic tale, . . . it is difficult to believe that so many disasters could happen to one human being. Everything turns out disastrously for Félicité" (260).

3. As Julian Barnes points out in *Flaubert's Parrot* (16–22; also see Lottman 286 and 382, n. 25) there currently exist not one but two stuffed parrots with a claim to be the one Flaubert borrowed. The former of these birds resides in the Flaubert Museum, Hôtel-Dieu, Rouen, while the latter can be found in the smaller Flaubert Pavilion in Croisset.

4. Starkie (245–247) summarizes some of the reading Flaubert did for *Saint Julian*, reading which probably included medieval devotional texts as well as works dealing with hunting and animals.

5. Defoe's authorship of this work, while accepted by many, has been

strongly challenged as well. When the *General History of the Pyrates* first appeared, it was credited to a Captain Charles Johnson. It was not attributed to Defoe until the twentieth century.

*Chapter 5.* **Dead Parrot Sketch**

1. One occasionally finds this line attributed to Shaw in the popular media, as for instance at the website of the Parrot Society UK ("Verse by George Bernard Shaw"). However, Shaw has often been credited with *bons mots* he did not in fact coin, and this would seem to be a case in point. It is certainly not to be found in his plays and prefaces. My limited search of his nondramatic prose has also failed to turn it up there (*pace* the Parrot Society, he didn't write verse); likewise, the professional Shavians whom I have consulted have not recognized the line.

# Bibliography

Aelian. *On the Characteristics of Animals*. Trans. A. F. Scholfield. 3 vols. Cambridge, Mass.: Harvard University Press, 1949.

Aesop. *The Complete Fables*. Trans. Olivia and Robert Temple. London: Penguin, 1998.

Amours, F. J., ed. *Scottish Alliterative Poems in Rhyming Stanzas*. Edinburgh: William Blackwood and Sons, 1897.

Andrade, Mario de. *Macunaima*. Trans. E. A. Goodland. New York: Random House, 1984.

Anthony, Katherine. *Dolly Madison: Her Life and Times*. Garden City, N.Y.: Doubleday, 1949.

Apicius. *Cookery and Dining in Imperial Rome*. Trans. Joseph Dommers Vehling. Chicago: Walter M. Hill, 1936.

Apuleius. *Apologie. Florides*. Ed. and trans. Paul Valette. Paris: Société d'Edition *Les Belles Lettres*, 1960.

Aristotle. *History of Animals*. Ed. and trans. Arthur Peck and D. M. Balme. 11 vols. Cambridge, Mass.: Harvard University Press, 1991.

Arrian. *History of Alexander and Indica*. Trans. P. A. Brunt. 2 vols. Cambridge, Mass.: Harvard University Press, 1976.

Ashdown, Dulcie M. *Princess of Wales*. New York: Charles Scribner's Sons, 1979.

Athenaeus. *The Deipnosophists*. Trans. Charles Burton Gulick. 7 vols. London: William Heinemann, 1951.

Atwood, Margaret. *Oryx and Crake*. New York: Doubleday/Nan A. Talese, 2003.

Audubon, John James. *My Style of Drawing Birds*. Ardsley, N.Y.: Overland Press, 1979.

———. *Ornithological Biography*. 5 vols. Edinburgh: Adam Black, 1831.

Babrius. *Babrius and Phaedrus*. Trans. Ben Edwin Perry. Cambridge, Mass.: Harvard University Press, 1965.

Barnes, Julian. *Flaubert's Parrot*. London: Picador, 1984.

Barton, Anne. *Ben Jonson, Dramatist.* Cambridge, UK: Cambridge University Press, 1984.

Baynham, Elizabeth. *Alexander the Great: The Unique History of Quintus Curtius.* Ann Arbor: University of Michigan Press, 1998.

Bedini, Silvio A. *The Pope's Elephant.* Nashville: J. S. Sanders, 1998.

Belon, Pierre. *L'histoire de la nature des oyseaux.* Paris, 1555.

*Bestiary, Being an English Version of the Bodleian Library, Oxford MS Bodley 764 with all the Original Miniatures Reproduced in Facsimile.* Trans. Richard Barber. Woodbridge, UK: Boydell, 1993.

Bibesco, Princess Marthe. *The Green Parrot.* Trans. Malcolm Cowley. New York: Harcourt, Brace, 1929.

Boccaccio, Giovanni. *Genealogiae.* 1494; rpt. New York: Garland, 1976.

———. *Eclogues.* Trans. Janet Levarie Smarr. New York: Garland, 1987.

Bonner, Stanley F. *Education in Ancient Rome: From the Elder Cato to the Younger Pliny.* London: Methuen, 1977.

*The Book of Beasts, Being a Translation from a Latin Bestiary of the Twelfth Century.* Trans. T. H. White. 1954; rpt. New York: Dover, 1984.

Booth, Joan, ed. and trans. *Ovid: The Second Book of "Amores."* Warminster, Wilts.: Aris and Phillips, 1991.

Bosworth, A. B. *Conquest and Empire: The Reign of Alexander the Great.* Cambridge, UK: Cambridge University Press, 1988.

Bowles, Paul. *Their Heads Are Green and Their Hands Are Blue.* New York: Random House, 1957.

Burger, Joanna. *The Parrot Who Owns Me: The Story of a Relationship.* New York: Random House, 2001.

Butler, Arthur G. *Foreign Bird Keeping.* London: Feathered World, n.d.

Butler, Robert Olen. *A Good Scent from a Strange Mountain.* 1992; rpt. New York: Grove Press, 2001.

———. *Tabloid Dreams.* New York: Henry Holt, 1996.

Butler, Samuel. *Hudibras.* London, 1761.

Cabral, Pedro. *The Voyage of Pedro Alvares Cabral to Brazil and India.* Ed. And trans. William Brooks Greenlee. London: Hakluyt Society, 1938.

Callimachus. *Fragments.* Trans. C. A. Trypanis. Cambridge, Mass.: Harvard University Press, 1975.

Cantimpré, Thomas of. *De Rerum Natura.* Ed. Luis Garcia Ballester. 2 vols. Granada: University of Granada, 1974.

Catullus. *Carmina*. Ed. R. A. B. Mynors. Oxford: Clarendon, 1958.

Chaptman, Dennis. "UW Coach's Son Gets Ten Days for Parrot's Microwave Death." *Milwaukee Journal Sentinel*. December 10, 1999.

Chaucer, Geoffrey. *The Riverside Chaucer*. Gen. ed. Larry D. Benson. Boston: Houghton Mifflin, 1987.

Chopin, Kate. *The Awakening and Selected Stories*. Ed. Sandra M. Gilbert. Harmondsworth: Penguin, 1986.

Church, Richard. *The Royal Parks of London*. London: H. M. Stationery Office, 1965.

"The Churchwardens' Accounts of the Parish of Saint Mary Thame, Commencing 1442." Ed. W. P. Ellis. *Berkshire, Buckinghamshire, and Oxford Archaeological Journal* 9 (1903–1904): 45–68.

Claudian. *Claudian*. Trans. Maurice Plantnauer. 2 vols. Cambridge, Mass.: Harvard University Press, 1956.

Colette. *Ripening Seed*. Trans. Roger Senhouse. 1955; rpt. London: Penguin, 1959.

Columbus, Christopher. *The Log of Christopher Columbus*. Tran. Robert H. Fuson. Camden, Me.: International Marine Publishing, 1992.

Conrad, Joseph. *Nostromo*. New York: Signet, 1964.

Cortes, Fernando. *Fernando Cortes: His Five Letters of Relation to the Emperor Charles V*. Trans. Francis Augustus MacNutt. 2 vols. Cleveland: Arthur H. Clark, 1908.

Crabbe, George. *The Complete Poetical Works*. Ed. Norma Dalrymple-Champneys and Arthur Pollard. 3 vols. Oxford: Clarendon, 1988.

Crinagoras. From *The Greek Anthology*, trans. W. R. Paton. 5 vols. London: Heinemann, 1925.

Cruttwell, Maud. *Andrea Mantegna*. London: George Bell and Sons, 1901.

Cushion, John P. *Animals in Pottery and Porcelain*. London: Cory, Adams and Mackay, 1966.

Custis, Eleanor Parke. *George Washington's Beautiful Nelly: The Letters of Eleanor Parke Custis Lewis to Elizabeth Bordley Gibson, 1794–1851*. Ed. Patricia Brady. Columbia: University of South Carolina Press, 1991.

Dalby, Andrew. *Empire of Pleasures: Luxury and Indulgence in the Roman World*. London: Routledge, 2000.

Defoe, Daniel. *Robinson Crusoe*. Ed. Harvey Swados. New York: Penguin, 1961.

———. *A General History of the Pyrates*. Ed. Manuel Schonhorn. 2 vols. Mineola, N.Y.: Dover, 1999.

Devoti, Donata. *L'arte del tessuto in Europa*. Milan: Bramante, 1974.

Díaz del Castillo, Bernal. *The Discovery and Conquest of Mexico*. Trans. A. P. Maudslay. New York: Grove Press, 1956.

Doane, Bonnie Munro, and Thomas Qualkenbush. *My Parrot, My Friend: An Owner's Guide to Parrot Behavior*. New York: Macmillan, 1994.

Douglas, Norman. *Birds and Beasts of the Greek Anthology*. New York: Jonathan Cape and Harrison Smith, 1929.

Dupin, Jacques. *Joan Miró: Life and Work*. New York: Harry N. Abrams, n.d.

Du Quesnay, I. M. Le M. "The *Amores*." *Ovid*. Ed. J. W. Binns. London: Routledge and Kegan Paul, 1973. 1–48.

Elliott, Mike. "Environment, Resources, and Development Committee: Native Fauna." Http://sa.democrats.org.au/parlt/budget99/0728_k.htm.

Enciso, Martin Fernandez de. *A Brief Summe of Geographie*. Trans. Roger Barlow. Ed. E. G. R. Taylor. London: Hakluyt Society, 1932.

Esquemeling, John. *The Buccaneers of America*. Ed. William Swan Stallybrass. London: George Routledge and Sons, 1936.

Ferguson, James. *Lectures on Select Subjects*. London: A. Millar, 1760.

Ferguson, John. "Catullus and Ovid." *American Journal of Philology* 81.3 (1960): 337–357.

Fish, Stanley. *John Skelton's Poetry*. New Haven: Yale University Press, 1965.

Flaim, Denise. "Polly Gets a Crackdown." nyNewsday.com, February 9, 2003.

Flaubert, Gustave. *Three Tales*. Trans. A. J. Krailsheimer. New York: Oxford University Press, 1991.

———. *Correspondance*. 8 vols. Paris: Louis Conard, 1930.

Fleming, Victor. *Treasure Island*. Hollywood, Calif.: Metro Goldwyn Mayer, 1934.

Ford, Walton. *Tigers of Wrath, Horses of Instruction*. Texts by Steven Katz and Dodie Kazanjian. New York: Harry N. Abrams, 2002.

Forshaw, Joseph. *Parrots of the World*. Melbourne: Lansdowne, 1973.

Franklin, Alfred. *La vie privée d'autrefois; arts et métiers, modes, moeurs, usages des Parisiens du XIIe au XVIIIe siècle*. 23 vols. Paris: E. Plon-Nourrit, 1887–1901.

Fried, Michael. *Courbet's Realism*. Chicago: University of Chicago Press, 1990.

Garber, Marjorie. *Academic Instincts*. Princeton: Princeton University Press, 2001.

García Márquez, Gabriel. *One Hundred Years of Solitude*. Trans. Gregory Rabassa. New York: Harper and Row, 1970.

————. *Love in the Time of Cholera*. Trans. Edith Grossman. New York: Penguin, 1989.

Gardner, Erle Stanley. *The Case of the Perjured Parrot*. New York: Pocket Books, 1939.

*Sir Gawain and the Green Knight*. Ed. J. A. Burrow. New Haven: Yale University Press, 1972.

Gesner, Conrad. *Historia Animalium Liber III. Qui est de avium natura*. Frankfurt, 1604.

Gittner, Cory H. *Miami's Parrot Jungle and Gardens: The Colorful History of an Uncommon Attraction*. Gainesville: University Press of Florida, 2000.

"Good Bird Jokes!" Http://www.plannedparrothood.com/jokes.html.

Gopnik, Adam. "Power and the Parrot." *New Yorker* 76 (February 5, 2001): 44–47.

Gorra, Egidio. "La novella della dama e dei tre papagalli." *Romania* 21 (1892): 71–78.

*The Greek Anthology*. Trans. W. R. Paton. 5 vols. London: William Heinemann, 1925.

Hakluyt, Richard. *The Principal Navigations Voyages Traffiques and Discoveries of the English Nation*. 12 vols. New York: Macmillan, 1904.

Hanke, Lewis. "Pope Paul III and the American Indians." *Harvard Theological Review* 30 (1937): 65–102.

Harrison, C. J. O. "The Earliest Parrot: A New Species from the British Eocene." *Ibis* 124.2 (April 1982): 203–210.

Hartmann, Cyril H. *La Belle Stuart: Memoirs of Court and Society in the Times of Frances Teresa Stuart, Duchess of Richmond and Lennox*. London: Routledge, 1924.

Heaton, H. C., ed. *The Discovery of the Amazon According to the Account of Friar Gaspar de Carvajal and Other Documents*. Trans. Bertram T. Lee. New York: American Geographical Society, 1934.

Herrera, Hayden. *Frida: A Biography of Frida Kahlo*. New York: Harper and Row, 1983.

Herrick, Robert. *The Complete Poetry of Robert Herrick*. Ed. J. Max Patrick. New York: W. W. Norton, 1968.

Heyerdahl, Thor. *Kon-Tiki: Across the Pacific by Raft*. Trans. F. H. Lyon. Chicago: Rand McNally, 1950.

Historical Manuscripts Commission. *Report on Manuscripts in Various Collections*. Series 55, volume 7. London: His Majesty's Stationery Office, 1914.

Hoccleve, Thomas. *Hoccleve's Works. II. The Minor Poems in the Ashburnham MS Addit. 133*. Ed. Israel Gollancz. London: Early English Text Society, 1925.

Hockney, David. *David Hockney by David Hockney*. New York: Harry N. Abrams, 1977.

*Holy Bible: Authorized Version*. Cleveland: World, n.d.

Holzberg, Niklas. *Ovid: The Poet and His Work*. Trans. G. M. Goshgarian. Ithaca, N.Y.: Cornell University Press, 1998.

Humboldt, Alexander von. *Personal Narrative of Travels to the Equinoctial Regions of the New Continent*. 7 vols. London, 1821.

Hyman, Susan. *Edward Lear's Birds*. London: Trefoil, 1980.

International Union for Conservation of Nature and Natural Resources (IUCN). *2002 IUCN Red List of Threatened Species*. Cambridge, UK: IUCN, 2002.

Isidore of Seville. *Etymologiarum sive Originum Libri XX*. Ed. W. M. Lindsay. 2 vols. Oxford: Clarendon, 1911.

[Jehan.] *The Marvels of Rigomer*. Trans. Thomas E. Vesce. New York: Garland, 1988.

"Joke Dictionary: The A-Z Jokes Collection." Http://www.jokedictionary.com.

Jonson, Ben. *Ben Jonson*. Ed. C. H. Herford and Percy and Evelyn Simpson. 11 vols. Oxford: Clarendon, 1925–1952.

"Judges Hear Evidence from Nuisance Parrot." Http://www.ananova.com/news/ story/ sm_498489.html.

Juniper, Tony. *Spix's Macaw: The Race to Save the World's Rarest Bird*. London: Fourth Estate, 2002.

Juniper, Tony, and Mike Parr. *Parrots: A Guide to Parrots of the World*. New Haven: Yale University Press, 1998.

Keller, Otto. *Die Antike Tierwelt*. 2 vols. Hildesheim: Georg Olms, 1963.

Kelly, Niall. *Presidential Pets*. New York: Abbeville Press, 1992.

Kingsolver, Barbara. *The Poisonwood Bible*. New York: HarperCollins, 1999.

Kinney, Arthur. *John Skelton: Priest as Poet*. Chapel Hill: University of North Carolina Press, 1987.

*The Knight of the Parrot*. Trans. Thomas M. Vesce. New York: Garland 1986.

Knight, Michael. "Birdland." *New Yorker* 74 (November 9, 1998): 82–89.

Ktesias. *Ancient India as Described by Ktresias the Knidian*. Trans. J. W. McRindle. 1882; rpt. Delhi: Manohar Reprints, 1973.

LaFay, Laura. "Born Wild in the USA." Parrotchronicles.com, March–April 2003.

Langland, William. *The Vision of William Concerning Piers the Plowman in Three Parallel Texts*. Ed. Walter W. Skeat. 2 vols. Oxford: Clarendon, 1886.

*Latham v. Wal-Mart Stores, Inc.* 818 S.W. 2d 673 (Mo. App. E.D. 1991).

Léry, Jean de. *History of a Voyage to the Land of Brazil*. Trans. Janet Whatley. Berkeley: University of California Press, 1990.

Lévi-Strauss, Claude. *Tristes Tropiques*. Trans. John and Doreen Weightman. New York: Atheneum, 1974.

Lindsay, Sir David. *The Works of Sir David Lindsay of the Mount*. Ed. Douglas Hamer. 2 vols. Edinburgh: William Blackwood and Sons, 1931.

*Lives of the Later Caesars*. Trans. Anthony Birley. Harmondsworth: Penguin, 1976.

Locke, John. *An Essay Concerning Human Understanding*. Ed. John Yolton. 2 vols. London: J. M. Dent and Sons, 1961.

Loisel, Gustave. *Histoire des ménageries de l'antiquité à nos jours*. 3 vols. Paris: O. Doin et Fils, 1912.

Lottman, Herbert. *Flaubert: A Biography*. Boston: Little, Brown, 1989.

Luria, Maxwell S., and Richard L. Hoffman, eds. *Middle English Lyrics*. New York: W. W. Norton, 1974.

Lydgate, John. *Poems*. Ed. John Norton-Smith. Oxford: Clarendon, 1966.

MacDonogh, Katharine. *Reigning Cats and Dogs: A History of Pets at Court Since the Renaissance*. New York: St. Martin's, 1999.

Macrobius. *Ambrosii Theodosii Macrobii Saturnalia . . . [et] In Somnium Scipionis*. Ed. Jacob Willis. 2 vols. Leipzig: B. G. Teubner, 1963.

*Mandeville's Travels*. Ed. M. C. Seymour. Oxford: Clarendon, 1967.

Martial. *Epigrams*. Trans. D. R. Shackleton Bailey. 3 vols. Cambridge, Mass.: Harvard University Press, 1993.

Martyr, Peter. *The Decades of the New World or West India*. London, 1555.

———. *De Orbe Novo*. Paris, 1587.

Mayer, Alfons. "Der Waldensische Physiologus." *Romanische Forschungen* 5 (1890): 392–418.

Mayr, Gerald, and Michael Daniels. "Eocene Parrots from Messel (Hessen, Germany) and the London Clay of Walton-on-the-Naze (Essex, England)." *Senckenbergiana Lethaea* 78 (1998): 157–177.

McLynn, Frank. *Robert Louis Stevenson: A Biography*. New York: Random House, 1993.

Mearns, Barbara, and Richard Mearns. *The Bird Collectors*. San Diego: Academic Press, 1998.

Menzhausen, Ingelore. *Early Meissen Porcelain in Dresden*. Trans. Charles E. Scurrell. London: Thames and Hudson, 1990.

Millar, Oliver. *Van Dyck in England*. London: National Portrait Gallery, 1982.

Mirk, John. *Mirk's Festial: A Collection of Homilies*. Ed. Theodor Erbe. London: Early English Text Society, 1905.

Montagné, Prosper. *Larousse Gastronomique*. Ed. Nina Froud and Charlotte Turgeon. London: Paul Hamlyn, 1971.

Monty Python [Graham Chapman, John Cleese, Terry Gilliam, Eric Idle, Terry Jones, and Michael Palin]. *Monty Python's Flying Circus*. London: British Broadcasting Corporation, 1969–1974.

Morison, Samuel Eliot. *The Great Explorers: The European Discovery of America*. New York: Oxford University Press, 1978.

Mozley, J. H., ed. and trans. *Statius*. 2 vols. Cambridge, Mass.: Harvard University Press, 1982.

Müller, Karl, ed. *Fragmenta Historicorum Graecorum*. 4 vols. Paris: Firmin-Didot, 1928.

Murphy, Kevin. "Outrage Greets Man Accused of Killing Parrot." *Milwaukee Journal Sentinel*. May 14, 1999.

Musch, Irmgard, Rainer Willmann, and Jes Rust. *Albertus Seba: Cabinet of Natural Curiosities*. Cologne: Taschen, 2001

Myers, Norman. *Deforestation Rates in Tropical Forests and Their Climatic Implications*. London: Friends of the Earth, 1989.

Nashe, Thomas. *The Works of Thomas Nashe*. Ed. R. B. McKerrow. 7 vols. Oxford: Basil Blackwell, 1958.

Neckam, Alexander. *De Naturis Rerum et De Laudibus Sapientiae*. Ed. Thomas Wright. London: Longman, Green, Longman, Roberts, and Green, 1863.

"Our Favorite Pirate or Parrot Jokes." Http://nce.aaris.net/our.htm.

Ovid. *Amores. Medicamina Faciei Femineae. Ars Amatoria. Remedia Amoris*. Ed. E. J. Kenney. Oxford: Clarendon, 1961.

Oviedo, Gonzalo Fernandez de. *Natural History of the West Indies*. Trans. Sterling Stoudemire. Chapel Hill: University of North Carolina Press, 1959.

Parrot Society UK. "Verse by George Bernard Shaw." www.theparrotsocietyuk .org/poem2.htm

Pepperberg, Irene. *The Alex Studies: Cognitive and Communicative Abilities of Grey Parrots*. Cambridge, Mass.: Harvard University Press, 1999.

Persius. *Satirarum Liber*. Ed. Fridrich Dubner. 1833; rpt. Osnabruck: Biblio Verlag, 1972.

Peterson, Roger Tory. Introduction. In John James Audubon, *The Art of Audubon: The Complete Birds and Mammals*. New York: Times Books, 1979. ix–xi.

Petronius. *Petronius*. Trans. Michael Heseltine. Cambridge, Mass.: Harvard University Press, 1969; rpt. 1987.

Pliny the Elder. *Histoire naturelle*. Ed. and trans. E. de Saint Denis. 32 vols. Paris: Société d'Edition *Les Belles Lettres*, 1961.

———. *Letters and Panegyricus*. Trans. Betty Radice. 2 vols. Cambridge, Mass.: Cambridge University Press, 1969.

Plutarch. *Plutarch's Moralia*. Trans. Harold Cherniss. 15 vols. Cambridge, Mass.: Harvard University Press, 1957.

Poe, Edgar Allan. "The Philosophy of Composition." *Graham's Magazine* 28.4 (April 1846): 163–167.

"Poison Plan for Flocks." *Herald Sun*. Thursday, March 25, 1999.

Pope, Alexander. *"The Rape of the Lock" and Other Poems*. Ed. Geoffrey Tillotson. London: Routledge, 1993.

*Psittacorum regio, the land of parrots, or, The she-lands*. London, 1669.

Purchas, Samuel. *Hakluytus Posthumus or Purchas his Pilgrimes*. 20 vols. New York: AMS, 1965.

Rhys, Jean. *Wide Sargasso Sea*. 1966; rpt. New York: W. W. Norton, 1982.

Robbins, Louise E. *Elephant Slaves and Pampered Parrots: Exotic Animals in Eighteenth-Century Paris*. Baltimore: Johns Hopkins University Press, 2002.

Roosevelt, Theodore. *Theodore Roosevelt's Letters to His Children*. Ed. Joseph Bucklin Bishop. New York: Charles Scribner's Sons, 1919.

Rowland, Beryl. *Birds with Human Souls: A Guide to Bird Symbolism*. Knoxville: University of Tennessee Press, 1978.

Schafer, Edward H. *The Golden Peaches of Samarkand: A Study of T'ang Exotics*. Berkeley: University of California Press, 1963.

Shakespeare, William. *The Riverside Shakespeare*. Ed. G. Blakemore Evans et al. Boston: Houghton Mifflin, 1997.

Shell, Marc. "The Family Pet." *Representations* 15 (Summer 1986): 121–153.

Shepard, E. "The Castle Mall Archaeological Project, Norwich." Http://www .eng-h.gov.uk/archcom/projects/summarys/html96_7/1053rec.htm.

Skelton, John. *The Poetical Works of John Skelton*. Ed. Alexander Dyce. 1843; rpt. New York: AMS, 1965.

Solinus. *The Excellent and Pleasant Worke Collectanea Rerum Memorabilium.* Trans. Arthur Golding. 1587; rpt. Gainesville, Fla.: Scholars' Facsimiles and Reprints, 1955.

Starkie, Enid. *Flaubert the Master.* New York: Atheneum, 1971.

Statius. *Statius.* Trans. J. H. Mozley. 2 vols. Cambridge, Mass.: Harvard University Press, 1982.

Steele, Richard. *The Tatler.* 4 vols. London, 1797.

Stern, Jane, and Michael Stern. "Parrots." *New Yorker* 66 (1990): 55–73.

Stevenson, Robert Louis. *Treasure Island.* New York: Heritage Reprints, 1941.

Stidham, Thomas A. "A Lower Jaw from a Cretaceous Parrot." *Nature* 396 (November 5, 1998): 29–30.

Stresemann, Erwin. *Ornithology from Aristotle to the Present.* Trans. Hans J. and Cathleen Epstein. Cambridge, Mass.: Harvard University Press, 1975.

Surtees Society. *The Publications of the Surtees Society, Volume 4. Testa Eboracum, or Wills Registered at York. Part I.* London: J. B. Nichols and Son, 1836.

———. *The Publications of the Surtees Society, Volume 99. Extracts from the Account Rolls of the Abbey of Durham. Volume I.* Durham: Surtees Society, 1898.

*Susannah: An Alliterative Poem of the Fourteenth Century.* Ed. Alice Miskimin. New Haven: Yale University Press, 1969.

Taylor, Jane H. M. "The Fourteenth Century: Context, Text, and Intertext." *The Legacy of Chretien de Troyes.* Ed. Norris J. Lacy, Douglas Kelly, and Keith Busby. 2 vols. Amsterdam: Rodopi, 1987. 1:267–332.

Taylor, John. *All the Workes of John Taylor the Water Poet.* 1630; facs. London: Scolar Press, 1977.

———. *Works of John Taylor the Water Poet.* New York: Burt Franklin, 1876, rpt. 1967.

Thevet, André. *The New Found World, or Antarcticke.* London, 1568. Facs. Amsterdam: Da Capo, 1971.

Thomas, Keith. *Man and the Natural World: Changing Attitudes in England, 1500–1800.* London: Allen Lane, 1983.

Toynbee, J. M. C. *Animals in Roman Life and Art.* London: Thames and Hudson, 1973.

Trevisa, John. *On the Properties of Things: John Trevisa's Translation of Bartholomaeus Anglicus "De Proprietatibus Rerum."* Ed. M. C. Seymour et al. 3 vols. Oxford: Clarendon, 1975.

Truman, Margaret. *White House Pets.* New York: David MacKay Company, 1969.

Twain, Mark. *The Adventures of Huckleberry Finn*. Berkeley: University of California Press, 1985.

Tyndale, William. *Obedie[n]ce of a Christen Man*. [Antwerp,] 1528.

Varro. *On Agriculture*. Trans. William Davis Hooper. Rev. Harrison Boyd. Cambridge, Mass.: Harvard University Press, 1934.

Walcott, Derek. *Remembrance and Pantomime*. New York: Farrar, Straus, and Giroux, 1980.

Waldman, Diane. *Joseph Cornell: Master of Dreams*. New York: Harry N. Abrams, 2002.

Waldseemüller, Martin. *Cosmographiae Introductio*. Trans. Joseph Fischer and Franz von Wieser. Ann Arbor: University Microfilms, 1966.

Walters, Lori J. "Parody and the Parrot: Lancelot References in the *Chevalier du papegau*." *Translatio Studii: Essays by His Students in Honor of Karl D. Uitti for his Sixty-Fifth Birthday*. Ed. Renate Blumenfeld-Kosinski et al. Amsterdam: Rodopi, 1999. 331–344.

*The Wars of Alexander*. Ed. Hoyt N. Duggan and Thorlac Turville-Petre. Oxford: Oxford University Press, 1989.

Washington, George. *The Papers of George Washington. Retirement Series*. Ed. Dorothy Twohig et al. 5 vols. Charlottesville: University Press of Virginia, 1998.

Waugh, Evelyn. *The Loved One: An Anglo-American Tragedy*. Boston: Little, Brown, 1948.

Wendorf, Richard. *The Elements of Life: Biography and Portrait-Painting in Stuart and Georgian England*. Oxford: Clarendon, 1990.

Woolf, Virginia. *To the Lighthouse*. San Diego: Harvest, 1981.

Wotke, Friedrich. "Papagei." *Paulys Real-Encyclopädie der Classischen Altertumswissenschaft*. Waldsee: Alfred Drückenmuller Verlag, 1949. 18.3: 926–934.

Yapp, Brunsdon. *Birds in Medieval Manuscripts*. New York: Schocken, 1982.

Zall, P. M., ed. *A Nest of Ninnies and Other English Jestbooks of the Seventeenth Century*. Lincoln: University of Nebraska Press, 1970.

Ziolkowski, Jan M. *Talking Animals: Medieval Latin Beast Poetry, 750–1150*. Philadelphia: University of Pennsylvania Press, 1993.

# Index

# Acknowledgments

A book this wide-ranging couldn't be written without equally wide-ranging help, and I've been fortunate in both the quantity and quality of assistance to have come my way while I worked on it.

My first and deepest thanks go to Jerry Singerman, best of editors, who conceived of this project long before I did, and who won me to his vision with patience, humor, and insight.

Various friends and colleagues have commented on this book either entirely or partly in manuscript. These include Diane Roberts, Bob Butler, Marshall Brown, Sara Van Den Berg, and Annabel Patterson (these last three in connection with an early version of Chapter 3 that appeared in *Modern Language Quarterly* for 1997). Joanna Burger read the entire manuscript with care, wisdom, and encouragement. I cannot thank her enough.

Others have contributed research suggestions and specialized information drawn from their various areas of expertise. These include Ernst Badian, Kevin Barton, Bruce Bickley, Wendy Bishop, John and Mary Bradford, Barbara DeMent, David Freeda, Paul Freedman, Laurel Fulkerson, Amy Gorelick, Hunt Hawkins, Richard Hoffman, Cynthia Hollis, Dean Newman, Susan Seeley, Chris Shinn, Chris Spelling, Jeff Tatum, and Lori Walters. More is their due than more than all can pay.

As she did with this book's predecessor, Trish Thomas Henley has helped me organize the illustrations and permissions for the present volume. I'm fortunate, and relieved, to have been able to rely on her efficiency. I'm also grateful to Noreen O'Connor for her copyediting and to Ted Mann for his help in coordinating the illustration program of the book.

The English Department of Florida State University has given me money for research trips, reproduction fees, and general silliness, this last being the most important element of any scholarly project. No one has supported my trips, fees, or silliness more faithfully than my current department chair, Hunt Hawkins, for whom I have no adequate words of thanks, and never will.

Although nothing in this book is being reprinted, I've published articles and read papers on related subjects in a number of venues, including *Modern Language Quarterly* 59.2 (June 1998): 171–193; *Shakespeare Among the Animals* (New York: Palgrave, 2002): 99–132; the 1997 meeting of the Shakespeare Association of America; the Alumni Lecture Series sponsored by the English Department of the University of Texas at El Paso (November 12, 1997); the Florida State University English Department's Works-in-Progress Colloquium; the University of Mississippi's 2003 Renaissance Colloquium; and the 2003 meeting of the Group for Early Modern Cultural Studies. I'm grateful to these publications and events, and their respective audiences, for allowing me to develop and present my research.

Finally, I'm indebted beyond measure to the friends and relations who have endured and abetted my fascination with parrots over the years. Without them, a work like this would have been unthinkable. And most of all, I owe this book about art and literature to my wife and best friend, Linda Hall, who has shown me how a real artist acts, thinks, and works.

\